UNIVERSITY OF ST. THOMAS LIBRARIES

D1779851

"The infamous American actress Mae West once said: "An ounce of performance is worth pounds of promises." Finally, a book that goes beyond "promises" but gives greater clarity about the essential contributing factors of high performance organizations. This pioneering work of Dr. de Waal is a must read for people interested in this subject."

Manfred F. R. Kets de Vries, Clinical Professor of Leadership and Organizational Change at INSEAD and The Raoul de Vitry d'Avaucourt Chaired Professor of Leadership Development, and one of the world most influential thinkers

"I met André in 2007 when I was engaged in a major turnaround. The HPO methodology provided a perfect means of benchmarking where we were, telling us what good looked like, the things that we really needed to focus on, a target to aim for and the means to measure our progress – excellent. On a personal basis I really enjoyed working with André, bright, perceptive and always challenging – always adding further polish to the HPO mirror!"

Huw T. Owen - President, BT Global Health

"As the oldest airline in the world, KLM has always invested in the continuous improvement of its performance. Through an ever innovative approach towards people, processes and technique, the company searches on a daily basis for ways to further strengthen the quality of its services and of it's financial results. Examples of such an approach to business can be found in abundance in the book What Makes A High Performance Organization. André de Waal has done a wonderful job in researching high performance scientifically and then turning his findings into tangible ideas that managers can use immediately."

Peter Hartman, KLM Royal Dutch Airlines President and CEO

"A recurring problem with many books in the field of high performance is that these describe theoretical models which have not been tested extensively in the real world, and are therefore of limited practical value to managers. The HPO Framework of André de Waal, described in this well-written book, is based on solid scientific and practical research and its working has been tested at actual organizations. This makes De Waal's framework the first one to actually help managers improve in a sustainable manner. André de Waal has delivered a strategic plan for us all that not only promises to succeed, but that has been

proven to do so. If his five factors are observed and practiced, your company is bound to reach optimum levels and stay there. This is a business book with value for one and all."

Henk W. Broeders, Corporate Vice President Capgemini S.A.

"Andre de Waal has delivered a strategic plan for us all that not only promises to succeed, but that has been proven to do so. Thanks to his extensive research, the road to achieving High Performance Organization status has been clearly marked. If his five factors are observed and practiced, your company is bound to reach optimum levels and stay there. This is a business book with value for one and all."

Suzanne Bates is CEO of Bates Communications, author of three books including the bestseller "Speak Like a CEO" and "Motivate Like a CEO" and an expert in business communications and leadership, appearing in hundreds of publications including the New York Times, Forbes Magazine and Business Week.

What Makes a High Performance Organization: Five Validated Factors of Competitive Advantage that Apply Worldwide

What Makes a High Performance Organization

Five Validated Factors of Competitive Advantage that Apply Worldwide

ANDRÉ DE WAAL

© André de Waal 2012

Apart from any fair dealing for the purpose of research or private study, or criticism or review, as permitted under the Copyright, Designs and Patents Act 1988, this publication may only be reproduced, stored or transmitted, in any form or by any means, with the prior permission in writing of the publisher, or in the case of reprographic reproduction in accordance with the terms and licences issued by the Copyright Licensing Agency. Enquiries concerning reproduction outside those terms should be addressed to the publisher. The address is below:

Global Professional Publishing Ltd
Random Acres
Slip Mill Lane
Hawkhurst
Cranbrook
Kent TN18 5AD
Email: publishing@gppbooks.com

Global Professional Publishing Ltd believes that the sources of information upon which the book is based are reliable, and has made every effort to ensure the complete accuracy of the text. However, neither Global Professional Publishing Ltd, the authors nor any contributors can accept any legal responsibility whatsoever for consequences that may arise from errors or omissions or any opinion or advice given.

ISBN 978-1-906403-82-9

Printed in the United Kingdom by Bell & Bain

For full details of Global Professional Publishing titles in Management, Finance and Banking see our website at:
www.gppbooks.com

Contents

Chapter 1	**Introduction:**	
	Starting the journey toward HPO	1
	Toyota: an HPO in crisis	8
	Umpqua Bank (USA): a passion for excellence	16
Chapter 2	**Foundations of the HPO:**	
	research that spans the world	21
	The bonus as hygiene factor: the role of reward systems in the HPO	32
	International bank (the Netherlands): management makes the difference	43
	Retail International Group (Europe/Asia/South America): learning from the 'best countries'	51
	Ministry of Local Governance and Social Affairs (Rwanda): working on HPO in government	58
Chapter 3	**HPO factor 1 – Management Quality:**	
	without good management there is no HPO	63
	Longfellow Benefits (USA): even a full-blown HPO can improve	96
	De Beers Marine (South Africa): dealing with the past through the HPO Framework	104
Chapter 4	**HPO factor 2 – Openness & Action Orientation:**	
	less communication, more dialogue	111
	Vietnamese banking industry (Vietnam): identifying the HPO characteristics of an industry	130

vii

	Iringa University College (Tanzania): improving through applying the HPO Framework	133
	Palestine Polytechnics University (Palestine Territories): working on HPO in difficult circumstances	140
Chapter 5	**HPO factor 3 – Long-Term Orientation: stakeholder thinking trumps shareholder management**	**145**
	The myth of economic growth	148
	Creating HPO interactions with customers	155
	The relationship between Corporate Social Responsibility and the HPO Framework	166
	Two mining multinationals (Peru): using the HPO Framework for corporate social responsibility purposes	169
	Archway Marketing (USA): flipping the organizational pyramid to become HPO	172
Chapter 6	**HPO factor 4 – Continuous Improvement & Renewal: keep improving … and be truly innovative**	**183**
	Amanco Plastigama (Ecuador): emphasizing corporate social responsibility as part of HPO	199
	Two diamond companies (Europe): strengthening the value chain through HPO	204
	Temping Agency (Europe): looking internally for best ideas	208
Chapter 7.	**HPO factor 5 – Employee Quality: without good employees the HPO can never be achieved**	**215**
	Atrion Networking Corporation (USA): being HPO in inconspicuous surroundings	229
	South American College of Higher Education (South America): balancing growth with stability	235
	Nabil Bank (Nepal): achieving the sector's top position	240

Chapter 8.	The HPO transition process:	
	make it happen	245
	Reasons for starting an HPO Diagnosis	249
	ATLAS Consortium (UK): creating a successful partnership	265
	The HPO Framework: guideline for mergers	275
	Grohe (the Netherlands): achieving success during times of crises	279
Chapter 9.	Benefits of the HPO Framework: it pays to use it	287
About the author and the HPO Center		295
Acknowledgments		299
References		301
Notes		315
Index		323

Visit the book website

www.whatmakesahighperformanceorganization.com

Enter login code: AdWHPO12

to obtain more free HPO articles, cases, interviews and other HPO information.

For the HPO Leadership Toolbox app go to:

http://itunes.apple.com/app/hpo-leadership-toolbox/id543205661

Chapter 1
Introduction: *Starting the journey toward HPO*

A leader's journey toward high performance

"We felt we had stayed in our comfort zone for too long. Our organization had been doing quite well in recent years and would continue to do so – or, at least, that's what we thought. However, various changes in the environment started to hurt us more and more, making it painfully clear that we were losing our value to clients. We, as management, realized that it was not us but the employees who were the decisive factor for the results of the organization. Our people at the counters took a decision every six minutes, that is 80 decisions per day per person. And with 400 counter clerks that meant 32,000 decisions any given day! Such a number could never be regulated by protocols or instructions from 'above' so clerks had to take these decisions autonomously. And if they would simply follow a checklist provided to them by us, they would not be thinking about client needs while making decisions and we would never create added value for our clients. We became aware of the need to build an organization that would facilitate employees making good decisions and turn the work floor into the most important layer of the organization. We needed to become a high performance organization. But the sixty-four thousand dollar question was: how?

WHAT MAKES A HIGH PERFORMANCE ORGANIZATION

First we had to get out of our comfort zone, which required us to abandon the old traditional idea of wanting to achieve higher turnover and profit growth. We had to broaden our horizon and get used to thinking about new ways to deliver ever increasing quality and made-to-measure services to our clients, which would eventually translate into growth and profitability. This meant we had to work 'smarter', be more entrepreneurial, listen better to our clients, and develop a true service-minded attitude. As management, we had to move from giving top-down instructions and always wanting to be in control – creating uninspired employees and killing creativity – to being managers who could facilitate, coach and inspire people and by that increase our value to employees. Speaking about myself, I had some tough questions to answer: What did I need to do? How was I going to approach the upside-down pyramid? What would it mean for me personally? I felt that I had to confront my fears: Did I really want this? Was I capable of doing this? Where would we end up? At the same time I knew it would be a lonely journey, certainly at the beginning, as the organization wasn't really welcoming change. In addition, I realized that the course would be uncertain and that others could and probably would react negatively. As a leader you just have to accept these uncertainties and dare to tackle them. Only after I had faced up to this reality could I start my journey to make the organization a high performance organization."[1]

The above was compiled from interviews with Jonard Speijer, former chief executive officer of Dactylo. With 120 branches nationwide, Dactylo was one of the largest temporary employment agencies in the Netherlands. Dactylo specialized in deploying flex workers in administrative, industrial and technical positions in different types of industries. Dactylo is now part of the Randstad Group, the second largest temping agency in the world. Before Jonard Speijer decided to take on the journey toward a high performance organization (HPO), he and his fellow management team members had been endeavoring for quite some time to improve the temping agency's performance. And they had not been alone in this. At the HPO Center we frequently meet senior executives who feel the same pressure to make their organizations high performing, in the current business environment, which can be characterized by the following:[2]

- *The economic balance of power in the world is shifting.* While Western economies are still recovering from the recent financial and economic crises, upcoming economies are growing rapidly and gaining significance in the world economy. The Western business world changed in 2007-2008 when the credit crisis hit, eventually causing the most severe recession since the 1930s and creating continuous low growth rates. At the same time emerging economies like China, India and Brazil but also many countries in Africa are steadily growing causing them to become the economic motor of the world.

- *Economic globalization will continue.* As competition nowadays can be expected from every corner of the world, companies are forced to operate in many different countries and cultures. To deal with this, mergers are created resulting in large global corporations that are often more powerful than countries. Concurrently, regional economic blocs such as ASEAN and NAFTA form strong economic bases around the world.

- *The gap between the affluent and the deprived is widening.* National wealth continues to be distributed inequitably in both developing and developed countries. This causes tension between communities and increases the risk of conflicts.

- *Changes in the environment and demographics create uncertainty.* Global warming and environmental pollution are two of the major problems the world is facing today. They create economic and political tensions between countries over scarce resources such as water, yet a solution to these problems still doesn't seem to be near. Concurrently, the world population is increasing to an expected population of 9 billion people. The population in developed countries is rapidly ageing while birth rates are going down, causing a struggle for job openings to be filled adequately. In developing countries, on the other hand, the population is young and many jobs will need to be created for them in the near future. It is still unclear whether the economic growth in developing nations will create enough jobs for young people in their own countries and whether economic migration will decrease as a result of that.

- *The impact of technology on business and society continues.* The rate at which new technology is invented and put to use is still accelerating, creating new opportunities and at the same time, new unforeseen threats. Ultra modern materials and manufacturing techniques, such as nano-technology have the potential to disrupt complete industries.

- *The demand for more transparency and information increases.* Analysts, banks, shareholders and society are monitoring more actively what an organization is doing and not doing. At the same time, the possibilities to generate data and the social media are causing increasing difficulties for governments worldwide to control the flows of information, and the same is valid for the top management of a company.

As managers are expected to realize the goals of the organization by achieving outstanding performance in their organizational unit, they are constantly under pressure to deal effectively with the current business environment. At the same time, they are always short on time because of the numerous demands on them and therefore they need a strong focus on what really matters to improve the performance of the organization. As a consequence, managers have become strongly interested in knowing the characteristics of high performance as these will help them in their quest for excellence.

1.1 Introducing the High Performance Organization Framework

To help managers find ways to improve their organizations, the HPO Center started a five-year research project into the factors of sustainable high performance. The result of this research, the High Performance Organization (HPO) Framework, is one of the subjects discussed in this book as are many real-life examples illustrating the workings of the HPO Framework at organizations worldwide. As opposed to many previous publications on organizational performance, this book describes not just a theory on high performance but also a vast number of case studies in which this theory was put into practice. Successively it goes into the search for the factors of sustainable high performance, the construction of the HPO Framework, and the positive effects of applying the HPO Framework at all types of organizations worldwide. Also, in contrast to previous studies into HPOs, longitudinal research was performed in which companies were followed and studied while they worked with the HPO Framework. This allowed establishing the benefits of applying the HPO Framework in terms of better financial and non-financial results, and consequently the HPO Framework currently is the only improvement methodology that has been scientifically validated to help organizations achieve better performance. Therefore managers can take the lessons learned by the case study organizations using the HPO

INTRODUCTION

Framework and the best ideas of the HPO Leaders that are interviewed throughout the book, to heart in the knowledge that these can and will help them to turn their organizations into HPOs.

> ### *What is the HPO Framework?*
>
> The HPO Framework is a conceptual, scientifically validated structure which practitioners can use for deciding what to do to improve organizational performance and make it sustainable. It isn't a set of instructions or a recipe which can be followed blindly. Rather it is a framework that has to be translated by managers to their specific organizational situation in their current time, by designing a specific variant of the framework fit for their organization. This is bad news for bad managers, as the HPO Framework doesn't provide a blueprint. It is however good news for good managers, as they can put in their own experience, expertise and creativity while transforming their organizations into HPOs.

1.2 Defining the high performance organization

The HPO Center defines an HPO as follows:

> *A High Performance Organization is an organization that achieves financial and non-financial results that are exceedingly better than those of its peer group over a period of time of five years or more, by focusing in a disciplined way on that what really matters to the organization.*

This definition consists of several interesting parts worth discussing:

- High performance is relative. In other words, performance can only be denoted as 'high' when it is compared to a peer group. This peer group comprises competitors, in the case of profit companies, or comparable organizations, in the case of non-profit organizations or governmental agencies.

- Organizations which have done well for a period of only one, two or three years are not considered to be HPOs. High performance is characterized by sustainable good results over a prolonged period of time. So an HPO not just performs well because it was lucky but because it has been doing the right things right.[3] The limit of five years was chosen because the assumption was that most organizations have a strategic plan, with an average time horizon of three years, aimed at increasing performance and beating the peer group. After five years it can be evaluated in retrospect whether the organization has indeed achieved its aim of doing better than the peer group. Another reason for choosing five years was that the average life span of an organization is approximately 12 and a half years and is still going down. Thus, if an organization performs much better than its competitors for almost half of the expected life span of a 'normal' organization, it can rightfully be said to be an HPO.[4]

- Recent research shows that it is very difficult for organizations to achieve consistent growth, even at modest rates. The case studies in this book reveal that HPOs know what makes them prolonged successful. They have the discipline not to be distracted by the newest management fad but to stick to their knitting. This means that they continue to do what made them successful (processes, systems, behavior) and that their improvement efforts will always be aimed at making these continuously better. The main reason for HPOs to start something different is if they see an opportunity to strengthen their core capabilities and competences. HPOs also know that deviating from this path may mean getting into trouble and declining performance, so management is keen on keeping the discipline.[5]

1.3 Benefit of HPO and the HPO Framework

What is the benefit of being an HPO? Table 1.1 shows the financial returns of an HPO compared to its peer group. The figures are based on results of HPOs provided in the literature. The returns are given as ranges rather than single numbers because they differ per industry, as each industry has its own financial profile. For instance, a profitability margin of 4 percent in a supermarket would be very good, while in the banking industry (at least, in the old days) it would be substandard. Only those financial returns have been included in the range which have been reported in more than one HPO study. The estimation of the range is conservative, therefore overly large outcomes have not been included in the listing. On the basis of the comparison, an organization can theoretically expect the following improvements versus its competitor when it becomes an HPO: revenue growth will be 4 to 16 percent higher; profitability 14 to 44 percent better; ROA, ROE, ROI and ROS 1 to 26 percent higher; and TSR 4 to 42 percent higher.

Type of financial return	Return of HPO versus peer group (in %)
Revenue growth	+ 4 to 16
Profitability	+ 14 to 44
Return on assets (ROA)	+ 1 to 12
Return on equity (ROE)	+ 9 to 25
Return on investment (ROI)	+ 15 to 26
Return on sales (ROS)	+ 2 to 18
Total shareholder return (TSR)	+ 4 to 42

Table 1.1: The returns of an HPO versus its peer group

It is somewhat difficult to compare the non-financial performances of HPOs against its peer groups because non-financial indicators tend to differ per industry. However, several HPO studies give clear indications that HPOs generally have higher customer satisfaction, higher customer loyalty, and higher employee satisfaction, higher quality, less complaints, more innovative products and services, and a better reputation than non-HPOs.

In Chapter 9 the benefits of applying the HPO Framework will be discussed, based on the numerous case studies. At this time it can already be said that the practical experience at case organizations in many different countries shows that applying the HPO Framework indeed helps an organization to achieve better financial and non-financial results. Not only does the framework help organizations pinpoint its current status and strong and weak points, but it also provides clear indications and suggestions for organizations which need to be addressed in order to become an HPO. The HPO Framework has been so extensively tested in sector comparative studies and in longitudinal research, that it can be safely stated that it pays to apply the framework to become an HPO!

Toyota: an HPO in crisis

'On August 28th, 2009, Toyota, the world's largest and most profitable car manufacturer, stopped being an HPO'

On that day the first accident happened with a Toyota, which triggered a recall of more than 10 million vehicles in 2009 and 2010 and a loss of more than US$4 billion for fiscal year 2009. In San Diego, USA, the gas pedal of a Lexus got stuck under the floor mat causing the car to run out of control and of the road, killing its occupants. However, the accident did not set off a whole series of improvements at Toyota, as it once would have done in a manner which gained the company a reputation for its world-class processes.[6] But Toyota was no longer the robust company of the earlier days, the company which had risen from the brink of bankruptcy in the fifties and had achieved a stretch of 50 consecutive years of profitability – a record unheard of in manufacturing industries – to become the biggest car manufacturer in the world. A company known for its excellence in manufacturing processes and its continuous improvement culture, collectively known as the Toyota Way.[7] Toyota was in 2010 rapidly losing its reputation as HPO and everyone wondered: what happened?

The answer was given by Akio Toyoda, president of Toyota Motor Corporation:[8] "Toyota has, for the past few years, been expanding its business rapidly. Quite frankly, I fear the pace at which we have grown may have been too quick. I would like to point out here that Toyota's priority had traditionally been the following: first, safety; second, quality; and third, volume. These priorities have become confused and we were not able to stop, think, and make improvements as much as we were able to before, and our basic stance to listen to customers' voices to make better products has weakened somewhat. We pursued growth over the speed at which we were able to develop our people and our organization, and we

INTRODUCTION

should sincerely be mindful of that." Subsequent analysis by both Toyota and outside researchers revealed weaknesses in the once so strong company. Because of the rapid growth and the tendency that had developed among Toyota's management to put quantity above quality in order to achieve the top spot in car manufacturing, the company had lost its intense focus on understanding customers concerns, taking these seriously and addressing them as quickly and best as possible. In addition, the company had become bureaucratic with outdated lines of communication, decision and accountability, and a tendency towards smugness so it took too long to respond to issues. And to make matters worse, several business practices which had served the company well for so many years were no longer applied, such as only building what was sold so no inventory would build up, and only expanding when there was enough trained personnel to do so in a quality controlled manner. In conclusion, the company no longer practiced what it had preached and what had made it so successful: the relentless focus on quality. Management no longer had the discipline to withstand the economic pressures of selling more at the expense of quality.

Will Toyota become an HPO again? It lost its position to General Motors as the world's largest car manufacturer, it has not returned to its former profitability yet, and severe damage was done to its reputation and brand. However, it seems that the company has seized the crisis to go back to its old ways and culture and that it is doing now more of what it had been doing right in all those decades before the recall crisis began. This is a promising sign and hopefully the company will become 'the poster boy' of HPOs once again.

1.4 Setup of this book

What Makes a High Performance Organization: Five Validated Factors That Apply Worldwide is meant for anyone interested in improving organizations, using a scientifically validated framework instead of depending on the latest management fad. The book consists of nine chapters. After introducing in Chapter 1 the HPO and the HPO Framework and their accompanying benefits, Chapter 2 concentrates on the research done by the HPO Center to develop the HPO Framework for practitioners to improve organizational performance. Five factors of high performance – the HPO factors – are introduced as well as several factors that during the research turned out to be of lesser importance than always thought for becoming an HPO. In this chapter the question is also raised, and answered, whether the five HPO factors will remain the same through time and thus whether they will still be relevant for managers in the future. Chapter 2 concludes with the practical application of the framework by introducing the HPO Diagnosis. The working of the diagnosis is illustrated by the experiences at two case companies. Chapters 3 through 7 go in more detail into the five HPO factors. They describe the underlying characteristics of high performance, and ideas to get started – originating from the HPO research and other recent organizational studies – with improving the characteristics. Chapter 8 gives the steps which need to be taken to make the transition to an HPO. Finally, in Chapter 9 the added value of the HPO Framework is discussed, based on the experiences of organizations and researchers while working with the framework.

Introducing the HPO leaders

In the past years the HPO Center undertook many case studies to study the workings of an HPO, the experiences of organizations with the HPO Diagnosis, and how organizations go about the transition to HPO. Many of these case studies can be found scattered in between the chapters. In preparation for this book the HPO Center also conducted interviews with 11 HPO Leaders, managers who were either working at an HPO or who were turning their organizations into HPOs. They were willing to share their experiences and ideas with us. Each chapter contains quotes from the interviewees to illustrate the subject matter treated in the chapter. We interviewed the following managers:

- *Air France – KLM Royal Dutch Airlines, France/the Netherlands: Arend de Jong, senior vice president Internal Audit & Internal Control* – KLM Royal Dutch Airlines is the airline of the Netherlands and is part of the Air France-KLM group. KLM

INTRODUCTION

operates worldwide scheduled passenger and cargo services to more than 90 destinations. Its hub and spoke system is based at Amsterdam Airport Schiphol and its core business is the transfer of passengers from origins to destinations both inside and outside of the Netherlands. KLM is the oldest airline in the world still operating under its original name and has approximately 30,000 employees. In May 2004 the merger of KLM with Air France created Air France-KLM. Arend de Jong started as assistant controller and later became corporate controller of KLM. Currently he is senior vice president internal audit and internal control of the Air France – KLM group.

- *HP, United Kingdom: Huw Owen, former CEO of HP Defense & Security* – HP (formerly Hewlett-Packard) is one of world's largest technology services providers, delivering flexible technology, applied innovation, collaborative expertise and service excellence to organizations. As part of HP, HP Defense & Security has provided technology to UK forces which allows NATO-compatible information sharing at the frontline, ensuring that soldiers, sailors and airmen can do their jobs. HP Defense & Security partners with the UK Ministry of Defense through the ATLAS Consortium to help transform business administration processes within the British Armed Forces. HP Defense & Security is leading this consortium charged with delivering the new Defense Information Infrastructure. Hugh Owen led the ATLAS Consortium and at the time of the interview was the chief executive officer of HP Defense & Security. At both organizations he was working with the HPO Framework.

- *Microsoft, USA: Rik van der Kooi, Corporate VP, Advertiser and Publisher Solutions* – The story of Microsoft is well-known. Established in 1975 by Bill Gates and Paul Allen in Albuquerque New Mexico, the company has grown to the largest and one of the most profitable and well-known IT providers in the world, now under the leadership of Steve Ballmer. The company has succeeded in consistently being at the forefront of developments in the industry while being a first choice employer for graduates and being very profitable. Rik van der Kooi is based at Microsoft's headquarters in Redmond, Washington, where he joined in 2005 as chief financial officer of the Online Services Division. Currently he is Corporate Vice President of Advertiser and Publisher Solutions, in charge of Microsoft's digital advertising business.

- *Microsoft, the Netherlands: Theo Rinsema, general manager Microsoft the Netherlands* – Microsoft Netherlands is the pioneer of the New Way of Working concept, which aims at achieving time and location independent working. This means that it does not matter when or where Microsoft employees work, they have almost complete freedom in this as long as they achieve the agreed upon targets. Because of the flexibility this provides it is easier for employees to combine work and private life, which works as a big morale booster. This New Way of Working requires a new way of managing as people do not keep regular office hours and are not that often in the building anyway, so the factor trust has become increasingly important in the relation between manager and employee. Physically the New Way of Working takes shape in the building of Microsoft Netherlands which does no longer have offices or cubicles but consists of open spaces, concentration rooms and a sophisticated coffee bar. Theo Rinsema is the person who introduced the New Way of Working concept at Microsoft.

- *SABMiller, Europe: Alan Clark, managing director* – SABMiller plc is one of the world's largest brewers, with brewing interests and distribution agreements across six continents. The group's wide portfolio of brands includes premium international beers such as Pilsner Urquell, Peroni Nastro Azzurro, Miller Genuine Draft and Grolsch, as well as leading local brands such as Aguila, Castle, Miller Lite, Snow and Tyskie. SABMiller is also one of the world's largest bottlers of Coca-Cola products. SABMiller Europe's brewing operations cover 10 countries, and in the majority of these countries the company is the number one or two brewer by market share. The company also exports significant volumes to a further eight European markets of which the largest are the United Kingdom and Germany.

- *Schuberg Philis, the Netherlands: Pim Berger, founder/managing director & Ilja Heitlager, information officer* – Schuberg Philis is an IT outsourcing company which offers the highest service quality for mission critical applications of organizations, fully committing to a 100 percent uptime. This means that the customer is guaranteed that its IT systems which are critical for its operations will function 24/7 365 days per year, without exception. After fully analyzing the risks with customers, Schuberg Philis takes full responsibility for the systems. In case of issues, Schuberg Philis will suffer financial penalties which are taken without discussion. Schuberg Philis has the best reputation in the industry, has the most active promoters among its customers, is seen by the most customers as a strategic partner, and thus achieves the best financial results in the industry.

INTRODUCTION

- *Svenska Handelsbanken, Sweden: Mikael Sørensen, general manager the Netherlands* – Svenska Handelsbanken is a Swedish bank with branches in Sweden, the United Kingdom, Western and Eastern Europe, Russia, Asia and USA, and approximately 10,000 employees. The bank has for more than 40 years consistently outperformed other European banks on performance indicators such as return on equity, total shareholder return, earnings per share, cost-income ratio and customer satisfaction. The bank is successfully obtaining its goal year after year, which is to have a higher profitability than the average for its competitors. In the process, Svenska Handelsbanken has been the first bank of choice for graduates for years and has the lowest turnover in the industry; it has the highest customer satisfaction, the least complaints, the lowest credit losses in the industry, and the best financial results in the industry.

- *Tata Steel, the Netherlands: Jan Maas, Director Change Supply Chain Transformation* – In 1999 Koninklijke Hoogovens N.V., based in the Netherlands, merged with British Steel Plc to form Corus, which was subsequently taken over in 2007 by Tata Steel. Tata Steel Group manufactures, processes and distributes steel products and services to customers worldwide. The company is now Europe's second largest steel producer with annual revenues of around £12 billion and a crude steel production of over 20 million tons. Jan Maas was, at the time of the interview, director services at Tata Steel in IJmuiden, the Netherlands, in charge of IT, logistics, security, maintenance, buildings, and third party vendors.

- *Umpqua Bank, USA: Lani Hayward, executive vice-president Creative Strategies* – Umpqua Bank is one of North America's most successful banks. Established in 1953 in Oregon as the National Bank of Oregon, it transformed from a small, solid but rather inconspicuous bank with five branches in Oregon into a company with US$7 billion of assets, 120 branches in several states, high profitability and large market share, extremely loyal employees who are hardly ever ill and almost never leave, and a product portfolio formula which has won several prices. The bank also did not suffer too much during the credit crisis because it had been focusing not only on its shareholders but on its stakeholders as well, thus taking decisions which were in the long-term interest of all parties involved. Lani Hayward is executive vice-president in charge of developing and executing creative strategies.

- *Unilever, Europe Middle East Asia: Lennard Boogaard, vice president Human Resources, Unilever Turkey, Israel, Iran & Central Asia* – One of the best-known companies in the world is Unilever, the British-Dutch organization that owns many of the world's consumer product brands in foods, beverages, ice cream, cleaning agents and personal care products (for example: Ben & Jerry's, Dove, Colman's, Slim-Fast, Lipton and Vaseline). Unilever has operating companies in more than 100 countries, owns more than 400 brands, achieves a turnover of US$40 billion, and has some 200,000 employees. The company focuses its marketing efforts mainly on its billion-dollar brands, a limited number of brands that achieve annual sales in excess of US$1 billion. Well-known brands include Blue Band, Dove, Flora/Becel, Knorr, Axe/Lynx and Hellmann's. From its origin Unilever always put much emphasis on creating a social working environment. Lennard Boogaard is in charge of the human resources of Unilever's operations in Turkey, Israel, Iran and Central Asia.

- *Ziggo, the Netherlands: Martine Ferment, former vice president Ziggo Customer Relations* – Ziggo is a Dutch media and communications services provider, serving approximately 3.1 million households, 1.5 million broadband Internet customers, 1.8 million digital television customers and 1.2 million telephone subscribers. In addition, business-to-business clients use services as data-communication, telephony, internet and television. The enterprise owns a next-generation-network through which it can supply bandwidth for all future services expected at present. Martine Ferment was interim vice president of Ziggo Customer Relations, the unit that deals with servicing customers. She has used the HPO Framework to transform Ziggo Customer Relations into an HPO.

INTRODUCTION

KEY POINTS CHAPTER 1

- In the modern highly complex business world, managers feel a great pressure to make their organizations high performing. This is why there is a strong interest among managers in knowing the characteristics of high performance organizations. These characteristics can serve as a guideline for improving the organization and achieving sustained high performance.

- A High Performance Organization (HPO) is defined as: *an organization that achieves financial and non-financial results that are exceedingly better than those of its peer group over a period of time of five years or more, by focusing in a disciplined way on that what really matters to the organization.*

- In 2003 the HPO Center started a research project to examine the determinant factors of sustainable high performance. In five years time, people from 1,470 organizations in 50 different countries spread across five continents participated in this project. It resulted in the HPO Framework, a conceptual, scientifically validated structure which practitioners can use for deciding what to do to improve organizational performance and make it sustainable.

- Since 2007, the HPO Framework has been applied in many different industries in different countries. The case studies described in this book show that organizations which use the framework actually start to perform better than they did before.

Umpqua Bank (USA): a passion for excellence

KEY MESSAGE

Although many competing banks have visited Umpqua Bank to see how they could copy what the bank was doing, none of them has yet succeeded in reproducing its success. Copying a successful organization does not automatically create an HPO. An organization can learn from an HPO, but at the same time it has to develop its own HPO vision and tailor it to the organization's specific requirements and circumstances.

In the Pacific North-West of the United States there is a mid-sized bank which is extremely successful and which has hardly been affected by the financial crisis. Umpqua Bank was established in 1953 in Oregon by six people who worked at that time in the logging industry. For decennia the bank, at the time called National Bank of Oregon, was a little-known, small bank with moderate profitability. This changed when in the 1990s Ray Davis was appointed as chief executive officer. Under his inspired leadership, Umpqua Bank transformed into a company with almost US$12 billion of assets, 186 branches in several states, high profitability and large market share, extremely loyal employees, and a product portfolio formula which has won several awards.

How did Davis accomplish this turnaround? Fortunately he has not kept his approach a secret as Davis has described it in his stimulating book titled *Leading to Growth*.[9] A striking fact in the story of Umpqua Bank is that the bank's strategy is unique in the sector: the bank considers itself a retail business rather than a financial services provider. That is why its branches are fitted out as if they are stores and its employees are send on 'training missions' to large successful American retail trading companies and hotel chains like Ritz-Carlton to learn how to behave in a customer friendly way with clients. Everything within Umpqua Bank (processes, products, reward systems, training courses) is aimed at executing this unique strategy as best one can. Initially Davis was laughed at by his peers because of his deviant approach but later on the same people were queuing to visit Umpqua Bank's stores. Another success factor at Umpqua Bank is the quality of the management and more specific the fact that managers function as role models for employees. Umpqua Bank's managers feel a true passion for their clients, employees and society (that is, the areas in which the stores are situated) and have a firm discipline to always look out for the interests of these stakeholders. They give their employees a lot of responsibility and at the same time address the results they achieve, and swiftly deal with non-performers. The core skills the company is looking for in an excellent manager can be described as follows: (1) develop a broad view on the business; (2) have the discipline to stick to the plan; (3) have a clear vision on the future of the company; (4) lead the way in change; and (5) implement the strategy successfully. Further, it is allowed to make mistakes as long as people learn from these.

It is therefore no wonder that Umpqua Bank likes to experiment with ways to make itself more appealing to its clients. In the last chapter, Davis states the essence of his book very succinctly: "In this book I have focused on leading for growth – not because getting bigger is the goal, but because getting better is. Growth means many different things. On a personal level, it means developing maturity, self-insight, even wisdom. In an organization, it means developing a deeper understanding of your organization and the markets you serve, increasing your bench strength, improving your products and services, and much more. Every organization has to be committed to the relentless pursuit of progress if it wants to stay vibrant and relevant. Making progress is a never-ending journey, one with no finish line."[10]

Does the above sound too good to be true? To investigate this we travelled to Portland, to visit the Umpqua Bank store in Pearl Street, downtown Portland. This is our report on the visit. "When you enter a store of Umpqua Bank initially you don't notice anything remarkable. Yes, the store is spacious and decorated in a non-standard, local theme. There is free freshly brewed coffee and comfortable seats to relax and even computer terminals with free internet access. Ray Davis already wrote in his book that people of many competing banks visited Umpqua Bank stores and then quickly concluded that they could perform the same tricks as Umpqua Bank. The comfortable seats have by now been copied in every bank in the United States, there is free coffee and also free internet for customers. But still, these banks do not resemble Umpqua Bank in the slightest. That is because it takes you a while before you start to notice what 'it' is that makes Umpqua Bank different. For instance, when you enter the building there are no counters with people who look at you with a gaze of 'What are you doing here?' Nobody notices you taking a second cup of free coffee. We see a business man entering hastily to plug in his mobile phone to recharge it as he is expecting an important call and his battery is almost dead. He then grabs a cup of coffee and sits down to answer his call and ... not one of the Umpqua Bank associates (as store employees are called) bothers him. At a computer terminal two elderly gentlemen are printing stuff and occasionally speak to each other. A moment later two business women enter. It turns out they just met on the street and decided to enter the store to sit down in a quiet corner to chat to each other and do some business. We suddenly perceive it: all these people feel at home in the Umpqua Bank store, something we would never have dreamed to happen at a bank. These people use the Umpqua Bank store as a part of their daily life and routine, the store is part of their community. It provides them with a place to meet people, drink coffee, and, oh yeah, do some banking business.

From the sitting room only one Umpqua Bank associate is visible. He stands next to a sort of counter, looks at everybody with a friendly gaze, nods at the people he knows, which is most of them. He talks to some of them, not so much about banking business but about their daily life. This makes him part of the people's lives, he knows when you go on holiday or when somebody is sick in your family. He tells us how much he enjoys his job. He worked in the restaurant business for 15 years and the skill he has learned there, to make contact with people without being pushy, he uses at the Umpqua Bank store every day. He mainly listens and knows how to put you and your affairs central in the conversation. Through following training courses he has learned the banking business and it is no problem if sometimes he doesn't know all the details, he can ask any of his three colleagues in the store. He introduces us to his colleagues, who are positioned behind open counters at the back of the store. These associates all have different backgrounds: one originates from the hotel industry, the second used to work in supermarkets, and the third turns out to have experience in banking. When we leave the store we know that we have really connected with Umpqua Bank, we now know what makes this company so special."

Chapter 2
Foundations of the HPO: *research that spans the world*

This chapter describes the research that resulted in the development of the HPO Framework, a conceptual structure which managers can use to improve organizational performance. The framework provides a definition of the concept of the HPO – which was discussed in Chapter 1 – and five factors of high performance – the HPO factors – with their 35 underlying HPO characteristics. The research indicated that some activities in organizations which most people consider important for achieving high performance, were not really distinguishing for becoming an HPO. After a brief list of those activities, one of these, the implementation of bonuses and reward systems, is discussed in more detail. The sections that follow discuss why the HPO factors are important both now and in the future, and how the HPO research and the HPO Framework differ from previous research on high performance. The chapter concludes with a description of the HPO Diagnosis, a practical tool to apply the HPO Framework, used to evaluate how far along the path to high performance an organization is.

2.1 Global HPO research

The HPO Framework was developed after a two-phased research project to examine the determinant factors of sustainable high performance. It consisted of a descriptive literature review (Phase 1) and an empirical study in the form of a worldwide implemented questionnaire (Phase 2).[11] Phase 1 started with collecting the studies on high performance and excellence that were to be included in the literature review. The criteria used were:

(1) The study was aimed specifically at identifying HPO factors or best practices.

(2) The study consisted of either a survey with a sufficient large number of respondents, allowing generalization of the results, or in-depth case studies of several companies, which meant the results were valid for more than one organization.

(3) The study employed triangulation by using more than one research method.

(4) The study included written documentation containing an account and justification of the research method, research approach and selection of the research population, a well-described analysis, and retraceable results and conclusions allowing assessment of the quality of the research method.

The literature review covered 290 studies which satisfied one or more of the four criteria. These studies formed the basis for identifying the potential HPO characteristics, which were required for developing the questionnaire in Phase 2. The studies were put in several study categories depending on the rigor with which the study had been conducted (e.g. from purely scientific to 'based on my experience'). The identification process of the HPO characteristics consisted of a succession of steps. First, elements were extracted from each of the publications that the authors themselves regarded as essential for high performance. These elements were then entered in a matrix. Because different authors used different terminologies in their publications, similar elements were placed in groups under a factor and each group – later to be named 'characteristic' – was given an appropriate description. Subsequently, a matrix was constructed for each factor listing a number of characteristics. A total of 189 characteristics were identified. After that, the 'weighted importance', i.e. the number of times a characteristic occurred in the individual study categories, was calculated for each of the characteristics. Finally, the characteristics with a weighted importance of at least 9 percent were designated characteristics that potentially make up an HPO. A cut-off percentage of 9 percent was chosen as there was a natural gap around this percentage: several characteristics scored considerably below 9 percent while the next closest scoring characteristics scored considerably higher than 9 percent. The cut-off resulted in a list of 53 potential HPO characteristics. The research in Phase 1 was partly replicated by Cranfield University, which confirmed the conclusion.[12]

In Phase 2 of the HPO research the 53 potential HPO characteristics were included in a questionnaire which was presented to managers and employees during lectures and workshops all over the world. The respondents of the questionnaire – originating from profit, non-profit and governmental organizations from

Figure 2.1: Graphic representation of the HPO Framework

50 countries –were asked to grade how well their organization performed on the various HPO characteristics on a scale of 1 (very poor) to 10 (excellent) and also how their organizational results were, compared to those of peer groups. The questionnaire yielded 2,515 responses. With a statistical analysis, 35 characteristics with both a significant and a strong correlation with organizational performance were extracted and identified as the HPO characteristics. The statistical analysis also revealed that these 35 characteristics could be categorized into five factors, the HPO factors. These are described in the section 2.2.

The HPO research showed that there is a direct and positive relationship between the five HPO factors and competitive performance: the higher the scores on the HPO factors (HPO scores), the better the results of the organization, and the lower the HPO scores the lower the competitive performance. The research also showed that all HPO factors need to have equal scores. If for instance four HPO factors score an 8 (out of 10) and one factor a 5, the organization will not be able to function as an HPO because it is out of balance. An easy way to visualize this is to imagine a child's propeller (Figure 2.1). When exposed to the wind, it spins around at a constant speed. However, if one of the strings breaks, the propeller will no longer turn around smoothly and will eventually break down. It illustrates that an organization should distribute its attention evenly across the five HPO factors to make sure none of these will be 'broken' and hold back the organization. Working on just one HPO factor, or only a few characteristics, without paying attention to the other HPO factors or characteristics in due course, will not help the organization in the long run.

2.2 Five factors of high performance

This section briefly describes the five factors of high performance – the HPO factors. A more in-depth explanation of each factor is provided in Chapters 3 to 7. Table 2.1, at the end of this section, lists the 35 HPO characteristics that underlie the HPO factors, in order of importance within a factor.

HPO factor 1: Management Quality

In an HPO, managers at all organizational levels maintain trust relationships with employees by valuing their loyalty, treating smart people with respect, creating and maintaining individual relationships with employees, encouraging belief and trust in others, and treating people fairly. Managers in an HPO work with integrity and are a role model to others, because they are honest and sincere, show commitment, enthusiasm and respect, have a strong set of ethics and standards, are credible and consistent, maintain a sense of vulnerability and are not self-complacent. They are decisive, action-focused decision-makers, avoid over-analysis and propose decisions and effective actions, while fostering action-taking by others. HPO managers coach and facilitate employees to achieve better results by being supportive, helping them, protecting them from outside interference, and by being available to them. Management holds people responsible for results and is decisive about non-performers by always focusing on the achievement of results, maintaining clear accountability for performance, and making tough decisions. Managers in an HPO develop an effective, confident and strong management style by communicating the values and by making sure the strategy is known to and embraced by all organizational members.

HPO factor 2: Openness & Action Orientation

In addition to having an open culture, an HPO uses the organization's openness to achieve results. In an HPO, management values the opinion of employees by frequently having dialogues with them and involving them in all important business and organizational processes. HPO management allows experiments and mistakes by permitting employees to take risks, being prepared to take risks themselves, and seeing mistakes as an opportunity to learn. In this respect, management welcomes and stimulates change by continuously striving for renewal, developing dynamic managerial capabilities to enhance flexibility, and being personally involved in change activities. People in an HPO spend a lot of time on dialogue, knowledge exchange and learning in order to obtain new ideas to improve their work and make the complete organization performance-driven.

HPO factor 3: Long-Term Orientation

In an HPO, long-term gain is far more important than short-term profit. This long-term orientation is extended to all stakeholders of the organization, that is, shareholders as well as employees, suppliers, clients and society at large. An HPO continuously strives to enhance customer value creation by learning what customers want, understanding their values, building excellent relationships and having direct contact with them, involving them in the organization's affairs, being responsive to them, and focusing on continuously enhancing customer value. An HPO maintains good long-term relationships with all stakeholders by networking broadly, taking an interest in and giving back to society, and creating mutual, beneficial opportunities and win-win relationships. An HPO also grows through partnerships with suppliers and customers, thereby turning the organization into an international network corporation. Management of an HPO is committed to the organization for the long haul by balancing common purpose with self-interest, and teaching organizational members to put the needs of the enterprise first. They grow new management from their own ranks by encouraging staff to become leaders, filling positions with internal talents, and promoting from within. An HPO creates a safe and secure workplace by giving people a sense of safety (physical and mental) and job security and by using dismissal as a last resort.

HPO factor 4: Continuous Improvement & Renewal

The process of continuous improvement starts with an HPO adopting a unique strategy that will set the company apart by developing many new alternatives to compensate for dying strategies. After that, an HPO will do everything in its power to fulfill this unique strategy. It continuously simplifies, improves and aligns all its processes to improve its ability to respond to events efficiently and effectively and to eliminate unnecessary procedures, work, and information overload. The organization also measures and reports everything that matters, so it measures progress, monitors goal fulfillment and confronts the brutal facts. It reports these facts not only to management but to everyone in the organization, allowing all organizational members to access financial and non-financial information needed to drive improvement. People in an HPO feel a moral obligation to continuously strive for the best results. The organization continuously innovates products, processes and services, constantly creating new sources of competitive advantage by rapidly developing new products and services to respond to market changes. It also masters its core competencies and is an innovator in these core competencies by deciding on and sticking to what the company does best, keeping core competencies inside the firm and outsourcing non-core competencies.

HPO factor 5: Employee Quality

An HPO makes sure it assembles a diverse and complementary workforce and recruits people with maximum flexibility to help detect problems in business processes and to incite creativity in solving them. An HPO continuously works on the development of its workforce by training staff to be both resilient and flexible, letting them learn from others by going into partnerships with suppliers and customers, inspiring them to improve their skills so they can accomplish extraordinary results, and holding them responsible for their performances and with that encouraging them to be creative in looking for new productive ways to achieve the desired results.

FOUNDATIONS OF THE HPO

HPO factor 1: Management Quality	
1.	Management is trusted by organizational members.
2.	Management has integrity.
3.	Management is a role model for organizational members.
4.	Management applies fast decision making.
5.	Management applies fast action taking.
6.	Management coaches organizational members to achieve better results.
7.	Management focuses on achieving results.
8.	Management is very effective.
9.	Management applies strong leadership.
10.	Management is confident.
11.	Management always holds organizational members responsible for their results.
12.	Management is decisive with regard to non-performers.
HPO factor 2: Openness & Action Orientation	
13.	Management frequently engages in a dialogue with employees.
14.	Organizational members spend much time on dialogue, knowledge exchange and learning.
15.	Organizational members are always involved in important processes.
16.	Management allows making mistakes.
17.	Management welcomes change.
18.	The organization is performance driven.
HPO factor 3: Long-Term Orientation	
19.	The organization maintains good and long-term relationships with all stakeholders.
20.	The organization is aimed at servicing the customers as best as possible.
21.	Management has been with the company for a long time.
22.	New management is promoted from within the organization.
23.	The organization is a secure workplace for organizational members.

HPO factor 4: Continuous Improvement & Renewal	
24.	The organization has adopted a strategy that sets it clearly apart from other organizations.
25.	In the organization processes are continuously improved.
26.	In the organization processes are continuously simplified.
27.	In the organization processes are continuously aligned.
28.	In the organization everything that matters to performance is explicitly reported.
29.	In the organization relevant financial and non-financial information is reported to all organizational members.
30.	The organization continuously innovates its core competencies.
31.	The organization continuously innovates its products, processes and services.
HPO factor 5: Employee Quality	
32.	Management inspires organizational members to accomplish extraordinary results.
33.	The resilience and flexibility of organizational members is continuously strengthened.
34.	The organization has a diverse and complementary workforce.
35.	The organization grows through partnerships with suppliers and/or customers.

Table 2.1: The five HPO factors and their underlying
35 HPO characteristics

❝If your company is an HPO it will all be easier, more efficient, and more effective sailing. You will always have issues, however these will be issues that you will be capable of dealing with. If you are not an HPO, if you are not well aligned, if you don't have a common foundation, if everybody doesn't know where they are going and don't feel valued, people will not go the extra mile. As an HPO, you have got the ability to do an awful lot more than a non-HPO. Because people will step up and they will do more when required. So it means that you have got more agility, are more responsive, have got more fuel in your tank. If you have got an underperforming business where people are frustrated and bitter, they will do the bare minimum that they can get away with to get their pay check and go home. Which means that you are less agile and less effective. As a high performing business you have got a far greater chance of ploughing through the challenges with a minimal amount of disruption."

Huw Owen, HP D&S

2.3 Non-distinguishing factors

Below is a list of some of the techniques, methods and activities that organizations often apply to become high performing:

- defining a clear vision, mission and strategy
- enhancing trust in leadership
- putting more focus on customers
- creating better career development opportunities
- improving processes with an improved information technology structure
- selecting and putting in a different organizational structure ('reorganize')
- implementing competence management
- lowering work pressures
- introducing servant leadership
- appreciating employees more for their efforts
- developing better listening skills in managers
- creating more two-way communication with employees
- laying off poor-performing employees.

All these techniques, methods and activities seem reasonable things to do. For most of them there is however little scientific proof that they actually improve performance in the short term or the long term. It is therefore difficult to say which of them are important for achieving better performance. To find out more about this, the results of the HPO research described in the beginning of this chapter were further examined. The 189 potential characteristics of high performance found in the literature during Phase 1 were compared with the 35 HPO characteristics identified in Phase 2. The 154 characteristics which did not make it into the set of 35 were considered as factors which were not distinguishing for becoming an HPO. In the following paragraphs some of these factors are briefly discussed.

Organizational Design / Structure

None of the characteristics concerning organizational designs and structures were HPO characteristics. All of them showed no correlation with high performance and can therefore be considered non-distinguishing for achieving the HPO status. It seems to make no difference (neither positive nor negative) whether management chooses a functional design, a process design or a matrix design for its organizational structure. Consequently, launching a reorganization to boost performance is not advisable. In fact, research keeps finding that most reorganizations fail to yield long-term performance improvement.[13]

Employee Autonomy

It has been fashionable to empower employees but it does not necessarily contribute to high performance. The research results showed that a high level of autonomy had a negative correlation with competitive performance. Too much freedom for employees can lead to internal disorder and confusion if it is not backed up with sufficient means of coordination, and can thus seriously damage an organization. People want to have clarity about the goals, what is and what isn't allowed and what is expected of them. If they have that, they are happy to be empowered.

Strategy

With regard to strategy, it turned out that it is not so much the chosen strategy that is important – as all characteristics concerning cost leadership, product differentiation and customer intimacy strategies showed no correlation with high performance – but the uniqueness of the strategy compared to competitors in the same industry. Adopting merely a 'me-too' strategy is thus not enough to become an HPO.

Technology/ICT

No correlation was found between technology/ICT and high performance. This may come as a surprise as many organizations spend a lot of time and resources on implementing new information and communication (ICT) systems with the intention to improve organizational performance. This will however not necessarily make them HPOs. Although several of the HPO factors – especially Continuous Improvement & Renewal – cannot be improved without ICT systems, the implementation of new systems and technology in itself does not make the organization perform better for over a longer period of time; such implementations have to support at least one of the HPO factors.[14]

Benchmarking

The study results showed that benchmarking was less effective than expected for improving an organization. When an organization embarks on a benchmarking project it usually aims to identify best practices, emulate these and attain – at best – the same level as the industry's best. HPOs, however, have a completely different view on best practices. They regard competitors' best performance merely as the baseline for performance, a starting point from which HPOs distance themselves as much as possible.[15]

Communication

We often hear top managers saying "We have to communicate more ... then they will understand." However, employees are usually not interested in understanding, they want to be heard. Thus it is not about communication – which can be defined as one-way traffic from manager to employee – but about dialogue. The HPO research showed that communication from managers to employees is not distinguishing for becoming an HPO, but dialogue between managers and employees is. In a dialogue there is two-way communication with listening and hearing on both sides, exchanging ideas and working towards mutual understanding and common understanding. In other words, less soap box speeches and town hall meetings and more round tables.

Bonuses and reward systems

There is a continuous interest in the topic of bonuses and reward systems. The HPO research results show however that such systems are not distinguishing factors for creating and sustaining HPOs but merely hygiene factors. The organization needs to have an appropriate reward system (whether or not including bonuses) which is considered by employees to be fair and equitable. If such a reward system is not in place, the organization will run into trouble and opposition from employees, and becoming an HPO will then be virtually impossible. If such a system is in place – and it does not seem to really matter what type of reward system as long as it is appropriate for the organization in question – employees will consider it normal and will be content, so the organization can start thinking of turning itself into an HPO.

The bonus as hygiene factor: the role of reward systems in the HPO

Ever since the financial scandals that rocked the business world and the worldwide financial crisis that followed, the debate on the effects of bonuses on the performance of especially managers and the role of reward systems in organizations has divided academics and practitioners alike. On one side are the proponents of bonuses, who state that use of bonuses and emphasis on monetary rewards increases productivity and organizational performance. On the other side are the opponents of bonuses and monetary rewards, who state that bonuses create higher pay inequality with as result greater manager and employee turnover, and the long-term effects of bonuses do not seem unequivocal positive. In the polemic between proponents and opponents a key question regarding bonuses is often overlooked: How important is handing out bonuses for an organization to become and stay successful for a longer period of time? A way to obtain an answer to this question is by studying the results of research into the characteristics of HPOs.[16]

In Phase 1 of the HPO research, 12 potential HPO characteristics with respect to bonuses and reward systems were identified:

(1) *A fair reward and incentive structure:* employees have to see that reward systems pay out a fair compensation and that the reward system should value the employees.

(2) *Reward systems that reinforce core values and strategy:* the best organizations devise and implement reward systems that reinforce their core values and strategies.

(3) *Pay and incentives linked to long-term performance:* linking employee pay and incentives to long-term performance of the organization has a positive link with productivity.

(4) *Rewards based on relative performance:* success should be rewarded based on relative performance versus competitors.

(5) *Group compensation:* reward systems should emphasize group performance over individual performance.

(6) *Creative and flexible rewards:* reward systems should reflect the flexibility in the market.

(7) *Pay-for-performance:* people should be rewarded on the basis of performance-based pay, that is, only for the results they achieve.

(8) *Emphasis on intrinsic rewards:* monetary rewards should be restrained in favor of more meaningful intrinsic rewards like fun, personal development, teamwork, challenge, accomplishment.

(9) *Employee stock as incentive:* employees should be rewarded with stock in the company, increasing their commitment and financial interest in the company.

(10) *A minimum threshold for incentive pay and no cap on pay-outs of incentives:* reward systems with a minimum threshold for incentive pay reduce costs whereas reward systems without a cap on pay-outs increase motivation to achieve extraordinary results.

WHAT MAKES A HIGH PERFORMANCE ORGANIZATION

(11) *Skill-based pay:* reward systems should support employees in strengthening their skills by rewarding employees when they develop their knowledge and skills.

(12) *Rewards for results, not efforts or seniority:* employees should be rewarded for their performance and not automatically for getting a year older or for just doing their best.

For the 12 characteristics the weighted importance was calculated and it became apparent that only one characteristic surpassed the threshold of a weighted importance of 9 percent: *a fair reward and incentive structure*. During the empirical study (Phase 2) this remaining characteristic did not show a significant correlation with competitive performance, which means that this characteristic in the end also was *not* related to organizational performance. This leads to the conclusion that having bonuses and reward systems is not a distinguishing factor for creating and sustaining HPOs. Thus, well-performing organizations are as likely to use bonuses or certain types of reward systems as they are not. Using bonuses will therefore not help nor hurt organizations in achieving sustained high performance.

❝At Svenska Handelsbanken we do not have bonuses. We have a profit-sharing system, which is completely different from a bonus system. If the bank reaches the corporate goal – which is to have a higher profitability than our competitors – then part of the profit is set aside for the employees. It is a fixed amount for every employee, no matter if you are CEO or a first year assistant. It is put into a fund where it stays until the employee retires, which gives you a long-term perspective instead of the short-term focus bonuses create. You are interested in how the bank performs in five and ten years because you will not get the money before you retire, in twenty or thirty years. The money is invested on the market with the biggest investment being in Handelsbanken shares. This keeps the interest of employees in the bank's performance. And even if you leave Handelsbanken before you are 60, the money will remain in the fund for you until you are of that age. **"**

Mikael Sørensen, Svenska Handelsbanken

To prevent any misunderstanding: the HPO research does not show that the above-mentioned techniques, methods and activities are not important, some of them actually are. For instance, every organization needs a strategy, no doubt about it. Otherwise there is no course for people to follow. However, merely having a strategy does not make an organization an HPO because competitors also have strategies. The HPO research shows that having a *unique* strategy is distinguishing for becoming an HPO (see also section 6.1).

2.4   HPO factors: evergreens?

An important question is: will the HPO factors presented in this book stand the test of time? [17] Or in other words: will the HPO factors remain basically the same in the years to come and will the HPO Framework be useful in the foreseeable future? Especially the latter is important as managers want to be sure they are doing the right things to ensure the continuation of their organizations. Because HPO research studies by definition look at past experiences of organizations, the results of these studies should not be adopted indiscriminately. Circumstances change and other factors may have come into play. To find out whether the HPO factors and underlying HPO characteristics remain basically the same in the course of time, the HPO Center looked back on the period surrounding the rise of the 'new economy' in the mid-1990s. The 290 studies on high performance, that were examined in Phase 1 of the HPO research, were divided into two groups: studies performed in or before 1995; and studies performed after 1995. The year 1995 was chosen as dividing line because according to general consensus the 'new economy' started around that year. Globalization expanded significantly in the late-1990s, not in the least because of the rapid developments in ICT. At the same time, people became better educated and more articulate. Consequently, the business environment changed: the speed of business increased, competition intensified landscape and employees became more demanding, all of which placed higher demands on management. As an illustration: from 1972 to 1995 the average growth rate of output per hour (a measure of labor productivity) in the USA was around one-percent per year. However, in the early years of the 'new economy' (1995-1999) the average growth rate rose to 2.65 percent.[18]

The HPO characteristics found in the pre-1995 studies were compared with those found in the post-1995 studies. It turned out that almost 90 percent of the characteristics found in the first group were also present in the second group.[19] Thus the HPO characteristics had remained basically the same in a period in which the overall business environment had changed considerably. This is a strong indication that the 35 characteristics of the HPO Framework are most likely 'evergreens of management' and can be regarded as characteristics that are always important for creating and maintaining an excellent organization, and to which managers always have to pay attention when devising the actions they need to undertake to lead their organizations to excellence and superior results. This outcome in itself is not surprising as many researchers state that, even though business environments of organizations change a lot, the competitiveness of the business environment and the work that managers perform do not.[20] The results of the comparison thus give a strong indication that the HPO Framework will be relevant for the future and can be used by organizations with the confidence that it will support them in their transition to HPO.

2.5 What makes the HPO Framework unique?

Since the 1960s practitioners and academics alike have become interested in what makes organizations perform better. This 'quest for excellence' received a major boost by the work of researchers such as Tom Peters and Jim Collins, who wrote best-sellers on high performance.[21] Since their pioneering work many publications on excellence and high performance have appeared. The literature review that was part of the HPO research described in this book encompassed already 290 publications over the period 1960s to 2007 and since that time an estimate of another hundred books and articles have appeared on this topic. So what makes the HPO Framework unique compared to previously developed high performance models?

The main difference concerns the selection of research subjects. Many researchers selected their research population based on financial analyses of organizations that perform excellently in a certain sector and then compared these with competitors that did not perform so well. They then determined the characteristics of high performance on the basis of these comparisons. Making such a selection always brings with it an element of chance: was the correct information available and was the selection based on the right criteria? What if the organizations that were not selected had interesting and maybe even distinguishing characteristics, were these ignored? How can we be sure we have included all the relevant research subjects? In recent years this type of approach to high performance research of comparing the 'good' and the 'bad' is in academic circles considered inadequate.[22] In addition, most of the previous studies concentrated on the Western – predominantly North American – profit market while non-Western countries, including emerging markets and developing countries, and non-profit and governmental organizations were usually not taken into account. This limits a worldwide generalization of the results of these studies as well as the applicability in other than Western organizations.

In the HPO research described in this book no selection was made prior to research. In Phase 1, the studies that were going to be included in the descriptive literature review were not selected beforehand on the basis of 'good' and 'bad'. A broad set of studies from many different scientific disciplines and also the professional literature were studied. It was the most comprehensive literature study ever conducted,[23] which incorporated many different elements about organizational structure, human, emotional, strategic, material, resources, HRM, and the like. In Phase 2, the empirical part of the HPO research, the organizations that participated in the study were not selected in advance. Data were collected through questionnaires and interviews with organizations in many profit, non-profit and government sectors, in Western and non-Western countries, and finally both high, average and low performing organizations were included in the study. The fact that no selection was made in advance made it possible to generalize the outcomes, making them valid for different organizations and in different contexts.[24]

Another way in which the HPO Framework differs from previously developed models of high performance concerns the transparency and completeness of reporting. The reviewed studies often did not provide an exact account of how the data were collected and processed (e.g. which statistical methods were used). Also there was in many of the studies no proof of peer review or expert validation (by other researchers or scientific institutions). In the HPO research, on the other hand, openness was observed during the entire process. It was meticulously documented how the study was conducted and how the data were analyzed and processed. In addition, the research results (both intermediate and final) were regularly presented at scientific conferences and published in academic and practitioner journals. This way, the research was criticized and validated, as is common practice in science, yet not always practiced by all.[25]

A third reason why the HPO Framework and previous models are different has to do with the claims of validity that are being made. Many researchers claim that their findings, which are usually transferred into a model, are always valid in every context. Unfortunately, as many organizations have discovered to their detriment, such a claim cannot be fulfilled as it is impossible to have a magic formula for excellence which will work anytime anywhere anyplace. Many of those models have not been tested over a longer period of time to see whether they actually help organizations create sustainable higher performances. The HPO Center, on the other hand, has included its findings in a framework, not a model. The difference between a framework and a model is that a model is normative, in the sense that it states a set of steps which an organization should follow to achieve better performance, whereas a framework indicates what is important, not how an organization should act. To many people, working with a model has a certain appeal because it looks very practical and rather easy. One only has to follow the steps meticulously – almost without thinking – to improve performance. The question is however: will performance really improve over the long run? Because models bring along a degree of uncertainty as they do not take into account the specific context and characteristics of the organization, such as company history, the features of the industry it operates in, the skills and creativity of its workforce, the culture of the country it is based in. Working with a framework, such as the HPO Framework, has a higher probability for creating high performance because the framework does take the circumstances of the organization into consideration. After the 'what' provided by the framework (as in 'we now know what is important'), the tailoring of the organization, the 'how' (as in 'how we should improve this depends on the organization'), is done by the organization itself. This tailoring as well as the involvement of organizational members increases the probability of high performance considerably. Working with a framework is therefore generally much more effective than working with a model. In addition, the workings of the HPO Framework have been tested in longitudinal research to evaluate whether organizations that used the framework actually experienced an increase in performance over time. It turned out that this was indeed the case (see Chapter 9). The fact that the HPO Framework has been tested repeatedly in real-life situations makes it unique and a proven framework with a high probability of transforming an organization into an HPO.

It is sometimes stated that the HPO factors are nothing new under the sun. The implication being that organizations often have already implemented various quality and improvement models such as the EFQM model, Great Place to Work, Six Sigma or the balanced scorecard in recent years, and with that already addressed several of the HPO characteristics. So what new has the HPO Framework to offer and why spend time, energy and money on it? The fact is however that a lot of these quality and improvement models, as stated before, are not based on scientific findings and have an unproven chance of sustainable success. One could state that the HPO research described in this book identified with the initial 189 characteristics 189 opportunities to improve performance. The HPO research indicates which opportunities are less likely and which are more likely to lead to success. The five HPO factors and the underlying 35 characteristics are thus the opportunities with the highest probability of success.[26]

> ❝The HPO Framework to me is a validated analysis of what makes an organization excellent. A validated framework means that we don't have to research this ourselves. We can use it with great confidence to start our own transition to HPO, to try to move the department as close as possible to the characteristics of the framework, with the idea that if you are able to do this, you will become an HPO. We also find the HPO Framework better validated and certainly more elaborated than other models and frameworks that we know, so we could use it directly and easily.❞
>
> *Martine Ferment, Ziggo*

2.6 Practical application: the HPO Diagnosis

As it has always been the intention of the HPO Center to make the results of the HPO research tangible and practical for organizations, to allow them to use the HPO Framework for improving themselves, the HPO Center developed an HPO Diagnosis, shown in Figure 2.2.

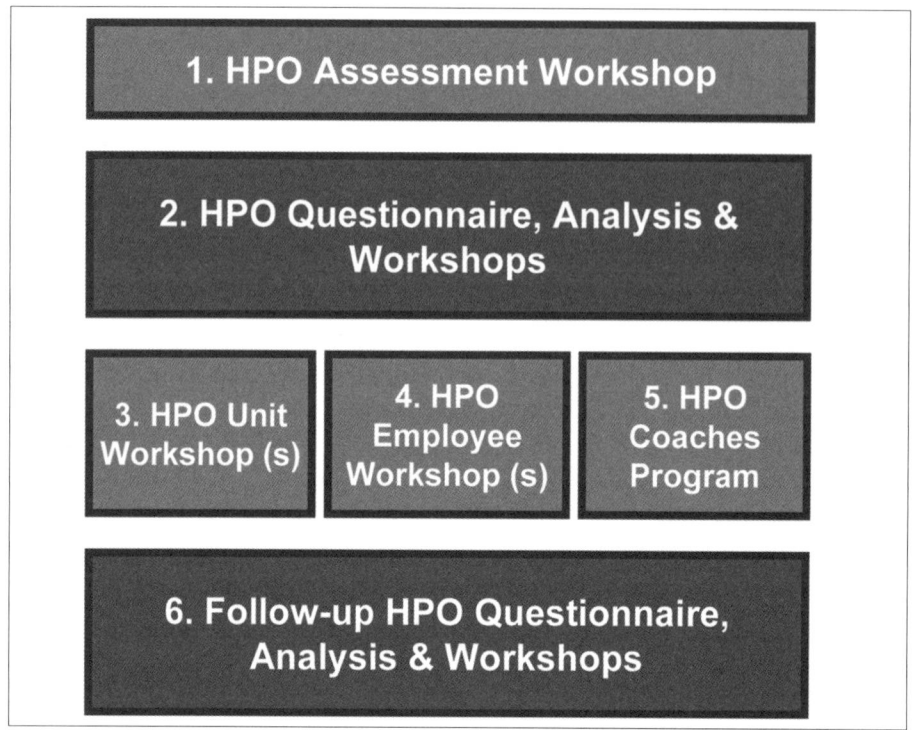

Figure 2.2: The steps of the HPO Diagnosis

The HPO Diagnosis consists of six consecutive steps, with steps 3, 4 and 5 being optional. Step 1 of the HPO Diagnosis consists of a workshop with senior executives in which a short HPO assessment is made of the organization, based on the views of the executives. As part of the assessment participants fill in the HPO Questionnaire, consisting of questions based on the 35 HPO characteristics with possible answers on an absolute scale of 1 (very poor) to 10 (excellent).[27] After this, the HPO scores are calculated and analyzed by the HPO Center. The scores for the five HPO factors (HPO scores) are visualized in a graph. This graph indicates whether the organization is an HPO or not; to be an HPO the average HPO score of each HPO factor has to be at least 8.5. The graph also shows which characteristics need to be improved to increase the performance of the organization. The HPO Framework, the results of the analysis and the HPO graph are discussed with senior executives.

Step 2 of the HPO Diagnosis is a full HPO analysis in which as many people at all levels of the organization fill in the HPO Questionnaire, to obtain a complete picture of the organization. The HPO scores are calculated for the whole organization, its business units and its organizational levels (senior managers, managers, employees). Subsequently, interviews are held by the HPO Center with a selection of staff from across the organization to 'get the stories behind the figures.' The data and interviews are analyzed, to identify the points which have to be improved and strengthened in order for the organization to become an HPO. The analysis results are shared then with senior executives and management in an awareness workshop to increase the understanding of those that will be working with the HPO Framework, as are the current HPO status of the organization and the 'HPO attention points'. This is followed by a call to action workshop in which senior executives, managers and the HPO Center discuss possible actions to address the HPO attention points and an action plan is drawn up. The action plan consists of two parts: (1) What improvement actions are needed to increase the quality of senior executives and managers and make them high performing individuals? (2) What improvement actions are needed to address the HPO attention points of the organization? Furthermore, the roll-out of the HPO Diagnosis in the organization is developed.

During step 3, the HPO Diagnosis is taken a level deeper into the organization. A detailed analysis of the HPO scores is made per organizational unit (department, business unit, country) and additional interviews are held, to identify the HPO attention points for each organizational unit. The analysis results are shared with management and unit heads in an awareness workshop and a call to action workshop. The action plan which is developed during the latter consists of three parts: (1) What improvement actions are needed to increase the quality of the managers and unit heads and make them high performing individuals? (2) What improvement actions are needed to address the HPO attention points of the organizational unit? (3) What improvement actions are needed to address the HPO attention points which lay outside the sphere of influence of the unit and have to be addressed on senior management level? Furthermore, the roll-out of the HPO Diagnosis to the employees in the unit is developed.

In step 4 of the HPO Diagnosis the employees get a full debrief of the HPO scores and attention points of their unit, conducted by the unit's managers and team leaders, coached by the HPO Center. This is again done in an awareness workshop and a call to action workshop. During the latter workshop an action plan is developed consisting of three parts: 1) What improvement actions are needed to increase the quality of the employees to make them high performing individuals? (2) What improvement actions are needed to address the HPO attention points of the organizational unit and what are employees going to contribute? (3) What improvement actions are needed to address the HPO attention points which lay outside the sphere of influence of the unit and have to be addressed on senior management level?

In step 5 a network of HPO Coaches is set up, consisting of people from different units and organizational levels. The task of the HPO Coaches is to promote the HPO culture and support management in its endeavors to make the organization an HPO. The HPO Center trains these HPO Coaches in getting an excellent understanding of the HPO Framework, its application, the organization-specific diagnosis results, and possible ways to improve the HPO attention points. The presence of HPO Coaches promotes HPO leadership in the organization and also makes sure the HPO knowledge stays alive in the organization after the HPO Center has left.

To evaluate which progress the organization has made, a second HPO Diagnosis is conducted in step 6 after 18 to 24 months. The activities of this step are the same as in steps 2, 3 and 4, with the difference that they are performed by the HPO Coaches, who are supported and coached by the HPO Center. The aim of the second diagnosis is not only to see in which units progress was made and in which not, but also to identify additional HPO attention points so further improvements can be achieved.

> "The moments when we saw that things started to become better in the organization came gradually. The first moment was the awareness workshops. During these workshops we talked, managers and employees together, about what was wrong in the organization and what should improve. We used the results of the HPO Diagnosis for that. Recognizing the improvements that needed to be made built a joint foundation. The second moment was the call to action workshops in which we asked people to think about what they could do to improve the situation and how we could set to work with the improvement suggestions put forward during the HPO Diagnosis. In this step we created the feeling that as individuals and as a group we would start to work toward HPO. And the third moment was conducting the so-called Go HPO sessions in which we said: We have made the plans and now we are really going to do it, we are going to work on the improvement suggestions and become HPO!"
>
> *Martine Ferment, Ziggo*

KEY POINTS CHAPTER 2

- The HPO Framework includes five factors of high performance: Management Quality, Openness & Action Orientation, Long-Term Commitment, Continuous Improvement & Renewal, and Employee Quality. Each HPO factor has several underlying HPO characteristics.

- By strengthening the HPO factors, an organization can significantly improve its performance and maintain a superior edge for a long period of time.

- The HPO factors can rightfully be called 'evergreens of management' as they will remain important through time for creating and maintaining an excellent organization. Managers will always have to pay attention to these factors when they devise actions to lead their organizations to excellence and superior results.

- The HPO Framework is not a rigid set of instructions or a blueprint. It is a general framework which managers need to tailor to their own specific organizational situation.

- An organization can identify which HPO factors need to be improved to become an HPO by conducting an HPO Diagnosis.

International bank (the Netherlands): management makes the difference

KEY MESSAGE

Despite the fact that the units of an organization use the same procedures, processes and systems and offer the same products and services, and even may operate in the same market circumstances, they can still achieve different results. A closer look reveals that management and employees of different organizational units focus on different things. The units that are paying specific attention to the HPO characteristics perform the best.

The HPO Center was invited to perform an HPO Diagnosis at a Dutch division of one of the largest multinational banks.[28] One of the bank's divisions sold a broad array of financial products to more than 1 million clients, with 2,500 employees distributed over 200 branches and headquarters. The division was divided into 13 regions, each headed by a management team who managed the sales teams which serviced clients. The sales process of the division consisted of several steps. First, the sales teams visited a (potential) client. After that, proposals were offered to a (potential) client. In the third step, proposals were accepted or declined by the (potential) client. And finally, if a proposal was accepted, a calculation was made of the financial value of the proposal, measured in achieved capital, and it was recorded in the division's ICT system. For example, two loans of €1 million at an interest rate of 2 percent would give an achieved capital of €2 million (and a deal margin of €40,000). The financial result of a region was calculated based on the total achieved capital and the total deal margins.

The HPO status of the division was assessed by distributing the HPO Questionnaire to managers and employees. For each of the

FOUNDATIONS OF THE HPO

13 bank regions the average HPO score was calculated by the HPO Center, and a ranking was made from the highest scoring region to the lowest scoring region. Then, the financial results over the past three years were collected for all 13 regions, and a ranking was made from the regions with the best financial results over those three years to the regions with the lowest financial results. Finally, the HPO Center matched both rankings. The result is given in Table 2.2.

	HPO ranking	Region	Region	Financial results ranking
highest	1	1	1	1
	2	12	3	2
	3	3	12	3
	4	9	10	4
	5	8	9	5
	6	13	13	6
	7	4	8	7
	8	5	4	8
	9	10	2	9
	10	2	5	10
	11	11	6	11
	12	7	7	12
lowest	13	6	11	13

Table 2.2: HPO ranking versus the financial results ranking for the 13 bank regions

The matching yielded a clear group of 'HPO leaders' which showed both the highest HPO scores and the highest results: regions 1, 3 and 12. The comparison also gave a clear group of 'HPO laggards' which showed both the lowest HPO scores and the lowest results: regions 6, 7 and 11. For many of the remaining regions the match between the HPO scores and the financial results was quite close. The context was the same for all regions as they all used the same management systems, products, processes and IT systems. All regions were therefore operating in the same manner and differences in HPO scores could only be explained by differences in management and employee quality in the regions and differences in the way they behaved and emphasized specific actions and issues. To evaluate whether this was really the case the HPO Center conducted a series of interviews at one of the leading regions (region 1) and one of the lagging regions (region 7). These regions were chosen as the HPO Center expected to find the strongest differences at the top and bottom of the ranking. The interviews revealed that the regions had different degrees of attention for the HPO characteristics. Below are a number of interview questions and answers from the managers of regions 1 and 7, to illustrate the differences in attitude and behavior.

How do you engage your employees in dialogue and important processes?

Region 1: "That is always difficult as you only have so many hours in a day. But I visit every branch at least every two months and then I stay a whole day. Not just talking to the branch manager, I arrive an hour early and then I walk around on the shop floor so I can easily speak with the employees. In those conversations you as boss have to take the first step by opening up about your affairs and what is going on in the region. This will build the trust needed for a good dialogue. You also have to be transparent about what you are doing with the suggestions and complaints you get from employees, you have to *show* you take these seriously."

Region 7: "Management used to sit here in their ivory tower, people hardly ever saw them let alone that management ever asked employees for ideas or suggestions. And even when the previous director spoke to them, they would normally give socially acceptable answers. When I came here I had a hard time getting straight, honest answers from employees. If people didn't agree with me they wouldn't talk to me but complain to each other, and I would hear about it indirectly."

How do you go about improving the region?

Region 1: "I have set up what I call an active moaning system. I put a lot of pressure on people to increase productivity and efficiency and I know that if something in the processes prevents them from achieving better results, they will start to moan about it to me. Then I know in which part of the process to focus the improvement effort and I can do something about it, quickly. An added advantage is that people see that I take their complaints seriously, so they are more motivated to help fix the problems. Sometimes you cannot implement certain improvements when managers higher up the hierarchy decide there are other priorities. Then you have to be honest and say 'Hey guys, this cannot be solved, so let's move on.' This way, you keep your credibility. Another thing we do when we are undertaking an improvement project is to have daily heartbeat sessions. In these sessions, we get management and employees together early in the morning and discuss the state of affairs: What is going right? What wrong? Have we seen any benefits of the improvements yet? What are the problems? Who is going to fix them? What happened to yesterday's problems? This way you keep on top of the improvement process."

Region 7: "To be honest, we kind of have a zigzag policy in this respect. One day we are doing this and the next day we are doing that. This is because we have an attitude of 'let's go!', if we have a good idea we go for it, right away. We don't really question the constant course changes as we are real go-getters. And if an improvement idea comes from headquarters we tend to wait out the storm and then go back to our own ideas."

How do you make sure your region services its customers optimally?

Region 1: "We have close relations with our customers. We make it our business to know as much as possible about customers and we talk regularly to them to keep up-to-date with their situation and possible needs, wants and demands. In addition, every year we choose a theme on which the region will focus. These themes always have to do with customers. This year, for example, we have the theme 'surprise the customer' where we look at ways to do something extra for the customers so they will be pleasantly surprised. And we all participate in this theme, not only the employees but also management who in fact start off the theme by surprising employees. At the last meeting, I had brought along a rose for every employee to let them experience what it is to be pleasantly surprised."

Region 7: "To be quite frank, we could be a bit more customer-oriented. I will give you an example that happened last Monday. Some people had made a mess outside at the cash machine during the weekend and no one had bothered to clean it up so customers couldn't use the machine. Somebody in the office said they had called the cleaning company who would come over later this afternoon but I said this was way too late. It concerns our customers and we have to treat them with all regards, and having a mess on the doorstep isn't that. It should have been fixed right away!"

Is your strategy different from that of your competitors?

Region 1: "One of the major differences with our competitors is that we're not looking for a quick buck but for long-term benefit. For example, despite the recession we have hired many sales trainees and we have given these a good education, while our competitors did exactly the opposite and send many trainees home. Now business is picking up and we have skilful and knowledgeable people in both our front and back offices while the other banks are struggling to hire new, qualified people. I also spend a lot of time explaining our strategy to the branches because it is especially branch people who have to know and understand the strategy. After all, they are the ones that make the difference to our customers."

Region 7: "Headquarters announces the strategy to us and we basically follow it. It frustrates me that people in the branches here are not that concerned about the strategy but worry more about what the other branches in the region are doing and how these are performing, and whether people at the other branches will get higher bonuses."

How do you increase the speed of decision-making and action-taking?

Region 1: "Short communication lines and discipline. If I decide this afternoon that we need a conference call the next morning at eight o'clock, I can contact my people directly and everybody knows he or she has to participate in the call, no exceptions. For this to be successful you need engaged people, people who are strongly committed to the company and in addition to that willing to go the extra mile."

Region 7: "We still have a culture of 'saying yes, doing no.' This is inefficient because it can take quite a while before you discover that the things you thought would be done have not been taken care of at all. Why make any agreements when half of the people are not sticking to it anyway? It leads to a sliding scale where more and more people think: why bother to do this when nobody else does?"

Not surprisingly, the general atmosphere at region 1, the leading region, was much better than at region 7, the lagging region; management was genuinely interested in employees and clients, and people focused more on improvement and integrity. On the basis of the HPO Diagnosis the division was able to discover 'best ideas', for example activities of regions which proved to be very successful and from which other regions could and should learn, not necessarily by copying these ideas but by thinking about the ideas, tailoring these to the specific situation of the region and then implementing the adapted idea.

Retail International Group (Europe/Asia/South America): learning from the 'best countries'

KEY MESSAGE

Because the HPO Diagnosis uses an absolute scale of 1 to 10, it is possible to compare the performances of multiple country divisions to identify which country divisions are 'more HPO' than others. Thus, best ideas for improving the HPO factors can be identified from 'the best' country divisions, from which other divisions can learn. At the same time, because the HPO Framework shows *what* is important without dictating *how* the HPO factors should be improved, each country division should tailor these best ideas to their local circumstances.

Retail International Group (RIG) is a retailer which operates in 21 countries in Europe, Asia and South America.[29] The company sells fashion accessories in more than 850 shops with almost 11,000 employees. The turnover of the group is over €1 billion. RIG's headquarters are based in Europe and consist of the board of management and several staff departments such as Corporate Controlling and Corporate Human Resources. The company has a highly decentralized structure in which responsibility for operations lays with the individual country divisions. These country divisions consist of regional headquarters, with management and support staff, and stores. Each store is manned by a store manager and store staff. Each country division typically carries several formulas, from a cheap brand to high-end luxury goods. Each formula has a different name but the information systems and logistical processes are the same for all formulas, while inventory is held in central warehouses in the different countries. The goods are designed both at corporate headquarters and at the country division and are manufactured in the Far East, after which they are directly shipped to the central warehouses in the different countries.

Each formula typically has some well-selling products which stay in the assortment for several years, and products which only last one season. In contrast to the standardized logistical processes, the management systems (for reporting, evaluation and rewards) are tailored to each country due to local (legal) requirements. RIG management characterizes the company with the words: customer focused, professional, ambitious and decentralized; and demands from its employees that they act with integrity, are open to each other, and are result oriented. Integrity is seen by management as a powerful replacement for expensive and elaborate control systems; if someone's professional or personal integrity is in question, that person will have to leave the company. For RIG to be a learning organization, openness is a precondition as people can only learn from one another if they are willing to share not only their experiences and successes but also their problems. Result-orientation is important because retailing is a low-margin industry with strong competition, which requires all people to focus on achieving their targets in order to survive and thrive.

RIG's chief executive officer explained the reasons why the group decided to do an HPO Diagnosis as follows: "The HPO Framework provides us with a comprehensive framework which allows us to: evaluate where we stand today and how we should progress, categorize the wide variety of improvement initiatives we have, structure the improvement opportunities, and highlights areas on which we have to focus more going forward. We need this as competition is mounting and good is not good enough anymore. We have spent the past years getting our house in order, it is now time to take the next step forward and to fulfill our potential. Getting RIG to the next level will not require bold changes but incremental improvements, and that's where the HPO Framework comes in. It is not a quick fix but promotes a steady and continuous improvement effort. The framework also gives us the opportunity to evaluate current improvement initiatives and to ask ourselves: Are these the right initiatives or should we be doing other things?"

FOUNDATIONS OF THE HPO

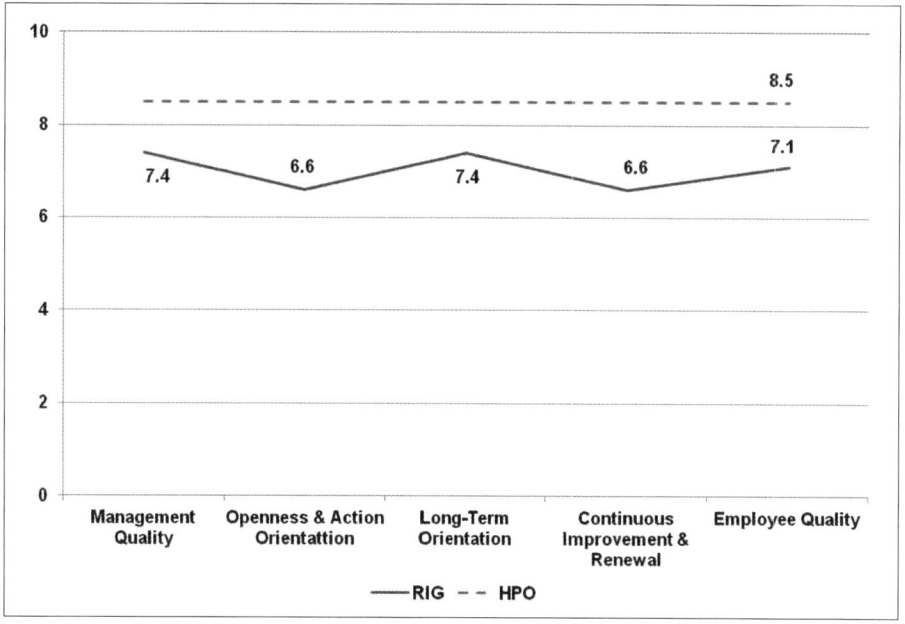

Figure 2.3: HPO status of Retail International Group

The HPO Diagnosis process was started by distributing the HPO Questionnaire among managers and employees in nine country divisions, both at regional headquarters and in the stores.[30] Additionally, interviews were held by the HPO Center at four country divisions. The data were analyzed by the HPO Center to determine the HPO status. Figure 2.3 shows that RIG, with an average HPO score of 7, was a well-performing organization but not yet an HPO.

For each of the nine country divisions the average HPO score was calculated by the HPO Center, and a ranking was made from the highest scoring country division to the lowest scoring country division. Then the financial results over the past five years were collected for the nine country divisions, and a ranking was made from the country divisions with the best financial results over those five years to the country divisions with the lowest financial results. Finally, the HPO Center matched both rankings. The result is given in Table 2.3

	Average HPO scores	Country divisions	Country divisions	Financial results ranking
highest	7,9	A	A	1
	7,8	F	F	2
	7,4	D	C	3
	7,3	C	D	4
	7,3	I	H	5
	6,4	G	I	6
	5,9	H	G	7
	5,8	B	B	8
lowest	4,9	E	E	9

Table 2.3: Average HPO scores versus financial results of nine country divisions

Table 2.3 shows that there was a direct link visible within RIG between the average HPO scores and the financial results: the country divisions that had the highest HPO scores (A, F) also had the highest financial results, and country divisions with the lowest HPO scores (B, E) had the lowest financial results. It showed that the performance situation at RIG had been assessed quite well with the HPO Diagnosis, and implementing the HPO improvements suggestions would mean the financial results of the country divisions were to improve substantially for a longer period of time. The results of the HPO Diagnosis, including strengths and weaknesses and improvement suggestions for the overall group and each of its country divisions and corporate headquarters, were presented by the HPO Center during a meeting with the entire management of the group. Subsequently the improvement suggestions were prioritized. The two most important ones are summarized below.

HPO improvement suggestion 1: Create a stronger and more visible management

During the interviews conducted by the HPO Center as part of the HPO Diagnosis, it emerged that employees were looking for stronger role models at all management levels of the organization. They also wanted better coaching from managers who should show more interest in humans and less interest in financial figures. This would increase employees' trust in management. An employee put it as follows: "We have seen a lot of new management, each time a new strategy, as if to prove they were in charge. But we would like to see that management sees what happens on the floor, visits us in the stores, listens to what we need. Management by walking around. Listen! And quick follow-up on the problems of employees is vital to improve confidence and trust." Thus, there seemed to be a real need for increased accountability and visibility of managers on the store floor. An employee commented: "I have an intense dialogue with regional management. However, I would like to see that top management visits the stores more. If they do that, different decisions would be made. For instance, it is easy to make the decision from a distance that some stores only need one employee. However, they don't know the consequences, how it feels to work alone while four customers are waiting. Since they don't know that feeling, the wrong decisions are easily made." A store manager had a nice idea: "When the regional manager comes in the store, he now gives everybody a hand and then takes me to a corner of the store and starts telling me all the things that have to be improved. What I would like him to do is to give me a hand when entering the store and then talk with the employees to ask them how it is going and what suggestions they have for improvement."

Evidently RIG's managers had to concentrate on better coaching and being more decisive in order to become high performing managers. They also had to start visiting stores more often and during these visits listen attentively to employees' questions and ideas and follow up on these.

HPO improvement suggestion 2: Make dialogue more sincere and 'richer'

Within RIG there seemed to be confusion about the meaning of the words 'communication' and 'dialogue'. A lot of meetings were being held all over the group but the HPO scores and interviews revealed that people of all organizational levels wanted more dialogue and better information sharing. There existed a feeling among people that they were not really listened to by higher levels. The newly appointed corporate HR manager commented: "When I started at RIG, I overheard store managers complaining about regional managers not listening enough to them, regional managers complaining about country managers not acknowledging them, country managers complaining about corporate managers only imposing all kinds of initiatives on them without giving them room for their own ideas, and corporate managers complaining about the supervisory board not listening to them enough. The need for better dialogue was very clear to me." A side effect of the lack of openness created by the lack of dialogue was that distrust started to arise which resulted in people blaming each other for their misfortunes. As an interviewee said: "When performance is poor the first reaction of people is to point fingers at each other. People insufficiently reflect on themselves and what the effect of their behavior is on others. We should give more constructive and positive feedback." As an almost logical consequence stores and also departments in country headquarters hardly did any knowledge sharing, as a manager pointed out: "Each unit tends to operate as a silo. This appears difficult to break through. Also employees want to be more involved and require more performance information about their own results and that of the company."

It was thus evident that RIG had to improve the openness of the organization, starting with a review of the reporting process, the meetings in which performance information was shared, and the performance information sharing process from corporate and country division headquarters towards the regions and shops. In this respect RIG had to look for ways to enhance both the formal and informal information processes by proactively encouraging people to share performance information. Furthermore, managers needed to concentrate on improving openness through sincere dialogues.

Looking back at the HPO Diagnosis and the subsequent actions that were taken, the Corporate Human Resources manager told us: "Because the HPO Framework caught on well within the company, we decided to make the HPO improvement suggestions part of our strategy and budget cycle for next year. This meant that country division management explicitly had to develop initiatives for the improvement suggestions, for which they were given budget. We also found that the HPO Framework worked as a management development tool because it focused the attention of management on the things that really matter which otherwise might have been overlooked or even ignored. The HPO Framework helped to develop the competency within managers to focus, prioritize and stay on course. To give an example of how important focusing was: our process improvement efforts. We were constantly improving and simplifying our processes but we had great difficulty managing these improvement projects, partly because there were so many of them. The HPO Framework learned us to prioritize: all improvement projects that did not support at least one of the HPO factors we should skip, and we did. And since the HPO Diagnosis, RIG experienced improved results. This might have been a coincidence but I don't think so."

Ministry of Local Governance and Social Affairs (Rwanda): working on HPO in government

KEY MESSAGE

The HPO database contains a lot of data from the governmental sector and the five HPO factors have also been validated for this sector. This means that the HPO Framework is, in addition to profit companies, also useful for governmental institutions to focus their improvement efforts. This is demonstrated by the case study of MINALOC.

The Republic of Rwanda is a small landlocked country of 26,338 km² with a population of more than 10 million people, in the Great Lakes region of East-Central Africa and bordered by Uganda, Burundi, the Democratic Republic of the Congo and Tanzania.[31] A country of fertile and hilly terrain, the small republic bears the title 'Land of a Thousand Hills'. As part of the Rwandan government, the main mission of the Ministry of Local Governance and Social Affairs (MINALOC) is 'promoting the well-being of the population by good governance, community development and social affairs'. The Ministry has several main objectives: putting in place decentralized administrative units in order to implement government programs locally; ensuring synergy and collaboration between government institutions so they can support the local units; strengthening the local units so they can execute the programs effectively; putting in place mechanisms for assistance of vulnerable groups, especially genocide survivors; and implementing coordination mechanisms to deal with disasters. The Ministry itself is comparatively small (approximately 60 people) but has several semi-independent units such as the National Electoral Commission (NEC), the Rwanda Governance Advisory Council (RGAC) and the National Assistance Fund for Needy Survivors of Genocide (FARG) to execute the programs. MINALOC is known in Rwanda as being one of the most effective ministries and as such the Public Secretary (the first civil servant after the Minister) was very interested in applying the HPO Framework in order to evaluate whether the framework could help MINALOC to improve its performance toward HPO.

During an HPO workshop representatives of the Ministry and its semi-independent units filled in the HPO Questionnaire. Figure 2.4 gives the scores of MINALOC on the five HPO factors. The average HPO score is 7.5 which shows that MINALOC was a good performing organization but not yet an HPO.[32] MINALOC's HPO curve was almost level which meant that it was a well-balanced organization. This constituted a good starting-point for improvement at MINALOC.

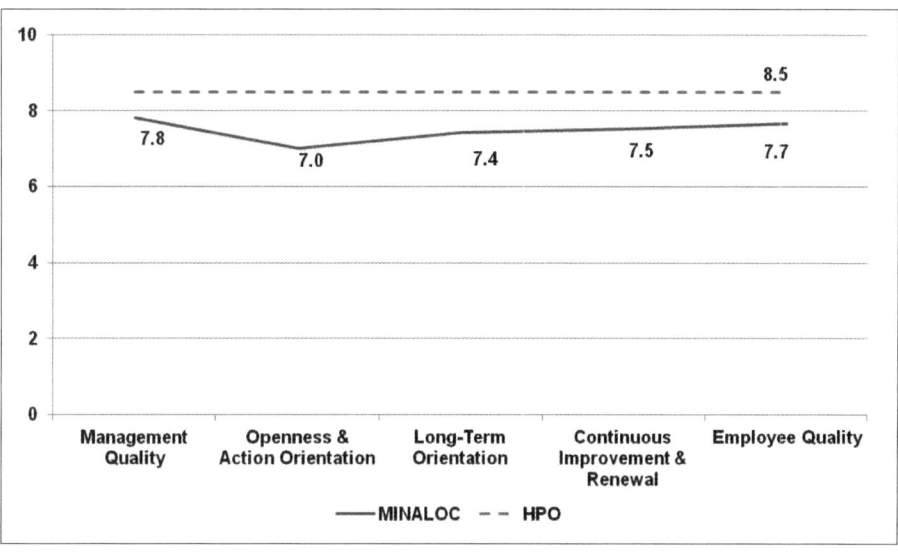

Figure 2.4: HPO status of MINALOC

During the HPO workshop three main attention points were discussed, which MINALOC needed to address in order to become a high performance governmental organization. Attention point 1 was that MINALOC had to improve its process improvement process. Although the ministry's processes were continuously improved, they were not simplified and aligned enough. The reason for this was that MINALOC was a complex organization of a small ministry with many semi-independent units and cooperations with other governmental institutions. Thus MINALOC had to perform a bundle of coordinating tasks on behalf of many parties, which made for many complicated processes which were difficult to simplify. Recommendations to deal with this attention point were to strengthen local authorities as they were the ones that should implement the programs; reinforce the decentralization process for other ministerial processes so that these ministries could deal with local units themselves and no longer needed MINALOC for that; and from now on only finish a limited number of improvement projects in time, within budget, with the required results before starting new process improvements.

Attention point 2 was that MINALOC had to improve its appraisal process as it allowed non-performers to stay too long and did not enough promote new management from within. One of the reasons for this was that poor performers were given too much time, often years, to improve themselves. Another reason was that there existed the possibility of performance appraisal bias so some low-performing employees got a performance rating which was too high. By law there was a limit for government employees: if they got three times a performance appraisal score below 70 they would be fired. It was therefore likely that management rated poor performers higher to prevent them from getting fired. Firing was generally not preferred because of its serious consequences to family well-being. Finally, labor laws limited promotion from within, vacancies had to be offered to people outside the organization to prevent nepotism. Because of this, well-performing people felt they had to leave the Ministry for real promotion opportunities. Recommendations to deal with this attention point were to make the performance appraisal process more objective and realistic and to use standards for the interpretation of rating scales. In a broader context, the labor law should be changed to allow internal promotions and to develop an internal promotion process that is transparent in order to prevent nepotism.

Attention point 3 was that MINALOC had to improve knowledge sharing. Employees did not sufficiently share knowledge with colleagues at other MINALOC units. The reason for this was that, in the decentralized MINALOC organization, the units still operated mainly independently and did not actively get together to share knowledge, ideas and experiences. In addition, there was so much work to do that there was not enough time available or taken for knowledge sharing activities. Possible solutions were to actively develop a culture which encouraged knowledge sharing skills and reward people for sharing knowledge. The representatives agreed that they were part of a bigger entity and that, even if individuals or units performed well but MINALOC as a whole was not performing well, no one at MINALOC was regarded successful by society.

The case study of MINALOC showed that the HPO Framework could be used to assess the strengths and weaknesses of a governmental organization. MINALOC's representatives stated that the HPO Framework provided them with the coordinating framework to direct and guide future improvement efforts.

Chapter 3
HPO factor 1 – Management Quality: *without good management there is no HPO*

MANAGEMENT QUALITY

Chapter preview

Managing comes down to dealing with people. It doesn't matter how many tools and techniques managers implement, if they cannot motivate people to use these for improving their performance, they haven't achieved anything. After all, the HPO research shows that the most important factor which determines whether the organization will become and remain an HPO is the quality of its management. The attitudes and behaviors of managers are essential for the success of the organization. Excellent managers are thus the foundation of the HPO.

This chapter discusses the 12 characteristics of the HPO factor Management Quality. A definition is given for each characteristic followed by a description of the behaviors of HPO managers and employees that is typical of the characteristic.[33] In addition, a number of 'ideas to get started' are listed to improve the characteristic discussed.[34] The application of the characteristics in practice is illustrated by recounting the behaviors of a successful catering manager with whom the HPO Center came into contact during the research into the characteristics of an HPO manager. This manager was appointed when the restaurant wasn't doing too well. Because of his notable way of working, the manager was able to create a smoothly running restaurant, with professional, motivated and happy employees and the highest profitability of all the restaurants in the restaurant chain. It turned out that the catering manager stressed many of the 12 characteristics belonging to the HPO factor Management Quality.[35] The story of the catering manager also illustrates the point that the HPO factor Management Quality is valid for every manager in the organization, not only top management.[36] In an HPO all managers at every organizational level have to be excellent performers.

3.1 Trust

Trust is defined as 'a firm belief in the reliability, truth or strength of a person.' The HPO research shows that being trusted is the most important characteristic for a manager to become a true HPO manager, and that in fact it is not possible to create an HPO without trusted management.[37] There is a strong connection between trust and the others characteristics of the HPO factor Management Quality and with many of the characteristics of the other four HPO factors. It turns out that when managers work on improving any of those HPO characteristics, they are at the same time working on increasing the trust of employees in them. And only if enough managers work on trust, a high-trust organization can be created.

HPO managers create trust among their employees by displaying behaviors such as: being honest[38] and forthright, showing respect, listening, learning, asking for help, showing trust themselves, and in general exhibiting elemental fairness in the way employees are treated by them. HPO managers endeavor to create and maintain individual relationships with their employees, by knowing and dialoguing with employees and staying in touch with them. When HPO managers feel the need to criticize employees they only do it when these employees are present and preferably in a bilateral conversation. HPO managers are fair during decision-making and in valuing contributions of employees and recognize these by giving credit.

HPO FACTOR 1 – MANAGEMENT QUALITY

The catering manager and creating trust

The catering manager we spoke to has worked for a long time in the catering industry and understands the work his employees are doing. The employees get clear guidelines from the catering manager in which they are free to operate as they like. In addition, the catering manager gives them responsibility to achieve their results and then trust them to do so, and he also listens to new ideas from the employees. They call the catering manager a trustworthy manager because of his vision on the restaurant, his consistency in operating, and the fact that he is often found on the shop floor to lend a hand when it is busy. During peak hours the catering manager is always, every day, present to work together with his people to manage the rush hours. Through this role model, the catering manager creates trust.

IDEAS TO GET STARTED TO CREATE TRUST DURING THE HPO TRANSITION

Trust is a characteristic that is difficult to improve as you cannot gain trust by asking for it or demanding it from your employees. In addition, as the saying goes, trust comes on foot and leaves by horse. It takes time to build a trust relation, trust has to be earned, but it can be easily lost. The good news is that you can actively work on creating and strengthening trust during the transition to HPO. This is what you can do: [39]

- You first need to find out what your employees know and do not know about HPO, how they feel about HPO and what their concerns about the transition are. This way you can address misguided opinions and thoughts that employees might have about HPO.

- You formulate together with employees objectives for the transition to HPO and the role of each person during the transition. This clarifies the objectives of the transition and everybody's role in it.

- You evaluate together with employees how HPO will affect everybody. You talk about how you will guide and support them during the transition.

- You determine together with employees the resources needed for the transition. Because there always is a lack of resources, this makes employees better understand what and how many resources can be made available.

- You make sure that everyone continuously receives information on the progress of the HPO transition and the results achieved so far. Continuous communication ensures that people do not spread rumors about the transition that may cause tension within the organization.

- You ask employees for feedback on any unclear issues and (potential) problems during the HPO transition.

- You regularly evaluate together with employees the progress of the HPO transition. The review gives you the opportunity to communicate with your employees about what is going on and discuss items which went wrong. It also entails checking whether both you and your employees have kept your promises about what everybody was going to contribute during the transition.

❝Trust is very important at SABMiller. If I trust someone, it means I can work with that person and I can ask honest questions. Because what I am basically testing is their thinking process, logic, insights, and how they arrived at those insights. I cannot go back and check the raw data, so if they say to me, "We are going to take a five percent increase on this brand, and this is the reason why I believe that we should do it, we have done elasticity studies and competitive benchmark surveys, and we have looked at the equity of our brand through our consumer research and our monthly tracking" then I have to trust their judgement. So I am checking the building blocks: how did they get to that decision? That is what I am probing the whole time. Am I comfortable that they have done a professional job of looking at the data and building up their case to get to this decision? All of that is based on trust that they do a good job and are open and honest to me. When that trust relationship breaks down, you cannot manage the business. We have ways of picking up if something is not right. The most obvious is in the actual governance: financial controls, an internal audit department. The other way is that we make sure – not because we are suspicious but because we believe it is a way of controlling integrity – that there is a mix of people in the organization. So we have people who are long term SABMiller managers who we put into the local organization quite quickly. And we know that they have a stronger loyalty to SABMiller than to the local operation and they will pull me to the side and say: "I think you should check this." When trust cracks, that is it, it is over. There are no second chances in our organization with trust. If you lose your trustworthiness: pack your bags and go, because we are going to end the relationship anyway."

Alan Clark, SAB Miller Europe

3.2 Integrity

Integrity is defined as 'moral uprightness.' HPO managers show their integrity by having a strong set of ethics and standards according to which they live and practice business. They practice what they preach and walk the talk, thereby displaying behavioral consistency. Employees and colleagues see them because of that as being credible and consistent. In addition, HPO managers ensure that the values of the organization are maintained and valued by everybody, thus creating a morally intelligent organization.[40] Finally, they do not try to win a popularity contest with employees and colleagues but treat everybody in the same way, always.

> ### *The catering manager and integrity*
> *Once, when one of the employees wasn't communicating very well with customers and colleagues, the catering manager took this employee aside and discussed the problem at length with him. Then they made a plan together to remedy the problem. The catering manager creates strict rules that are valid for everyone, thus he creates a clear playing field. One of these rules is that employees rotate among different work activities so that everybody every once in a while does the less desirable duties such as operating the sink. The catering manager is consistent in guarding the playing field and making sure everybody sticks to the agreements, including and foremost he himself.*

> ## IDEAS TO GET STARTED TO FOSTER INTEGRITY IN THE ORGANIZATION
>
> Integrity is, like trust, a characteristic that is difficult to improve. It seems you either have it or you don't. However, you can start creating an environment of integrity by doing the following:
>
> - Make 'integrity' one of the organization's core values and make sure everybody knows it.
> - Ensure that there is only one standard of integrity throughout the company. Ingrain this standard so much in the organization's DNA that the meaning of integrity is constant and not affected by the chief executive officer who is in charge at the time.
> - Install integrity procedures to describe how to develop, foster and maintain ethical decision making.

HPO FACTOR 1 – MANAGEMENT QUALITY

- Formulate integrity metrics for each business process. Hold managers accountable for positive results on these performance indicators.

- Discuss ethics and integrity frequently and openly during all kinds of meetings.

- Reward people for blowing the whistle on ethical and integrity breaches. Employees should not have to be afraid to hold their managers accountable for integrity problems.

- Check that there is no disconnection between the organizational targets and integrity, so that people do not have to resort to unethical activities to achieve the targets.

❝The issue with integrity is not so much about things going wrong – as in business there is always something going wrong – but about how one responds to that. So, you are not trying to check if people are doing things perfectly all the time. It is about whether they are open and transparent about what they do, that they do not hide their problems. There is an ongoing dialogue between us about what we are trying to achieve in this business. You know, conversations can get very heated, we can disagree. I can say, "Look, I have seen this data and this is your strategy, I disagree with that strategy and this is what you should be taking into account, and I really think you have ignored this and you need to go after this." And then, the manager either accepts what you just said and says, "I acknowledge we missed these things, we are going to change this", or the manager says, "You were here last week, you challenged these things. I have looked at it again and I am convinced that what I am thinking is the right thing to do." And frankly, most often my judgment will be to let the manager do what he has decided, I trust his integrity that he has done what he said. In fact, people here take bad performance personally, it literally upsets them. They have so much integrity that they are very determined to solve the issue, they have got to fix it, no matter what.*"*

Alan Clark, SAB Miller Europe

3.3 A strong role model

A role model is defined as 'a person looked to by others as an example in a particular role.' Research has shown that a member of the family is for most people their most important role model in life. The second most important role model however changes in the course of time: for people between 18 and 30 it is a teacher or a coach, for people over 30 it is a business leader. This business leader is not necessarily a top manager but more often a direct supervisor, thus the person to whom someone reports directly and works with daily.[41] This means that every manager at every organizational level has to be a good role model because they have the most influence on employees' motivation, loyalty, commitment and performance. Employees listen to what their managers do and not to what they say, so managers have to lead by doing and thus give the right behavioral example.

HPO managers set this example by always being committed, engaged, enthusiastic, positive. They act boldly in times of crisis while keeping a perspective, do not easily give up, put in the hard work themselves, and are always visible as a leader during trying times. HPO managers are not arrogant and in fact solicit for strong opinions and counteractions so their own ideas are challenged in a way that makes them better. They try hard to be a role model, not only for employees and colleagues, but also for partners and clients. In this way, the HPO manager creates a value chain with parties who trust each other completely.

> ### *The catering manager and being a role model*
>
> *As mentioned before, the catering manager has years of experience in the industry, among others as a cook. Because of this he has a lot of knowledge of food products, preparation techniques, and presenting the food attractively. Employees feel challenged by the catering manager to become as knowledgeable as he is. In addition, the catering manager*

HPO FACTOR 1 – MANAGEMENT QUALITY

shows through his actions that quality is number one to him. Not just quality of the products served by the restaurant but also quality of the way customers are treated. Instead of bombarding employees with his opinions on quality, he shows them through behavior what is important.

"At Microsoft our top managers are really seen as role models. Using interaction with our chief executive officer Steve Ballmer as an example, when you give him a presentation he flips through the slides and after two minutes he has internalized it and launches into discussion. Open, direct, and respectful. He expects feedback in the same manner, and is looking for healthy debate and dissonance. I also think he is very approachable. For example, if I need a one-on-one meeting with Steve because something is troubling me, I will be able to quickly get half an hour with him. And that is not because I'm an executive at the company, we simply have open and direct communication channels. Steve sets a good example, and one I am trying to follow. If people approach me I try to be as open and welcoming as Steve is. This openness is a core value of Microsoft."

Rik van der Kooi, Microsoft USA

IDEAS TO GET STARTED TO BECOME A ROLE MODEL

In order to become a role model, it is important that you do the following:

- Look for a role model for yourself. This can be a person inside or outside the organization – and maybe somebody from your past: a previous employer, a teacher or a professor – someone

> you highly respect and whose behavior inspires and enthuses you. Study this person, talk to this person and above all, learn from this person.
>
> - Develop emphatic behavior which makes it possible for you to put yourself in someone else's shoes. This way you can see and experience your behavior from that person's viewpoint. Thus, you can evaluate whether your actions have positive effects on employees and whether your behavior can be characterized as role model behavior.
>
> - Ask personal feedback from individual employees and colleagues in an informal and non-threatening environment. Let them comment on your behavior and whether they see you as a role model. Doing this regularly will give you frequent updates on your 'status' as role model.
>
> - Never forget you were once an employee yourself.

❝Quality of management has to come from the top. That is quite obvious naturally, but I mean that the longevity of the chief executive officer and the focus of that individual at the top is absolutely critical. And if that individual is successful in doing what he or she is setting out to do, it will spread far and deep, down to the front lines. Then you have your army out there. If it is living and breathing you have created a culture. I think the culture we have here really is what differentiates us and what keeps people here. Our chief executive officer, Ray Davis, developed a vision for the company. But in the 14 years he has worked here, it has gone beyond him. And that is good because the culture is now stronger than ever and has the ability to withstand change, even change in leadership.❞

Lani Hayward, Umpqua Bank

3.4 Fast decisions

Decision-making is defined as 'the process of deciding, in which a conclusion or resolution is reached.' Research has found managers basically use four decision-making styles:

- *Decisive*: a manager values action, speed, efficiency and consistency in decision-making and once a decision has been made he or she sticks to it and moves on to the next decision.

- *Flexible*: a manager values speed and adaptability, getting just enough information to choose a certain action and changing that decision when deviant information becomes available.

- *Hierarchical*: a manager values getting much information and first extensively analyzing that before making a decision that will be adhered to for a long time.

- *Integrative*: a manager values options and therefore taking broad decisions which leave many courses of action open.

It turns out that HPO managers change their decision-making style during their career. Early on, when they are a lower-level manager like a supervisor, they put emphasis on the decisive style. This is because the work they supervise is operational of nature and requires a focus on getting things done. When moving up the organizational ladder, HPO managers put less emphasis on the decisive style and more and more on the flexible and integrative decision-making styles. This is because decision-making at higher organizational levels is more about listening, understanding, the long term, getting cooperation and buy-in. Non-HPO managers however stick to the decisive style and therefore become less effective.[42] In addition, HPO managers make their decisions quickly. They do not suffer from 'paralysis by analysis': they do not overanalyze but balance thought and action. These managers take enough time for adequate decision-making but then turn their decisions quickly into actions to solve problems immediately.

IDEAS TO GET STARTED TO STIMULATE FAST DECISION-MAKING

It is important that the organizational structure supports rather than hinders the decision-making process, which means that it has to be clear which functions in which organizational units and levels have to make which decisions. To get the right decision structure in the organization, you have to do the following:

- Identify the organization's key decisions, which are the decisions that will have a major impact on value creation and therefore are critical to the success of the company. To this end, ask yourself for every decision: For which good business reason should we do this?

- Determine where in the organization those decisions should be taken.

- Organize the organizational chart around the places where value-influencing decisions are made.

- Decide what level of authority decision makers need to be able to make the value-influencing decisions quickly.

- Align other elements of the organizational system, such as information systems and processes, with the decision-making process to facilitate quick decisions.

- Help managers develop the skills that are necessary to make the value-influencing decisions quickly and well. Some of these skills are knowing what needs to be known for a quick decision; balancing thought and action while avoiding overanalysis; and being able to prioritize.

> ### The catering manager and making fast decisions and actions
>
> *The catering manager actively looks for new ideas from his people and when they put one forward he immediately discusses it and then takes action on it, either by implementing it in the restaurant or by discussing it with headquarters. He facilitates the idea generating process by regularly conducting meetings where he discusses opportunities and threats with the employees.*

3.5 Fast actions

Action-taking is defined as 'the process of doing.' Management is the art of getting things done, and therefore fast action-taking is very important. Unfortunately, research shows that only about ten percent of managers actually take purposeful and swift action. That is because many managers confuse being active with taking action. Being active means being busy, undertaking all kinds of activities with high energy and high commitment but without a strong focus on the desired or needed outcomes. In the end these managers are not very effective and actually get frustrated with their low added value. By contrast purposeful action is the conscious, intentional and goal-directed behavior that comes from a manager's personal involvement and willingness to go beyond getting things done and to achieve something meaningful. Such managers do not let themselves get distracted or overcome by all the demands placed on them by the organization but actively manage their environment in order to achieve the things they set out to do. They have the will power to get the right things done, which makes them HPO managers. [43] They also question themselves after every action whether it was good enough or if they have to take additional or remedial actions. HPO managers therefore continuously learn from what they are doing, and are not afraid to reverse decisions and actions if these turn out to be the wrong ones.

WHAT MAKES A HIGH PERFORMANCE ORGANIZATION

IDEAS TO GET STARTED TO STIMULATE FAST ACTION-TAKING

The best way to improve the speed of action-taking is to remove the obstacles that prevent you from taking action in the first place. These are the three types of obstacle and what you can do about them:

1. *Overwhelming demands.* You get overwhelmed by the demands and expectations put on you and the things you need to do to such a degree that you 'freeze' and are not able to do anything. To remove this obstacle, you have to consciously develop an agenda with both short-term, medium-term and long-term goals. Then you have to manage the expectations of others inside and outside the organization about what is possible for you to do in each time frame. Subsequently, you pace your schedule according to the agenda and start taking action.

2. *Unbearable constraints.* You get so locked in by all kinds of rules, regulations, budget restrictions and organizational limitations that you feel there is no room at all to take action. To remove this obstacle, you map the relevant constraints in relation to your agenda. You then concentrate on overcoming only those constraints that are relevant in terms of the agenda, selectively breaking rules and developing the capacity to tolerate conflicts and ambiguity in the course of making progress on your chosen actions.

3. *Tunnel vision.* Because of concentrating on immediate needs and requirements you develop a tunnel vision, you are unable to see things that are not straight in front of you, and you don't take the time to explore other than the obvious choices. To remove this obstacle, you have to learn to become aware of your

> choices and to enjoy having greater freedom in those choices. You then consistently work on expanding your opportunities and the choices you have, and you develop competencies to be able to create these choices and make them happen.

3.6 Coaching

Coaching is defined as 'the act of training and supporting employees.' HPO managers coach their employees by being supportive, facilitating them, protecting them from outside interference, and by being available for them when needed. They do not tell people how they should achieve their goals but do give them immediate and concrete feedback on their performance.

An activity that managers can undertake to support their employees and that is related to coaching, is mentoring.[44] Whereas coaching focuses on helping employees deal with activities in their current position, mentoring aims at the longer term. Mentoring should help employees develop to the next level in their career and therefore deals less or even not at all with 'the here and now' problems and issues. Also, the mentor does not have to be the direct supervisor of the employee as is the case with coaching. Often senior managers function as mentors, especially if the person mentored is a junior manager. Mentoring is therefore concerned with explicitly developing the competence and capacity in an individual in the context of a one-on-one relationship, where the mentor has a depth of expertise and experience in particular areas. Mentoring thus promotes personal growth and development and has an explicit professional development focus on building a career for the employee in a particular sector.

> ### The catering manager and coaching
> *Employees regularly talk with the catering manager about their personal development and possible improvements in their way of working. Outside of these fixed periodic conversations, the catering manager takes every opportunity to talk to employees about recent experiences, mistakes, good work and other possibilities for improving the quality of the restaurant. The catering manager actively supports employees in developing themselves.*

❝All through my career at Microsoft I have been coached, both in and outside the company. Many of the conversations focused on self-reflection. I have always benefited a lot from my coaches. Now, I have a mentor on the business side, somebody I can use as a sounding board. Although we are functionally on the same level I can learn a lot from this person. I also have an external coach who I see from time to time to get a fresh perspective. This emphasis on development and a desire to get better is also a core value of Microsoft. In turn I am a coach to other people, and I mentor eight people. How do I know I am a good coach? I wouldn't profess to say I am, but I do have a clear philosophy on leadership and the legacy of a leader. Building a sustainable, outperforming organization is the most important and satisfying task of a leader, well ahead of any functional capabilities. I spend much time on that and really enjoy that part of my role. Microsoft is serious about continuing to develop its talent and I feel responsible for helping the company to achieve that.❞

Rik van der Kooi, Microsoft USA

IDEAS TO GET STARTED ON EFFECTIVE COACHING

To become an effective coach, your coaching should aim at having the following traits:

- Coaching has to be goal oriented, in the sense that it has to take place in 'the here and now' situation that your employee is faced with. It should help your employees deal with current problems and issues in their current job.

- Put a strong emphasis on self reflection, which promotes self-directed learning and supports sustained behavioral change on the part of your employee.

- Do not provide answers or solutions to issues raised by your employee. You should assume that the person being coached has the necessary insights which your coaching should help bring to the surface. This way your employee will go through a learning process.

- Be not afraid to make critical comments when needed during the coaching or to bring taboo subjects into the conversation if necessary, as long as this is done in a positive way meant to help your employee grow.

❝It is very much a coaching role that I have. I have to make sure that the branches are successful, which is measured with the cost-income ratio, satisfied customers, development of employees, and that things are kept in good order. If the branches do a good job and are successful in those four things, then I leave them alone. But if there is one or several things in which they are not successful, then I have to coach and lead them to the right path.

And if that does not work, if I cannot do that, then the last option can be to change the branch manager. If a branch is successful, I spend very little time there, I do not want to interfere if they are doing well. However, in new branches I do spend more time in order to teach the new colleagues about the Handelsbanken way. If branches are not successful, there must be a reason for it. It can be that they do not work according to the Handelsbanken model, and I will therefore try to teach them how to work with our model. My prime goal is to ensure that we all go in the right direction on the highway called the Handelsbanken way. That we all move in the same direction, that nobody is moving faster or in the opposite direction, and nobody goes out into the fields but that they stay on that road."

Mikael Sørensen, Svenska Handelsbanken

"We spend a lot of time on coaching and we are particularly good at it on team level. I talk a lot with my team, about how they are doing, which way they are going, what help they need from me. I bring the team regularly together, either physically or virtually, so that people in different locations can exchange information and ideas. That is quite an enticer for them: participating in the meetings means you'll learn new stuff. In addition, I have the usual one-on-one conversations with individuals which are about the business but always also have a part where we talk more personal: how they are feeling, how happy they are, how they are coping, what their plans are, how the interaction between them and their team mates or subordinates is. I myself have two coaches, an internal one who is also my boss and an external one who has been coaching me for years."

Lennard Boogaard, Unilever

3.7 Results orientation

Results orientation is defined as 'the attitude of wanting to achieve outcomes.' HPO managers are strongly results oriented which shows by them being continuously working at achieving the goals and targets set by the organization, being proactive in looking for opportunities to achieve competitive advantage and better results, and streamlining the organization so it can become leaner and meaner and thereby more effective. HPO managers are intolerant of mediocrity and always strive for the best because they feel it can always be done better. They strongly dislike wasting time, energy and money, reject bureaucracy, and embrace simplicity.[45]

> **IDEAS TO GET STARTED TO DEVELOP A RESULTS-ORIENTED ATTITUDE**
>
> There are several things you can do to create results-oriented behavior in your organization:
>
> - Set high standards, both for the targets you want to achieve and the manner in which you want to achieve this. These standards should apply for your employees and for yourself, so you and your people will be challenged and have to stretch themselves.
>
> - Talk about HPO as the nirvana for the organization: the ideal state of the organization in which it will consistently deliver top-notch quality and service to the customers and consequently will be the envy of the competition and the role model for the industry. Then stress that people should be proud to be working for such an organization and that it is worth working hard for it.
>
> - Continuously fight complacency and inertia by stressing that the biggest danger for success is being successful, and by emphasizing that the organization can always do better.

- Realize that you cannot be good at everything. You do not have to adhere to the myth of the complete leader: the person at the top who knows everything, does not make mistakes and because of that is single-handedly responsible for the success of the organization.
- Live by the adage 'My weakness should be your strength.' Build a team of people around you which contains all the strengths needed for managing effectively.
- Value speed over perfectionism. Pay attention to detail but do not get bogged down by these.
- Guard against paralysis by analysis, and rather take a bad decision than waiting for all information to come in to take a perfect decision.
- Continuously and consciously balance quality with speed.

3.8 Effectiveness

Effectiveness is defined as 'the ability to achieve the desired result.' HPO managers are highly effective as they are good at sharing the vision and strategy of the organization with employees and then explaining the goals they are trying to achieve with the organizational unit. They keep on repeating this until the message is understood and supported by all employees. Subsequently, HPO managers focus on achieving the goals and do not rest until they have. To facilitate this, they create clear lines of accountability and make sure all information needed to do a good job is available. HPO managers are also good at solving conflicts in a constructive manner and dispelling concerns before these get out of hand. They spot both opportunities and threats early on and act on these. They pay attention to detail but ignore irrelevant issues that impede progress, and thus are very focused on what they need to achieve.

IDEAS TO GET STARTED TO BECOME MORE EFFECTIVE

An activity that most managers see as negative but which, if used in the right manner, can actually be very effective is conflict. You can deliberately use conflict as a means to spark creativity, make better decisions and foster collaboration. To be able to do this, you need to do the following: [46]

- Devise and implement a common method for resolving conflict. This will guide people in the organization as to how they should proceed when they encounter a conflict.

- Provide people with criteria for making trade-offs between conflicting priorities. These criteria spell out what is most important to the organization when conflicting priorities arise.

- When conflicts persist, you use these as an opportunity for coaching and helping employees to become better at solving conflicts.

- When a conflict is so serious that it cannot be immediately resolved and has escalated up the hierarchical line, you enforce three requirements: (1) that all parties in the conflict present their viewpoints about the conflict jointly so that all information is available for senior managers to make a good decision; (2) that the senior managers resolve escalated conflicts between themselves and do not individually pass the conflicts on to their superiors; and (3) that the senior managers explain the process of how they resolved the escalated conflict to their employees.

> **“**To be effective, managers have to be authentic when they come to work. They shouldn't be different at work than they are at home. If they check in part of themselves at the door or if they put on a mask, we get a weakened version of those persons, we don't get their full capacity and commitment. We use the slogan 'Be yourself' because that is why we hired you in the first place. And then these managers should strive for growing the business because growth is a law of nature. Something that doesn't grow anymore will wither and die and we don't want that to happen to our business; there are too many stakeholders depending on us. And finally, they should subscribe to the four themes which we all agreed upon several years ago: be deeply rooted in society, which is corporate social responsibility; be adaptive, so you can deal with changing circumstances and the things life throws at you; be excellent in the execution, because that is what our clients depend on we do; and create top talent by investing in your employees and improving them.**”**
>
> Lennard Boogaard, Unilever

3.9 Strong leadership

Strong leadership is defined as 'the ability of leading a group of people or an organization, which is not easily damaged or overcome, able to withstand opposition and has determination.' HPO managers exhibit strong leadership in tough times by not deviating from the pursued course, yet at the same time they are flexible in the ways to get where they want and need to be. They know there are many ways to Rome and they will get there. HPO managers are not afraid to seek out confrontation and to put their foot down if necessary, because they find achieving the agreed upon goals more important than maintaining the harmony in the organization (within reason). They will not hesitate to call employees or colleagues to account if agreements are not honored. During these confrontations HPO managers are calm, speak clearly and never become personal in order to not damage the other person. They always approach the confrontation from the stand of what is good for the organization and how the other person can contribute to that.

HPO FACTOR 1 – MANAGEMENT QUALITY

"Although we know that the required behavior at Umpqua works, we can still relapse if we take our eyes off the ball. That is because behavior is like a rubber band. You may stretch it quite a bit and sometimes because of the pressure, it will snap back to the old status. But if you have been here a while, you'll notice the relapse will not be that far. It is like two steps forward and one step backward. Then it becomes a case of how fast can you get people away from the wall and move them forward again."

Lani Hayward, Umpqua Bank

IDEAS TO GET STARTED TO COME ACROSS AS A STRONG LEADER

You are only a strong leader if you are perceived that way by your employees and your superiors. This means that you have to pay attention to the following:

- Make sure you have the cooperation of your employees and your colleagues. Without their consent and support you will not be able to achieve anything.
- Know what is going on in the organization. Create an early warning system which shows you when trouble is brewing so you can take timely action.
- Be predictable so people know they can depend on you.
- Give credit where credit is due.
- Be confidently humble.
- Check your ego at the door.
- Be results-oriented.

> "Excellent managers must be able to honestly say certain things to other persons about their performance and they must also be able to take the feedback themselves, if somebody says something to them about their functioning. Employees must have the feeling that managers will listen to them and deal fairly with their issues and possible mistakes. Communication skills are of course also important, with the employees and especially in the network of key-players throughout the company and in the value chain. Taking initiatives, daring to make choices, to take decisions and actions, being autonomous because there is nobody who will tell them how to run their business. But they should also be able to ask for help when they need it, they shouldn't try to fix problems which are over their heads when they could have easily asked for assistance from colleagues or their boss. They should be open if they have difficulty with certain things. In this company it will not make them seem weaker, it is seen as a sign of strong leadership."
>
> Jan Maas, TATA Steel

3.10 Confidence

Confidence is defined as 'a feeling and showing of reliance, certainty and self-assuredness.' HPO managers are confident enough that they can exhibit the right blend of humility and professional will to lead the organization while continuing to learn and develop themselves. They know their own strengths and weaknesses and recognize their limitations. HPO managers are authentic, self-conscience, self-disciplined and modest, emotionally robust and not arrogant. They use their power in an ethically responsive and positive way and have a people-centered approach. HPO managers also express confidence even if they don't really feel so sure. This is because many managerial decisions have to be made without the full picture being clear because of incomplete information. In order to move the organization forward nonetheless, the decision is taken with more aplomb than the manager might feel but showing this confidence is important because of the 'belief follows behavior' effect: the confidence of the manager inspires employees to act accordingly, which in turn helps to realize the decision. This 'pretending' is not the same as deceiving people as the alternative is stagnation. Employees need to feel that their managers are confident to move forward and take decisions, and they trust that managers will reconsider their decision if and when needed.[47]

> ### *The catering manager and being confident, strong and effective*
> *Employees call the catering manager a visionary with a strong drive for continuous improvement. They don't see him so much as their superior but more as one of them, someone who operates from a shared set of norms and values which is consistently guarded. Employees find that the catering manager conveys leadership at the moments when it is needed, by distancing himself from the group and then acting as their leader who takes corrective action. By asking many questions and listening to the answers, the catering manager radiates confidence. He is always present when the restaurant opens and is visible and approachable, to both customers and employees, during the time he is in the restaurant. The catering manager looks proactively for possible issues and doesn't wait for problems to arise. He talks to many customers, directs employees to the place they are needed most, and lends a hand if necessary. Customers see the catering manager as being strongly customer focused and service oriented.*

> ## IDEAS TO GET STARTED TO STRENGTHEN CONFIDENCE
> You can strengthen the confidence in the organization in the following ways:
> - Visibly believe in your people and in their power to make a difference, by investing in things that matter to them.

- Direct the energy tied up in negativity into positive actions. Focus your employees on a bigger cause and give them a chance to contribute to it.

- Make initiatives possible and desirable, by giving opportunities to your employees to contribute new ideas and by rewarding these and providing a support system for making these ideas happen.

- Look continuously for small wins, things which your employees can control and which let them experience success so they get a taste for it.

- Look for and create winning streaks, as winning fosters four types of confidence:

    1. *Self-confidence*: winning feels good and good moods are contagious, success makes it easier to be positive and to generate optimism which produces energy and higher aims.

    2. *Confidence in one another*: winning makes people feel more engaged with their tasks and with one another and people are more willing to cooperate, problems will be more likely caught and solved because people share information, take responsibility and admit mistakes.

    3. *Confidence in the system*: winning makes it likely to turn informal practices into formal traditions by building winners' habits of responsibility, teamwork, and initiative into routines, processes, and practices that encourage them.

    4. *External confidence*: winning makes it easier to attract financial backers, loyal customers and enthusiastic fans.

> "I use my time to connect to the people of the organization and I feel emotionally involved with a team and its people. People inspire me, and I get close to them, not to check or control but to participate and to contribute. I love to listen. I enjoy to sit in with groups and watch the dynamics and see what is really happening. I aim to interfere only if needed, trying to keep interventions to a minimum. If people dependent too much on their superiors to take decisions, one cannot build an HPO. We live in a time in which status and hierarchy will disconnect more and more. The more convincing and decisive you are as a leader, the higher the responsibilities will be placed in the company. However, in the complex world we live in, responsibilities should be placed as low as possible within the organization to ensure great capacity to action. Of course, this philosophy sometimes contradicts to being part of a worldwide organization like Microsoft working in a matrix system in which responsibilities can be placed on different levels in different countries. So, I see it as my task to teach people how to balance those challenges. It is a sign of maturity in an organization how well people are able to balance these different demands."
>
> *Theo Rinsema, Microsoft Netherlands*

3.11 Accountability

Accountability is defined as 'taking responsibility for one's actions and results.' HPO managers not only hold employees and junior managers accountable for their results but also their colleagues, their own superiors and themselves. They do this by making sure that everybody knows what they are accountable for by making the expected results crystal clear; establishing clear lines of accountability; making sure everybody has the resources and the power to influence their results; making sure everybody knows the consequences of non-performance; and then periodically calling people to account for their results, not their efforts. HPO managers themselves are visibly accountable for their own results and they take responsibility for their own mistakes and failures under all circumstances, without excuses.

IDEAS TO GET STARTED TO FOSTER ACCOUNTABILITY

If you want to transform your organization into an HPO, it is imperative that managers feel accountable for their results. However, there may be managers who try to evade their responsibilities and avoid taking accountability for the transformation of the organization. You have to quickly deal with these people before they have a negative effect on the HPO transition. But before you can do that, you need to be able to recognize the 'bad managers'. Look for these signs, so you can hold these managers accountable:[48]

1. Bad managers first clean up the mess of their predecessors, even when there is no mess. When appointed in a new position, bad managers claim that their predecessor has made such a big mess of the department that it will take at least one year, if not more, to get everything in order. They make clear that in that time they cannot be expected to work on the transition.

2. Bad managers always seem to be very busy. They are involved in so many projects that they don't have enough time for regular tasks, let alone the transition.

3. Bad managers like to manage from a distance. The further away they are from the day-to-day transition activities the easier it is for them to avoid involvement.

4. Bad managers always blame somebody else. They have a host of excuses as to why they didn't put enough effort in the transition activities.

5. Bad managers do not communicate. Bad managers feign interest in the transition and provide you with no or vague feedback on the status of their transition activities.

HPO FACTOR 1 – MANAGEMENT QUALITY

“When we evaluate each other, we are very critical of ourselves: What did we do well and what not? Are we innovating fast enough, or are we falling behind? Bill Gates in particular often asked: "Is this product successful because of our own work or are we just lucky?" We don't spare ourselves when we evaluate. What helps in these discussions is the fact that we are very data driven. There is a sense of 'In God we trust, all others bring data.' This is pervasive in our organization because of two things. Firstly, the beating heart of Microsoft is Product Engineering which is very fact based. In addition, we have a mathematical chief executive officer who is always looking for connections and cross correlations between items, and there you have our fact-driven culture. Don't forget that our chief executive officer was already working here when there were less than 100 employees, which means that the culture of Microsoft has been strongly influenced by this data-oriented approach; we really measure everything. Our culture is best described as one of continuous improvement; learning from mistakes; being modest about successes; measuring, measuring, measuring; and persistence, we never give up. We care about accountability: Did we achieve the result we signed up for? We do this by translating the company's top level goals into personal commitment sheets, against which we track performance on an ongoing basis. Our review system directly links to this philosophy. We have a clear rating system that connects the achievement of your goals to the way these were achieved, and to your proven capability over a longer period of time. Based on your rating against these, you will know if you are among the top achievers, somewhere in the middle of the pack, or at the bottom of the range. If you do end up at the bottom, this is a clear signal to improve performance or find a more fitting role inside or outside the company.”

Rik van der Kooi, Microsoft USA

3.12 Decisiveness toward non-performers

Decisiveness is defined as 'the ability to decide quickly and effectively.' HPO managers have an intolerance of mediocrity and therefore deal decisively with low-performers and non-performers. This is because they employ the 'bad apple principle': one bad apple will eventually spoil the whole basket, so it has to be removed as quickly as possible. HPO managers keep strict focus on the achievement of results and are not afraid to make tough decisions if people repeatedly do not achieve their targets. They carefully and thoroughly assess performance, evaluate whether there are organizational reasons for not performing (such as bad systems, bad procedures, unrealistic targets, insufficient support from management) and, if not, they hold employees and colleagues accountable for their disappointing results, and subsequently make sure these face the consequences of not performing. They do not let these non-performers muddle on but quickly help them to another position in the organization where their talents could come to better use or, if need be, place them outside the organization. HPO managers know that, as a side-effect, dealing decisively with non-performers will increase the motivation of the other employees as they see that management does not tolerate the behavior of non-performers while they themselves are working hard to achieve results.

> ### *The catering manager and accountability and dealing with non-performers*
>
> *The catering manager discusses with the employees which results have to be achieved in the next month, next quarter and at year-end and also makes agreements on who is responsible for achieving what result. Subsequently the catering manager actively and regularly holds the employees accountable for these results. The catering manager makes it clear to every new employee that there is a clear playing field and that, if someone leaves the field and crosses the boundaries, there will be consequences. Despite being careful when hiring new people, the catering manager knows there can always slip 'a bad apple' through and he is prepared to directly remove that apple.*

IDEAS TO GET STARTED WITH DEALING WITH NON-PERFORMERS

Many managers have problems confronting non-performers as they are not used to this process, have not been trained in it, dread the emotional aspects of the process, or do not want to be seen by employees as the 'bad guy'. You can help them deal with this difficult process by making sure the following is in place: [49]

- Adequate training in how to carry out the process of dealing decisively with non-performers (how to collect information about the employee that can be used in the process, how much time the process will take, what behavior is needed during the process).

- Enough time for the managers to conduct the process adequately.

- Adequate authority for the managers to deal with the non-performers.

- Adequate personnel systems that provide the information about the employee, needed in the process.

- Top management backing of managers.

Part of the aforementioned training should be helping managers recognize 'bad apples' by their behavior. In general, bad apples can be spotted by their behaviors of withholding effort, being free-riders; negativity, continuously expressing negative opinions, irritations and complaints; and being deviant, by tainting, embarrassing and scolding team members.

> "When you get a sense that things are not working, I am very willing to have a conversation with people, because it can happen at times that people become overwhelmed by the challenge. Sometimes you will make appointments with people in which you will take a risk, because they are not quite ready but, on the balance of things, they are the right individuals for the job. And then you are going to watch them quite closely. Now and then people might feel overwhelmed, then you have to think about what new support you can put in place to assist them. This organization is not a soft organization but a caring organization. We give a decent amount of time to non-performers to clean up their act because we are quite respectful of people. We make an effort to understand what is driving bad performance. If it is a case of someone who is like: 'I do not like this job, I do not want to be here, I am not excited when I come to work in the morning and I am not interested' you are going to deal with this person quite quickly. If it is somebody grappling to get to grips with the challenges of a new role and is perhaps not living up to expectations, we see this as a mutual responsibility. We appointed this person so there was something wrong with our judgment. Have we put him in the wrong job, have we overstretched him, did we misread his capability? In this case we are talking about redeployment rather than firing. We normally give, by the time you get to a performance counselling situation, the person six months and then it will either have corrected itself, or it is over."
>
> Alan Clark, SAB Miller Europe

3.13 Reflection: Is it all too much?

With the HPO factor Management Quality having 12 characteristics, it can safely be concluded that the HPO manager is of paramount importance to an organization. At the same time, with so many characteristics it seems an almost impossible task for managers to satisfy all these characteristics. In reality, however, it turns out to be easier than expected to fulfill the characteristics because these are often already present. Because of their attitude to working life, managers strive to be trusted and have integrity; from their position they already have to be decisive, action oriented, effective, responsible and results oriented; and often this type of person is confident by nature. Where managers often experience difficulties is with coaching, inspiring, being a role model, and holding people accountable, because during their studies and their first working years there often was not much attention for developing these characteristics. Also characteristics as communication, holding dialogues, daring to make and forgive mistakes, and being able and even welcoming change turn out to be arduous for managers because they, when they were still employees, rarely had bosses that set a good example in this respect. So these characteristics will require most of the work for managers to become HPO managers.

Interestingly, the HPO characteristics do not indicate which management style successful managers need to use. In practice, it means that there is not one specific management style for achieving high performance. HPO managers use different management styles depending on the organization's situation at a certain time. This is called situational leadership.

The catering manager and management style

The catering manager knows he cannot convey passion for the business, the restaurant and the customers to his employees while sitting in the office. His style is therefore to be as often as possible on the restaurant floor. He also knows that motivation of employees can be increased by giving them accountability for results and then not telling them what to do, that is their own responsibility. The catering manager has created a shared feeling of responsibility with his employees for making the restaurant a success and to be proud of that restaurant ... which everybody is and quite rightly so!

KEY POINTS CHAPTER 3

- The HPO research shows that, with twelve underlying HPO characteristics, the HPO factor Management Quality is the most important factor in the HPO Framework. In other words, it largely depends on the quality of management whether an organization will become and remain an HPO.

- The characteristics of the HPO factor Management Quality are: trust, integrity, a strong role model, fast decisions, fast actions, coaching, results orientation, effectiveness, strong leadership, confidence, accountability, and decisiveness toward non-performers.

- It seems a lot to introduce 12 characteristics for managers. In practice however some of these characteristics are often already present in the organization and introducing them therefore usually should not be too much of a problem.

- The HPO characteristics do not point to a certain management style that is best for achieving high performance. Typically, HPO managers use different management styles depending on the situation of the organization at a certain time.

HPO FACTOR 1 – MANAGEMENT QUALITY

Longfellow Benefits (USA): even a full-blown HPO can improve

KEY MESSAGE

Even a full-blown HPO can improve … and people inside the HPO can be acutely aware of this. A true HPO takes the need for such continuous improvement very serious, and never lets up.

You might not expect to find an HPO in an unassuming office building in the Back Bay area of Boston, Massachusetts, USA. But then you would be pleasantly surprised because on the tenth floor of an office on Huntington Avenue you can find Longfellow Benefits, a highly successful company and the winner of the annual Boston's Best Employer Award for six years in a row. Longfellow was founded in 1999 by four individuals who shared a common desire to create a service organization built upon the ideals of teamwork, accountability, and understanding. The company has been providing employee benefits consulting and advisory services to employers and individuals since its start. Longfellow is a broker (i.e. intermediary) that advises companies in choosing the best health insurance policy, retirement plan or executive benefit systems for a specific company. Until today, Longfellow is a privately held firm serving clients nationally and internationally. The company receives compensation in the form of commissions or fees for the services provided to clients. As it relates to commission income Longfellow may also receive additional compensation from carriers (the insurance companies) based on volume, growth, and other factors as determined by specific carriers. Longfellow does not participate in any special compensation arrangements beyond those normally used by carriers for their distribution channels. Longfellow's recommendations are always made in the best interests of its clients and their employees, and are not related to these compensation programs.

Currently Longfellow has over 200 corporate clients of whom the majority are 100 to 1,000 employees in size, and its client retention rate is at least 95 percent. The company employs 30 people and has been growing from a revenue of US$1.5 million in 1999 to more than US$9 million in 2010. Longfellow's mission is to listen to and advocate for clients; deliver superior, needs-based, service; be a caring and objective business partner; be a recognized industry thought leaders and constantly grow, improve, and innovate. Longfellow gives meaning to its mission by actively developing thought leadership in the industry – its associates have been published, recognized, or quoted more than 90 times since 2007 – and by partnering with its clients. The latter is achieved by providing to the client a team of dedicated professionals focused on service, strategy, prudent process, compliance, education, and communication. Longfellow has shown since its inception consistent growth and low employee turnover. The majority of their people have been with the company for more than ten years.

The HPO Diagnosis at Longfellow

In the true spirit of an HPO, Longfellow agreed to partake in an HPO Diagnosis. The HPO Questionnaire was distributed among the principals and employees of the company and after processing the data, interviews were held with seven people during a week spent by the HPO Center on the premises of Longfellow in Boston. This week was concluded by a presentation of the HPO Diagnosis results to representatives of Longfellow's management. Figure 3.1 shows the scores of Longfellow, compared to the average scores of the 20 US companies which were present in the database of the HPO Center at that time. The average HPO score for Longfellow was 8.7, which was higher than the cut-off score of 8.5 and considerably higher than the average HPO score of the 20 US companies, meaning that Longfellow qualified as an HPO.

HPO FACTOR 1 – MANAGEMENT QUALITY

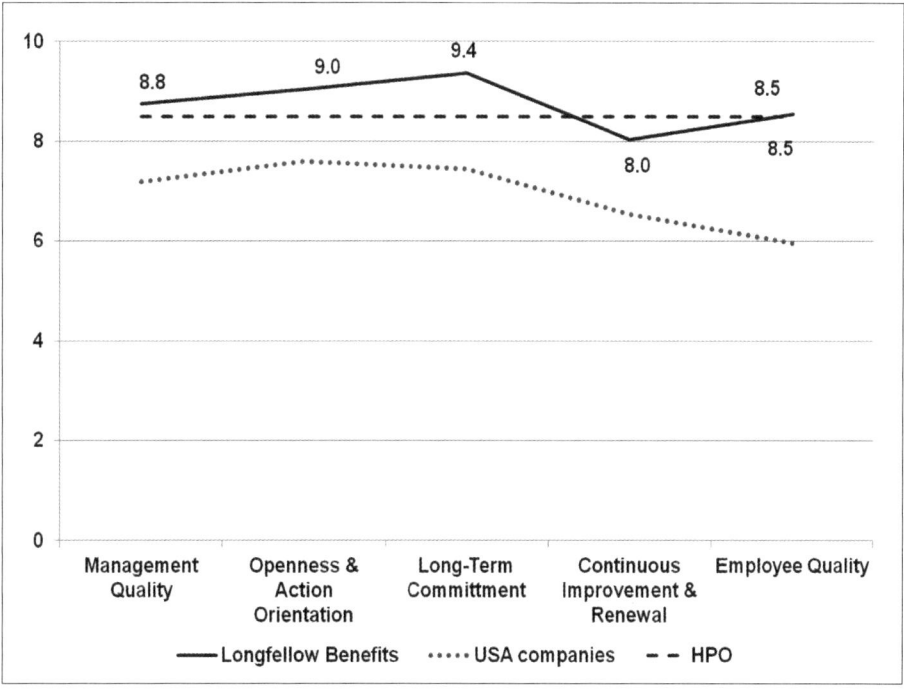

Figure 3.1: HPO status of Longfellow Benefits, compared with US companies

The interviews conducted at Longfellow concentrated on two questions: What made Longfellow Benefits great? and In which areas could Longfellow improve so it would not only remain an HPO but actually increase its HPO status?

What has made Longfellow so great can be attributed to four features. The first was Longfellow's service model. For every client Longfellow assembled a team of highly skilled people that was focused, dedicated and empowered to deal with the client in such a way that the client would always be satisfied. The team members had different skills which complemented each other, and there was always a principal in the team. The reason for the latter was elucidated by Joe Gray, managing principal of Longfellow: "Big companies get a partner in to sell but after that the client never sees the partner again, except for status meetings. At Longfellow this is not the case, the principal will always work side by side with our people and the client. This is good for the client and also for our people, who get mentoring on the job." The main task of the team was to create a ´sticky relationship´ with the client, which meant that they had to develop a long-lasting partnership between Longfellow and the client by meeting the needs of the client as best as possible. Craig Cerretani, one of the principals, told us: "We attract people that truly care about what they do and what they can achieve for their clients, and that resonates with our clients. Our people are very strong at relationship building. What also works great is the high degree of autonomy they get. They can make decisions themselves, for instance for additional investment. If the client wants to have something additional sorted out and this comes up during the conversation, the team members can directly promise to do this, without having to first check with a principal. Also, people work here not mainly for the money, which has to be okay of course, but for the learning opportunities. Professional honor is very important to our people."

The second feature that made Longfellow great was its business model. The company employed dedicated people for sales who didn't have to worry about running the business. At the same time, the client teams did not have to sell and could therefore fully concentrate on delivering quality service to the client without having to worry about achieving more turnover at the client and billing for every activity performed for the client. In this way, Longfellow had experts in both areas: people who were very good at selling and who brought in new clients which always created new energy and new learning opportunities; and technicians who were always up-to-date with regulatory and functional developments and who were creative in their solutions for a particular situation of a specific client. Both groups felt responsible for the client, as Craig Cerretani explained: "The clients are of the company, not of a principal or a sales person. Therefore there is no envy about who has which clients and who sold how much. We all share in the good fortune of the clients and Longfellow. Everybody has a healthy respect for the skills of others and there are no territorial battles."

Thirdly, Longfellow had a strong culture of empathy, honor, dignity and respect for each other, the client, and the carriers from whom the company obtained insurances. Kevin Ryan, VP Employee Benefits and newly appointed principal, put this succinctly: "At Longfellow you don't work *for* somebody but *with* somebody." Empathy was seen at Longfellow as putting oneself in the other's shoes so that the reaction on one's own actions could be anticipated upon and be dealt with in the right way. Empathy also made it possible to gauge beforehand who should be informed about what issues as they could have an interest in it. This culture had specific effects on leaders at Longfellow, as Craig Cerretani explained: "A great leader gives tough love and at the same time puts his arms around his people. He gets his hands dirty by being part of the teams that do the daily work and therefore has no distance to his people. In this way, he can be passionate about clients and employees because he knows both intimately."

Fourthly, Longfellow explicitly practiced an open book and open door policy. This created much openness in the company because achieved revenue was known to everybody in the organization, principals could easily be approached, there was an ability to discuss small mistakes before they got big, and during the weekly meetings anyone with a good idea could speak up and in fact was encouraged to do so, as an interviewee expressed: "If there is a better way to do it, we want to know about it." Another thing the company did was that directly after each client meeting the team sat down to evaluate the meeting, gave direct feedback to team members, and discussed opportunities for improvement. On the matter of mistakes, Kevin Gazda, senior VP Employee Benefits Operations, said: "If you make a mistake at Longfellow, you'll not lose your job. You don't have to look over your shoulder all the time here, you can learn from your mistakes, you will not be punished. It has to be this way anyway, a lot here is learning on the job because it is a creative job. We have to be like this if we want to offer tailor-made solutions to our clients."

Attention points for Longfellow

At the time of the HPO Diagnosis Longfellow found itself at a crossroads in its development. The organization had been growing steadily from small beginnings as an entrepreneurial group of four founders with loose control and an opportunistic view on the market in the sense that everything was an opportunity. Now Longfellow was turning into a more complex organization because there were more people employed from different generations; a greater demand for clarity of vision and structure; more need for guidance and coaching from the principals; a more difficult market place as competitors now took Longfellow seriously; and possible quality control issues which become inevitable with growth.

The crossroads therefore basically could lead to three possible routes: overcoming the issues and continuing with rapid growth (Route 1 in Figure 3.2), continuing on the current course by solving some problems while struggling with others (Route 2), or being overwhelmed by the situation and declining (Route 3). During the HPO Diagnosis two main attention points were formulated to which Longfellow had to pay attention to stay an HPO and continue on Route 1.

The first attention point was that the principals, together with the employees, had to create a vision of the future Longfellow. As mentioned before, Longfellow was becoming an organization which was too big and too mature to still be run as an entrepreneurship. Employees asked for more clarity, structure, vision and guidance, both for the organization and themselves, and the current growth and sales pressures negatively affected dialogue between management and employees in terms of having time for each other. Therefore everybody had to sit down and discuss options for the

HPO FACTOR 1 – MANAGEMENT QUALITY

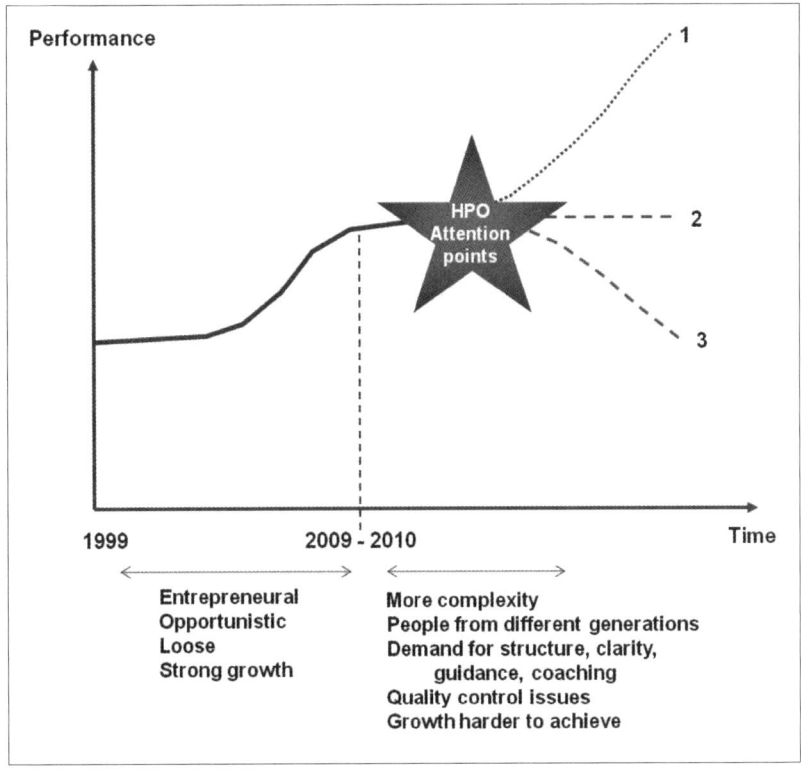

Figure 3.2: The development of Longfellow over time, including three possible future development routes

future, by answering questions like: How big should Longfellow become? What kind of clients does Longfellow want to service in the future? What type of leadership is needed to guide Longfellow into the future? and How can we grow old together as an HPO? Then decisions had to be made about the balances between more structure while maintaining flexibility, more empathy for clients and for each other while becoming more professional, and keeping the family culture while being more critical of each other.

The second attention point was to strengthen the process management. Longfellow experienced several times that its continuing growth came with some quality issues which had to be dealt with, while unfortunately its people were too busy to pay sufficient attention to this issue. The advice was that Longfellow should hire a 'Longfellow suitable' chief operating officer who would be in charge of systematic development and improvement of all processes while not putting everything in tight procedures as that would not work with Longfellow's employees. So flexible quality assurance procedures should be introduced and made the topic of regular discussion, and during these discussions people should develop a more critical and challenging attitude toward each other to unearth issues.[50]

De Beers Marine (South Africa): dealing with the past through the HPO Framework

KEY MESSAGE

Events that happened in the past can influence the HPO status of an organization for quite a long time. Management has to be aware of this when interpreting the results of the HPO Diagnosis and deciding on subsequent actions.

De Beers Group Services is a diamond exploration, mining and rough diamond trading company established in Kimberley, South Africa, in 1888. One of its subsidiaries is De Beers Marine (DBM), which mines for diamonds on the seabed. DBM's activities span the range of exploration, resource development, survey/geophysics, sampling, capital projects, building of marine mines, operation and maintenance of the marine mines and the associated support infrastructure, R&D, technical support and operations management. The vessels under management of DBM include the Coral Sea, the Douglas Bay, the Peace In Africa, two AUVs (autonomous underwater vehicles), and chartered vessels. DBM's headquarters are in Cape Town. Employees on the vessels work 28 days on and 28 days off, while shore-based employees are on normal office type conditions. DBM was established in 1983 with production starting in 1991 in Namibia. In 2001 a new entity, De Beers Marine Namibia (DBMN), was formed to manage the operations in Namibia. DBM's value chain is in the upstream part of the diamond pipeline, as the company's involvement ends at getting the rough diamonds from the seabed. Downstream activities are handled by the De Beers Group.

The HPO Diagnosis at DBM

The HPO Questionnaire was distributed among managers and employees of DBM and after processing the data, interviews were held with six people during a week spent by the HPO Center in Cape Town.[51] This week was concluded by a presentation of the HPO Diagnosis results to DBM's management. Figure 3.3 shows the HPO status of DBM. The average HPO score of the company was 6.4, which meant that DBM was an average performing organization and not yet an HPO. The HPO graph was almost level, which showed that DBM was a well-balanced company, a good starting-point for improving all HPO factors.

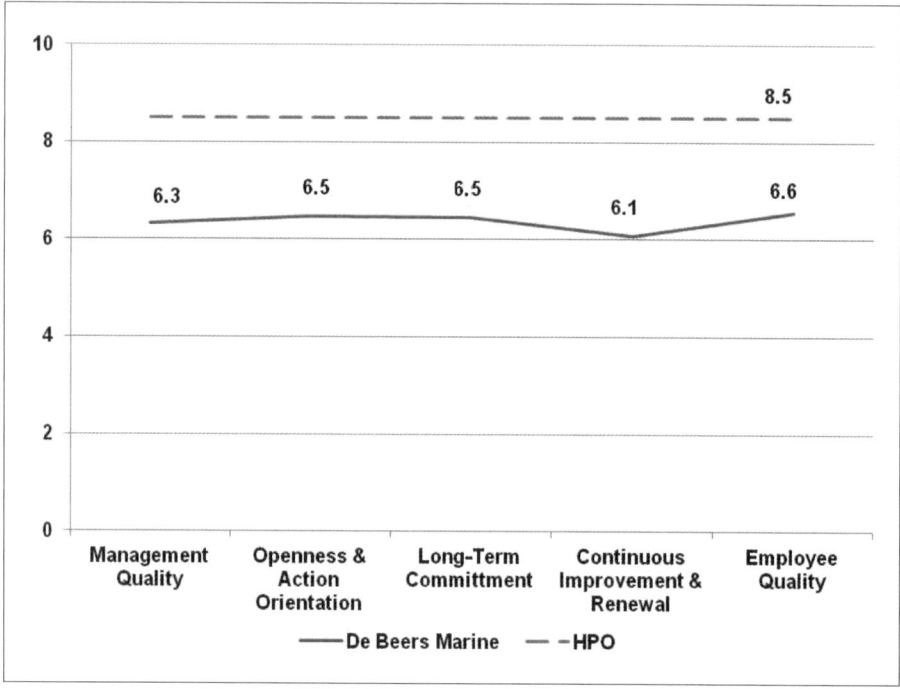

Figure 3.3: HPO status of De Beers Marine

The HPO status of DBM was heavily influenced by the history of the company. Until 2000, the situation of DBM was relatively stable, as the company was part of the 'De Beers family' and could count on a steady and predictable workload. After 2000, DBM was spun off as a separate entity which had to take care of its own income. This entailed that former colleagues in the De Beers family suddenly had to be treated as clients, and that DBM now had to obtain its

HPO FACTOR 1 – MANAGEMENT QUALITY

own sales and undertake its own ventures. This put a great deal of pressure on the organization because it had to develop sales and business capabilities while at the same time safeguarding the high quality of its technical processes. The HPO Diagnosis showed that DBM was a technically very proficient company with a historically strong focus on further development of the technical processes. The processes that could improve the HPO factors, on the other hand, did not get as much attention. Since 2006 the company had paid some attention to strengthening its business processes, but the rate of innovation and improvement in that area was still lagging behind that in the area of the technical processes. In addition, the worldwide crisis and subsequent recession affected the organization negatively which meant that a substantial number of the employees had to be laid off and several business functions were outsourced to reduce costs. After studying the HPO scores and the interview write-ups, the HPO Center identified four main HPO attention points which DBM had to address to make sure the company would continue on its route toward HPO.

Attention point 1: Increase the quality of management

As a consequence of the described changes in the organization, DBM had a fairly new management structure. Most managers came from within the De Beers family and were naturally more technically oriented than people oriented. These managers not only had to deal with organizational changes but also with the implementation of several new managerial tools, such as the Continuous Business Improvement (CBI) initiative. These tools were backed by many meetings between managers and employees. The effect was that potentially competent managers and good systems were present. However, managers had difficulty coping with all the changes, did not have enough time to coach their people, and as a result employees had not noticed much improvement. In fact, employees´ trust of management started to decrease because of the recent layoffs and outsourcing. One interviewee defined trust as: "Trust is following through with what you said you were going to do. It is a fundamental requirement that managers do what they say they will do and respect and trust are linked to that." Unfortunately, many meetings were attended by a rotating body of employees and each time chaired by different managers. Because of this, feedback mechanisms did not fully develop as each time different people met each other who might or might not know about previously made arrangements. This had a negative effect on trust in the organization. In addition, to many people, the longer-term future direction of DBM was not clear, causing an uneasy feeling among employees that management did not know how to set the company's direction. Finally, managers stacking improvement projects on top of the regular work of employees, in the hope that these projects would be inspirational to employees, did not help the trust issue either.

Attention point 2: Improve dialogue between management and employees

As mentioned before, many meetings between management and employees were organized at DBM. In fact, there were so many that a 'meeting-free Friday' was recently installed. However, the large number of meetings was not necessarily a guarantee for the quality of the meetings or whether real dialogue and knowledge sharing took place between people. The general manager used to inform everybody about the company status in a general meeting, which meant one-way communication with little feedback from employees. Later on, management team members started to have a monthly meeting with their departments to discuss the figures and to talk about the highlights and actions to be taken which was, communication wise, a large improvement but still did not constitute a real dialogue.

Attention point 3: Better manage the improvement process

There were many process improvement projects running at the time of the HPO Diagnosis, but the main focus of these projects seemed to be on technical improvement and not on business process improvement. The CBI, which was aimed at improving business processes, had only gotten into gear in Autumn 2009 and the effects had not been noticed yet. From the interviews however it became clear that CBI, although a promising and worthwhile initiative, was regarded by employees as a top-down initiative which had to be done on top of the regular work, so there was no clear commitment of employees to it yet.

Attention point 4: Create a culture of innovativeness in the whole company

The interviews demonstrated that the uniqueness of DBM consisted of the combination of generic engineering skills and marine knowledge, which created a set of unique skills. Coupled with the huge capital investment required for the offshore operations and stringent government regulations in regard to doing business in this industry made that DBM basically had no competitors. The technical nature of the company created an intrinsic drive for innovation, which was lead by R&D. DBM could therefore be characterized as a learning organization on the technical side where the company constantly pushed the limits. An interviewee described innovativeness: "We are constantly pushing the limit by finding ways to mine 10 percent better than the previous year, and continuously improving processes resulting in improved operational efficiency. What used to be a yearly production 27 years ago is nowadays a monthly production!" Almost by definition, R&D was allowed to make mistakes, but the interviews with people from other departments showed that management was much less lenient toward their mistakes. At the same time, many of the jobs at DBM (especially those at the ships) did not allow making mistakes because these would be dangerous. This was understood by employees but they were concerned about the way management in general reacted to mistakes which were all treated as 'bad.' The feeling was that DBM should take a hard look at whether its culture was really fostering an innovative climate throughout the whole company, not only in R&D, and whether this culture also concerned the business processes which would improve the HPO factors, and not just the technical processes.

Follow-up actions of DBM

The results of the HPO Diagnosis did not surprise DBM's management as they confirmed the findings of an earlier study on safety. The conclusion of that study was that the quality of management and processes needed to be improved, which was why the CBI initiative was launched. However, from the HPO Diagnosis it became clear that CBI alone would not be enough and that additional initiatives were needed to change the minds and attitudes of both managers and employees toward HPO thinking. Also, more room had to be created for initiatives from the work floor, which should be more supported than in former days by management. The recently introduced slogan 'Can do great things ... done' should get more content and follow-up. The first action management took was mapping out the route to get employee buy-in, and it was decided that business update sessions, in which management and employees meet to discuss current and future DBM affairs and ongoing projects, was an important mechanism to use in this respect. The second action was to put specific HPO actions in DBM's strategy. The third action was to develop a form that assessed managers' ability to Plan, Lead, Organize and Control in order to evaluate the leadership and management capabilities of DBM's managers. Subsequently almost all managers went through an assessment made by their employees. DBM then started to develop an E-learning module to assist managers to develop themselves to be higher-quality managers. In conclusion, DBM was very happy with the HPO Diagnosis and stated that it helped the company greatly in its pursuit of becoming an HPO.

Chapter 4

HPO factor 2 – Openness & Action Orientation: *less communication, more dialogue*

OPENNESS & ACTION ORIENTATION

Chapter preview

The HPO's motto is "a day not learned is a day not lived." That is because people in an HPO have an incurable curiosity about how the organization and its processes and people can be improved. Therefore they spend a lot of time on dialoguing, sharing knowledge and learning, which is for them a major reason why it is fun to work. It is all about developing oneself and one's organization.

This chapter discusses the six characteristics of the HPO factor Openness & Action Orientation. A definition is given for each characteristic followed by a description of the behaviors of HPO managers and employees that is typical of the characteristic. In addition, a number of 'ideas to get started' are listed to improve the characteristic discussed.

4.1 Dialogue

Dialogue is defined as 'discussion between people with different viewpoints, with the goal to improve decision-making and action-taking.' Not all communication is dialogue. In organizations, communication is often a one-way process in which senders (usually managers) convey messages to receivers (other managers and employees) with the purpose to inform them or influence them to do certain things and undertake certain actions. Although receivers usually may speak and make suggestions during the communication process, these are often not heard and acted upon by senders.

Conversely, dialogue is a two-way process. Senders and receivers exchange views and give content and quality to the subject by discussing its meaning and consequences, and improving it. HPO managers know that circulating information does not equal effective communication and they do not confuse meetings (bilateral, weekly operational meetings, management team meetings, quarterly reviews, town hall meetings etc.) with true dialogue. Senders need to listen to receivers and take responses into account while making plans or taking action. HPO managers use dialogue for creating commitment, spreading conviction and driving clarity deep into the organization. They do this by first listening before starting to send the message, so that the employees can help shape the message by providing input and ideas. They have humility in the sense that they acknowledge they don't have all the answers and that they need to consult the collective intelligence of the organization. They see the give-and-take nature of dialogue as an excellent vehicle for this. And then, when a message has been shaped, they present it with infectious passion and conviction while still being receptive to more suggestions. A nice tactic HPO managers use to promote dialogue is the 'open door policy' but with a different interpretation placed on it. As one HPO manager explained: "Open door policy for us means that the door is open for us, executives, to leave the office and to go to the work floor. People always feel a hesitation to enter the office of the chief executive officer so I need to come to them. I try to go to the production floor at least once of week to talk to people. And every morning I do my rounds on the office floor, to chat with people and see how they are doing."

HPO FACTOR 2 – OPENNESS & ACTION ORIENTATION

"A major road block that we have is the clay layer of change resistant middle management which prevents messages going down as far as the work floor. The way you break through it, when you are in an HPO transition, is to brutally and rapidly ensure that you have the right leadership team, work through the right strategy to move things forward, and then dialogue, dialogue and dialogue some more: this is where we are, this is where we need to be and this is how we are going to get there. Town halls, news letters, pod casts, diagonal slices, emails, direct meetings with managers and influencers. The story that everyone understands and their role in it, and what they can expect (rewards, recognition), and then visible everyday leadership from the top – then the ship will begin turning."

Huw Owen, HP D&S

"We have the Handelsbanken Knowledge Days. Once in a while we get round the table with a small group of managers and employees and we use the whole day to discuss the vision and model of the bank and nothing else. Even if you have worked here for 20 years it is still important to hear again why we work with this system. It is worth mentioning that in all these meetings there is always dialogue, never monologue."

Mikael Sørensen, Svenska Handelsbanken

"We put great emphasis on dialogue and therefore we spend much time on it. During our yearly Board Away Day when we go off site with board members to discuss important topics, we discusses the topic of dialogue: the principles of a good dialogue, what to do and what not to do, that it should adhere to the acronym ROLO: respect, open-mindedness, listening and openness. Another thing we do is to evaluate after a board meeting how satisfied we were with the dialogue during the meeting. Naturally dialogue constitutes a big part of our leadership training. In addition, I conduct special sessions on this. Last year during the global Human Resource conference we spent a day on the phenomenon of 'difficult conversations': what are topics of difficulty and how should you conduct this type of conversations. Another thing we do is 'fish bowl sessions' where for instance the board of management is placed in the middle of the room to discuss specific topics and around them people from all over the company are sitting to observe. When these people feel the need they can intervene and ask questions to board members in an open atmosphere. In this way, employees can skip four hierarchical levels because they address the chief executive officer directly. I will give you one other technique we use and which is quite confrontational: the family placing. You let the members of a group position themselves versus the others in accordance with the connection they feel with the other persons. So if you feel close to a person you stand physically close, if not than you create some distance. This way it becomes very visible if a person is not well connected in the group. You can then start the dialogue why this is and what we can do about it.**"**

Lennard Boogaard, Unilever

IDEAS TO GET STARTED TO CREATE AN EFFECTIVE DIALOGUE

You can benefit from the following, structured approach to obtain an effective dialogue: [52]

- Analyze the needs, wishes and capacities of employees in regard to dialoguing, and then match your dialogue style accordingly.
- Reduce the volume of communication, both in number of occurrences as in size of the communication, and simplify the

message. Create the right balance between global (what concerns the complete organization) and local (what concerns the local unit) and make sure employees get the right information about both.

- Do not strive for a perfect performance during the dialogue but keep it authentic. Seek for participation, listen to the others and create lively discussions.

- Measure the effectiveness of the dialogue by measuring the satisfaction of, understanding by and changing of behavior of employees. Regularly evaluate the participation level of employees to make sure they don't hold back during the dialogue.

"The Microsoft office at Amsterdam Airport Schiphol, the Netherlands, is designed to stimulate dialogue and collaboration. At the center of the office is a branch of the Coffee Company where any moment you can get the best coffees or other drinks. None of the employees or managers has a private office, including myself. Everybody has to find a parking space as well as a work space when they come in. Now we have this open plan office in which people work and come together whenever it suits them best, we experience that the content of meetings has changed. People meet nowadays to engage in dialogue and use the diversity of talents offered more. In the old days we had meetings to discuss and arrange 'the what' of our work, instead now we have dialogue on 'the how' and with many different people. An unexpected side-effect was that the new way of working affects my contacts with clients. I still visit four to five clients a week but the number of clients I engage with in this office has increased to many more every week, often in short five to ten minutes conversations. Gone are the days when making appointments was a struggle with a secretary as a gatekeeper. I did not plan for this benefit, but it is great it happened!"

Theo Rinsema, Microsoft Netherlands

"What helps the dialogue process is that we measure a lot. We are really fact-based and we don't discuss on rumours and perceptions but on the basis of hard facts. We cannot say "we heard somewhere that we might have a problem." No, you have to come with the facts and say either "there is no problem" or "look, the data shows we do have an issue.""

Lennard Boogaard, Unilever

4.2 Knowledge sharing

Knowledge sharing is defined as 'the activity through which the understanding of a subject is exchanged with other people.' Knowledge is considered to be one of the most valuable assets of present-day organizations as it embodies best practices, routines, lessons learned, problem–solving methods, and creative processes that are often difficult to replicate. People in an HPO therefore actively share information, knowledge and best practices organization-wide. Management makes sure there are infrastructures and a shared knowledge base present in the organization, to collect and translate knowledge and best practices company-wide and to create an efficient sharing process. In addition, HPO managers deliberately cultivate and utilize new ideas and knowledge from everyone anywhere in the firm. They do this by stressing the importance of lateral, cross-division, cross-function, and cross-rank knowledge exchange within the organization. This is important because research has shown that organizational boundaries (i.e. business unit, job function, office location) have a negative influence on who interacts with whom inside the organization. A pair of individuals that shares the same business unit, job function and office location communicates at an estimated rate of approximately 1,000 times higher than two people that are not within the same boundary and who are geographically separated! So if managers do not pay dedicated attention to regular knowledge sharing and exchange of experiences, they run the risk that their organization turns into a collection of organizational silos.[53]

HPO FACTOR 2 – OPENNESS & ACTION ORIENTATION

“As we are constantly looking for the maximum for our customers, there is a lot of going back-and-forth between teams and with customers, much interaction, asking for advice, sharing of knowledge. Some new people initially have difficulty with this as they are not used to it. At their former company they were sitting alone in their room, being brilliant, trying to solve problems on their own, with nobody seeing their mistakes. Because that is what is central here: you cannot hide your mistakes, you have to be vulnerable and don't hesitate to ask help when needed. And if you have announced with a lot of bravura that you will fix something on your own and then you don't deliver, then you are in trouble and will suffer the consequences. Because you don't have to act this way, everybody here is willing to help you and to accept your help.”

Pim Berger & Ilja Heitlager, Schuberg Philis

IDEAS TO GET STARTED TO PROMOTE KNOWLEDGE SHARING

The effective sharing of knowledge requires an actively managed process, which in this case is called knowledge management. It is defined as a strategy or a framework of systems designed to help organizations create, capture, analyze, apply, and reuse knowledge to achieve competitive advantage. To set up knowledge management in your organization, you need to install the following three processes:

1. Knowledge acquisition, during which new information is created and acquired, filtered, interpreted, and integrated with existing knowledge.
2. Knowledge dissemination, during which knowledge is transmitted to target receivers for absorbing and achieving

> better performance, and subsequently is shared between different receivers.
>
> 3. Responsiveness to knowledge, during which people take action in response to the knowledge gathered, filtered and interpreted. As knowledge is the only resource that increases by its use, this process is very important to constantly increase added value in activities such as continuously innovating products, processes, and services. These activities create new sources of competitive advantage. The more knowledge management is used, the more valuable it becomes for the people and the organization.

❝For learning and knowledge sharing among the various SABMiller units we use a combination of methods. Sometimes we say that there are some processes which are so important that they should be done in the same way in all units. Obviously, because of our decentralized nature, this doesn't happen very often and maybe it can be considered more of spreading common processes rather than real knowledge sharing. Then we have portals on the intranet. For example, all our global brewing standards are on the technical portal. They are available to everybody, so if you want to understand our standards on yeast management or on bottle mould specifications you can find them there. We have got a marketing portal. If there are best ideas going around about market segmentation, they are available, and you can contribute and join an internet chat, you can connect with people who developed it. Knowledge sharing also takes place through functional forums. For example, the Marketing Director has a Marketing Directors Forum every four months where all the European Marketing Directors get together to talk about processes that should be common, common problems that they might have, common strategies they might be pursuing, and in that way they are sharing. Another way is that I connect people. When I visit the Poland team which is struggling with a specific problem, I might suggest they should get into contact with the Czech team which dealt with a similar problem. A third way is through networks where people get to know each other over time and develop a bond, a collegial connection. To me that is actually the most effective method of knowledge sharing."

Alan Clark, SAB Miller Europe

4.3   Employee involvement

Employee involvement is defined as 'the act or instance of participation and sharing an experience by co-workers.' Recent research has shown that one of the top 10 differentiators between winning and non-winning organizations was that contributions of employees to the organization's success were always recognized at the winning organizations. Interestingly enough, this recognition not only manifested in monetary terms but also in the feelings of employees that they were taken seriously by management. For instance because managers not only listened to their ideas but also allowed employees to move forward with their ideas and put them into action, and a deliberate effort of management to include employees in every quality initiative undertaken in the organization. It turned out that greater commitment is created among employees when they are allowed to participate and have their say, and can feel co-owner of the decisions and actions that are taken. There are, however, some conditions which need to be met in order to create effective involvement: participation doesn't mean that everybody is entitled to participate in everything at the same level (being informed, join in the conversation, think along, take part in deciding, take part in executing); people who are participating must have enough knowledge to be able to usefully participate; the participants must be aware that they are participating for the greater good of the organization, not to serve the interests of their own departments; and participants must be able to deal with uncertainty and ambiguity, as there is no guarantee that their involvement will always influence the course of the process in the way they would like to.[54]

> "In the process to make sure we have good and safe flights nobody can work perched in their ivory towers without interacting with others, it is crucial to work together. And that means openness and involving everybody, which is therefore in our genes. Also, when there are developments we take great care to personally talk with our people at their workplace. So if we need to talk to the cargo loaders we will organize several meetings in the warehouses, one during every shift. When board members fly on one of our planes, they will take the time during the flight to talk to the crew. In other words, management is visible and the nice side-effect is that it creates trust. This openness makes taking action also easy: everybody knows why we are doing certain things and why we are doing them in a certain way. So we can be very action oriented and solve problems quickly."
>
> *Arend de Jong, Air France KLM*

IDEAS TO GET STARTED WITH INVOLVING EMPLOYEES

You can use these ideas to improve the effective involvement of employees:

- Involve employees always in activities that influence their work.

- Make clear that being involved does not mean that employees have a veto.

- Make sure you are prepared for the involvement: it has to be clear who should be involved in which processes when and in what way and what is expected.

HPO FACTOR 2 – OPENNESS & ACTION ORIENTATION

- Involvement and participation should be seen as part of the regular job.
- Make clear that someone is not only involved for the personal benefit but also for the benefit of others, by sharing experiences during the involvement.
- Make sure there is enough training, guidance and coaching to make the involvement as effective as possible.

❝One of the rules we uphold is consent: everybody should in principle agree with a decision, that is without having any substantial doubts. Even if only one person objects because he or she really has substantial doubts, irrespective of his or her function in the organization, we take this seriously. We discuss in-depth what the issue is because that person might have found a reason why a certain solution was not optimal for the customer. Hierarchy just does not fit in with this way of operating.❞

Pim Berger & Ilja Heitlager, Schuberg Philis

4.4 Allowing mistakes

Allowing mistakes is defined as 'permitting a person to do things incorrectly or make errors of judgment without consequences.' Research shows that organizations learn more effectively from their mistakes than from their successes and that knowledge from mistakes depreciates more slowly than knowledge from success. However, in general, people have difficulty owning up to a mistake and this is all the more true the higher up the organizational ladder. It seems that especially managers are afraid to set the right example by openly admitting they did something wrong or something went awry. HPO managers therefore actively promote undertaking experiments and learning from mistakes.[55] They permit employees to take risks, are willing to take risks themselves, and convey that mistakes are an opportunity to learn. HPO managers have a tolerance for failure and setbacks, they don't play the blame game, the focus is on remedying and improving. People do not need to cover up their mistakes but can openly discuss these and subsequently learn from them. Messengers of bad news are not punished for bringing the news, they are actually rewarded for their courage, while people who hide their mistakes are reprimanded. In the HPO nobody cares about why a mistake was made but about how it is going to be fixed and what can be learned from it. There is however in the HPO one type of mistake which is never allowed: the same! People in an HPO also know that if they never make a mistake, they are probably playing it too safe and are therefore not innovative enough.[56]

> ❝Our chief executive officer says it all the time: do your thing and if this thing eventually has to be changed or adjusted we will let you know, but start doing it anyway. People always have a bit of fear taking charge in this manner, they always want to do the right thing. Clearly some mistakes are harmful. In a highly regulated industry we have to draw the lines. We encourage being accountable, from making decisions when they're needed to calling out incongruent behavior when you see it. At the end of the day, it's about being engaged.❞
>
> *Lani Hayward, Umpqua Bank*

> ❝Being high performing doesn't mean you don't make mistakes! If we make one, we will genuinely own up to it and that is much appreciated by the customer. If something goes wrong and you are able to be open about it and fix it quickly and afterwards make sure you solve the root cause of the mistake, you will get many compliments from your customer. Perhaps the most difficult display of behavior to overcome in an organization and in the relation with partners and customers is the blame culture that kicks in the minute something goes wrong. We, from our very inception, have addressed the 'fingerpointing' issue by taking 100 percent responsibility for the availability of mission critical applications at the customer. Our company culture and natural attitude is to first

HPO FACTOR 2 – OPENNESS & ACTION ORIENTATION

solve an issue with all means possible and only afterwards, through fact based analysis, find the root cause and plan and execute fixing the problem structurally. Adopting this mindset frees up time and energy – which otherwise would be devoted to figuring out who is at fault or who is to blame – to productively diagnosing and solving problems. Consequently, a culture that avoids fingerpointing also prevents partners from defensively withholding information from each other. Information that may be important to their mutual and customers' success but which is not shared for fear that it might be used as evidence of incompetence or poor performance. Based on our collaborative attitude, behavior and culture we are capable of building high-trust relationships with all parties involved."

Pim Berger & Ilja Heitlager, Schuberg Philis

IDEAS TO GET STARTED TO CREATE A SAFE ENVIRONMENT FOR ALLOWING MISTAKES

You can build a psychologically safe environment for employees to make mistakes in the following ways:

- Create an understanding in the organization of the kinds of mistakes and failures that can be expected to occur in a given work context and why openness about the mistakes is important to be able to fix them and learn from them.

- Embrace messengers of mistakes openly, so that people who come forward with mistakes are rewarded rather than punished.

- Be open about the mistakes that you have made and that you cannot fix alone, this will encourage others to do the same. An interesting 'by-product' of owning up to your mistakes is that it actually increases trust of your employees in you.

- Invite participation by asking for observations and ideas and creating opportunities for people to detect and analyze mistakes and failures and promote intelligent experiments.

- Set boundaries to make clear what is and what isn't acceptable, and hold people accountable. If someone is punished, tell those directly and indirectly affected what happened and why it warranted punishment.

- Introduce 'the blunder of the week' on the agenda of meetings. All persons present have to state their biggest goof-up of the past week – which shouldn't be something minor like "I forgot to return your call"- and which should be accompanied with the things the person learned because of the mistake. The first person to always start owning up should be you, so that a climate of safety is created for everybody to speak freely.

❝We give people so much responsibility early on in their career that mistakes are bound to be made, you just expect them so that is not such a big deal. Making the same mistake twice, that is really not done because then you show that you haven't learned from the first time around. Tolerance for the same mistakes is just plain low here.❞

Lennard Boogaard, Unilever

❝We are the world's greatest bank, not the world's most perfect bank. Mistakes are going to be made, they just are. But it is a matter of how empowered one is: Is someone allowed to fix a problem at all cost, especially when it happened several times, and you're going to lose customers if you can't fix it at the end of the day? The important thing is that we talk about the opportunity around a mistake or a customer issue. There is more opportunity in issues than in the day-to-day transactions and being nice and giving service. If you are empowered to turn a bad situation into a good one, our frontline people will say: "I am going to see what I can do here" and they go to the ends of the earth. They are not always going to be successful with everyone, certainly, but they convey to customers that they try as hard as possible. We learned a lot from the Ritz-Carlton. A lot of their teachings say that it is not only about making the stay at their hotel really great and continuously surprising and delighting their guests, but about handling a complaint in such a way that guests are going to tell 20 friends: "Go over there and let them make a mistake because what they do to fix it is great."

Lani Hayward, Umpqua Bank

4.5 Welcoming change

Welcoming change is defined as 'the act of greeting or receiving the opportunity to become different.' Managers in an HPO stimulate change by promoting self-awareness in the organization, which encourages people to reflect on whether they need to change, and by developing capabilities to actually be able to change and to enhance flexibility. HPO managers are active leaders of change processes in the organization by being personally involved in these. They adapt without difficulty their leadership style if the change process requires so.

"We continuously challenge our people to come up with new ideas, work on changing and improving processes, structures or systems. Our people thus developed an inherent attitude that, even after coming to work for 20 years, they still want to try out something new."

Jan Maas, TATA Steel

IDEAS TO GET STARTED TO WELCOME CHANGE

To welcome change, you should do the following things:

- Set expectations explicitly. If people don't know what is expected of them there will be a lot of uncertainty among employees and colleagues about the change, which causes an a priori resistance to it.

- Assign responsibilities clearly. If it is unclear who's responsible for what, nobody feels accountable for the change to actually happen.

- Discuss roadblocks (e.g. systems and procedures) with your colleagues, employees and executive management. If obstacles persist, change will not happen.

- Free up resources. If people are not given the opportunity to work on the change, it is bound to fail from the start and people won't get involved.

- Install incentive systems that reward change in the own unit and the whole organization. Without these incentives people will not exert themselves for 'the bigger picture'.

- Do not punish people if they weren't able to achieve their own targets because they helped in organization-wide change projects. This punishment will induce them to never again give their support to 'the bigger picture'.

❝Good managers need to 'walk the talk' every single day and not see change and improvement as a project. As a leader you are going to have to stretch yourself and your people. Yes, you are going to have your moments where you bounce backwards, but you are going to have to continue making everybody uncomfortable with the current situation so they want to go into new realms. You have to keep them pumped up and motivated, which isn't easy. At Umpqua this attitude has spread far and wide in the company, and thus not only in divisions that deal with customers. If you look, for instance, at our chief financial officer, he and his finance group will look for opportunities to do things differently with our financial affairs. This is why we have unusual names for our divisions. It's not just to be cute, it's to think differently. So Accounting is called Financial Integrity Group. The human resources department is called Culture Enhancement. I do not work in the marketing department but the Creative Strategies Department. It paints a much clearer picture of what we are doing and what we stand for."

Lani Hayward, Umpqua Bank

4.6   Performance drivenness

Performance drivenness is defined as 'having a strong orientation to do things well and a need to achieve results.' People in the HPO do not assume that success is permanent. They realize that nothing lasts forever, and therefore they fight complacency and challenge the current status quo; focus strongly on achieving the highest form of excellence in everything the organization does; and stimulate each other to achieve high performance. They have a strong discipline in execution, yet at the same time they know and expect that disappointments will occur and consequently develop resilience to setbacks. Because of this attitude, they will eventually accomplish the agreed upon targets.

"Every month we make a ranking of the financial results that the branches have achieved. As long as branches show a continuous positive movement in the financial results and thus move up the ranking, they are okay. The idea is of course for branches to get above the average. Every branch wants to be above average, they want to be in the upper half of the ranking and be better than their peers. So everybody moves continuously up, and this creates a real performance-driven culture."

Mikael Sørensen, Svenska Handelsbanken

IDEAS TO GET STARTED TO BECOME MORE PERFORMANCE DRIVEN, BY PROMOTING COLLABORATION

One of the main roadblocks for creating a performance-driven organization is lack of collaboration between organizational units, leading to sub-optimal results. You can use 'the three steps of collaboration' to promote effective collaboration in your organization (based on Hansen, 2009):

1. Investigate and evaluate the possibilities for collaboration. You cannot just start from the assumption that all collaboration is good and worthwhile, you first have to make a business case for that. Establish the goal of the collaboration and determine the possible benefits (better innovation, more sales, less operational costs, other benefits). In addition, calculate the costs of the collaboration in terms of manpower, systems changes and other resources needed. Weigh the benefits and costs and if the outcome is positive, you should go ahead with the collaboration.

2. Identify the barriers for collaboration. There are four main barriers which can be expected:
   - not-invented-by-me: people don't want or seek the help of others when they don't feel a sense of ownership

> - hoarding: people are not willing to provide information;
> - search problem: people are not able to find the right information or the right people to help them;
> - transfer problems: people are not able to transfer complicated information and knowledge to each other.
> 3. Deal with the barriers, in a manner which is tailored to the specific situation in which the collaboration has to be realized.

❝In regard to being a performance-driven organization, 'sharing the load' is an important notion here: look around regularly to see if somebody needs your help. Another notion is 'it won't happen on my watch', meaning that it is the pride of the teams that they do not allow a problem to occur during their working hours, so they jointly make an effort to prevent it from happening. It is not only your own team's customer but it is a Schuberg Philis' customer which needs to be helped.❞

Pim Berger & Ilja Heitlager, Schuberg Philis

KEY POINTS CHAPTER 4

- The HPO factor Openness & Action Orientation concerns the manner in which managers and employees interact in the organization.

- The underlying characteristics of HPO factor Openness & Action Orientation are: dialogue, knowledge sharing, employee involvement, allowing mistakes, welcoming change and performance driveness.

- In the long run, improvement of these characteristics helps to develop trust in the organization and also creates the knowledge that is needed to practice continuous improvement.

- The HPO's motto is "a day not learned is a day not lived."

Vietnamese banking industry (Vietnam): identifying the HPO characteristics of an industry

KEY MESSAGE

Just as it can be done for a single organization, the HPO status can also be determined for a group of organizations within an industry. In addition, it is possible to identify the HPO characteristics that make the difference between becoming a leader or a lagger in a particular industry.

One of the challenges for Vietnam, since the country joined the World Trade Organization (WTO), was to restructure the banking industry in such a way that it would comply with the WTO requirements. Another reason for the restructuring was that, according to the WTO treaty, banks from other countries were finally allowed to do business in Vietnam with the same rights and privileges as local banks.[57] The Vietnamese banking industry could now be divided into two main categories: local banks (consisting of state-owned commercial banks and joint stock banks) and foreign owned banks. Because the onrush of the foreign owned banks, competition had increased considerably forcing local banks to look for ways to increase their performance and thereby improve their competitiveness. For this, they needed to know which HPO characteristics were most important for the Vietnamese banking industry. To find these characteristics, the HPO Questionnaire was sent to 26 local and foreign banks in Ho Chi Minh City and Hanoi. From the received questionnaires the average HPO scores for the two categories of banks was calculated. In addition, return on assets (ROA) and return on equity (ROE) financial data for the banks was collected for the years 2004, 2005 and 2006, and the mean values for the two types of banks for these three years was calculated.

	Local banks	Foreign banks	Difference
Management Quality	7.6	7.7	0.1
Openness & Action Orientation	7.0	7.4	0.4
Long-Term Orientation	8.1	8.4	0.3
Continuous Improvement & Renewal	6.8	7.6	0.9
Employee Quality	7.4	7.5	0.1
Average HPO score	*7.4*	*7.7*	*0.3*
ROA (%)	1.27	1.37	0.10
ROE (%)	14.18	14.20	0.02

Table 4.1: Average HPO scores and financial results for the foreign and local Vietnamese banks

Table 4.1 shows that the foreign banks had a slightly but significant higher HPO score than the local banks, and – as could be expected in terms of the HPO definition – they also had a slightly better financial performance than the local banks. The reason for the better performance of the foreign banks was that their parent companies had been practicing modern management for many decades while local Vietnamese banks had just started to learn over the past years what modern management was and how it should be applied in their organizations. The lead of the foreign banks however was smaller than might be expected and for this there are several explanations. A number of local banks were created by a dominant player in a specific Vietnamese industry to serve the needs of that industry in a closed loop, which meant foreign banks did not have access to that lucrative industry. Local banks had less complex organizational structures than foreign banks, which made it relatively easier for local banks to have fast decision-making and action-taking processes. In some local banks the senior members of the management repatriated from banks in foreign countries which made management quality levels somewhat more equal in the two types of banks. Larger numbers of managers at local banks had a greater number of years of service with the bank than was the case at foreign banks, as at the latter managers were often assigned to work in Vietnam for a couple of years and then returned to their home countries. Also, local banks had been striving to attract employees from foreign banks to switch to them. Local banks had a larger network in Vietnam than foreign banks. Most of the foreign banks only had one branch in Vietnam, while local banks had a much bigger network. Foreign banks hired many more expatriates and therefore had more expensive staff than local banks. Finally, obtaining a substantial market share was very important for foreign banks to gain a foothold in Vietnam, which meant they were less concerned with profitability at the time of the research. It could be said that, considering these advantages of local banks, it was almost a miracle that foreign banks still performed better.

On the basis of the results, it was evaluated whether the Vietnamese banks with the highest HPO scores focused on different HPO characteristics than the Vietnamese banks with the lowest scores. These characteristics then had to make the difference between becoming a leader or staying a lagger in the Vietnamese banking industry. The bank with the highest HPO scores (a foreign bank) and the lowest HPO scores (a local bank) were compared to identify the HPO characteristics with the biggest difference in scores. This comparison showed that the highest scoring Vietnamese banks paid more attention to the following HPO characteristics than the lowest scoring Vietnamese banks: the bank had adopted a strategy that set it clearly apart from other organizations; processes were continuously improved and simplified; the bank continuously innovated its core competencies, products, processes and services; management of the bank applied fast decision-making and fast action-taking; bank personnel was resilient and flexible; and the bank had a diverse and complementary workforce. This was important information for Vietnamese bank managers because they now knew on which these HPO characteristics they should focus to improve, in order to achieve the most added value for their organizations.

Iringa University College (Tanzania): improving through applying the HPO Framework

KEY MESSAGE

If an organization works in a disciplined manner on the improvement points identified during the HPO Diagnosis, it *will* – after a period of time – achieve a higher average HPO score during a second HPO Diagnosis. And this means better financial and non-financial results!

Iringa University College (IUCo) is one of the colleges of Tumaini University, which is owned by the Evangelical Lutheran Church of Tanzania.[58] The college has four faculties (Business and Economics, Arts and Social Sciences, Law, Theology); an Institute of Agriculture; a Directorate of Postgraduates, Research and Publication; and a Centre for Rural Entrepreneurship. At the time of the research, IUCo had 2,700 students which came from all over Tanzania and neighboring countries. IUCo had full accreditation status, granted by the Higher Education Accreditation Council. The college was headed by a Provost, who was the chief executive officer, reporting directly to the board of directors appointed by the Trustees of Tumaini University. The Provost was assisted by two line officers responsible for academic affairs and general administration, the deputy provost for academic affairs (DPAA) and the deputy provost for administration (DPA). Under the DPAA resorted the faculty deans, directors of various directorates, and heads of academic departments, while to the DPA reported the chief financial officer and various departments (accounting and procurement, personnel,

HPO FACTOR 2 – OPENNESS & ACTION ORIENTATION

students' welfare and recreation, catering, security and health). The planning, internal auditing and public relations functions reported directly to the Provost.

The reason for IUCO to conduct an HPO Diagnosis was that the university was facing many challenges. IUCo had to deal with a huge influx of students, from less than 1,000 in 2003 to more than 2,000 in 2007; stiff competition due to the increased number of universities in Tanzania; poor quality of the secondary school education resulting in many students with deficiencies; increased poverty level in the region; the great distance from the big city centre (Dar Es Salaam) making it difficult to attract qualified personnel; too highly priced accommodation for off-campus students; church politics and bureaucracy; high construction costs of new campus buildings; increased government support for private universities' expansion resulting in more competition for privately funded IUCo; and scarce availability of government loans for university students. IUCo's management stated that the quality of the internal organization of the university should not only be raised in order to deal with the aforementioned challenges, but also to increase enrollment, increase quality of teaching and research, and becoming financially more stable. To achieve this, management turned to the HPO Framework to guide its improvement focus and actions.

Results of the 2007 HPO workshop

IUCo's management visited the Maastricht School of Management in the Netherlands in August 2006, where IUCo's strategic plan was discussed and reviewed by management together with the author of this book. The results of the discussion were shared among IUCo staff members in a one day workshop organized by the Provost in Spring 2007. In July 2007 IUCo's management organized a four-day strategic plan workshop to advance the project. This workshop was facilitated by the author, and management and academic staff were present. During the workshop, the HPO status of the college was determined, IUCo's strategic objectives were reviewed and updated, and IUCo's performance management processes were discussed to identify improvements. To determine the HPO status of IUCo, the HPO questionnaire was distributed among managers and other staff. In this questionnaire respondents indicated how good IUCo performed on the various HPO characteristics, on a scale of 1 to 10. Their scores were then averaged. The bottom curve in figure 4.1 gives the HPO status of IUCo as of July 2007.

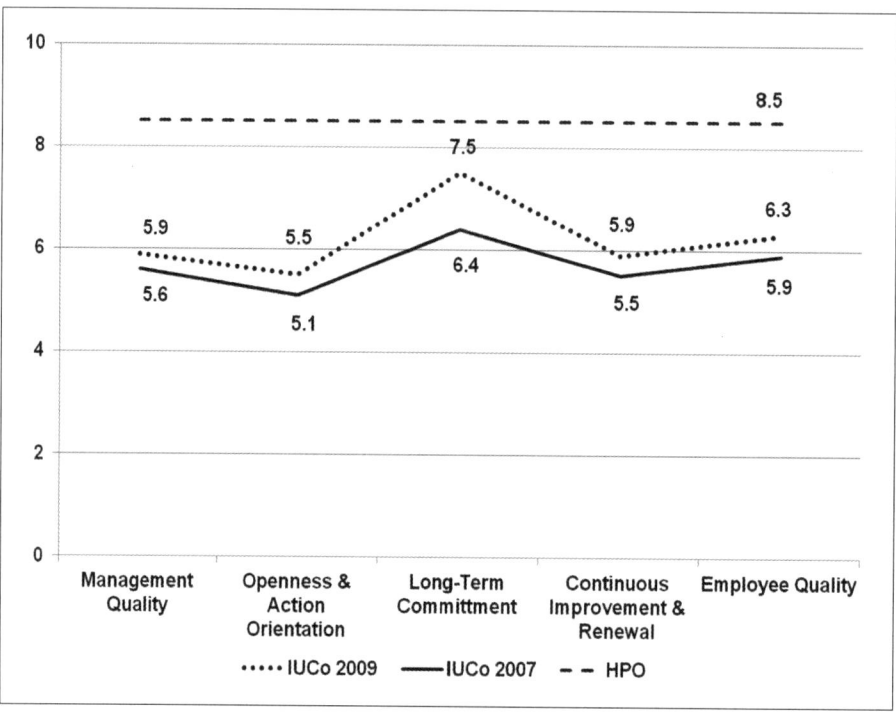

Figure 4.1: HPO status of Iringa University College in 2007 and 2009

It is clear from Figure 4.1 that IUCo had to improve all HPO factors considerably to achieve an excellent performance level. When looking into the individual IUCo scores of the HPO characteristics, a number of improvement themes were identified. First, the HPO factor Openness & Action Orientation (score: 5.1) had to be improved. IUCo's management did not frequently engage in a dialogue with employees (score: 4.3), IUCo's employees themselves did not spend much time on communication, knowledge exchange and learning (score: 4.7), and IUCo's management did not allow people to make mistakes (score: 5.0). Thus, to improve this HPO factor, IUCo had to become more open and courageous at all organizational levels. Open in the sense that there had to be more vertical dialogue between management and staff, and horizontal knowledge exchange between staff in the different departments. Courageous in the sense that management had to be willing to let staff experiment more and thereby probably start making more mistakes from which people could learn. At the same time, staff had to be willing to start experimenting and have the courage to start new things (and in the process make mistakes). Second, the HPO factor Management Quality (score: 5.6) had to be improved. IUCo's management had to become a role model for staff (score: 5.0) by, for instance, applying fast action taking (score: 5.1) and coaching staff to achieve better results (score: 5.0). This meant that IUCo's management had to become more inspirational. At the same time, staff had to improve also by becoming more resilient and flexible (score: 4.7) so they could be coached to better performance. Third, IUCo had to improve its focus on Continuous Improvement & Renewal (score: 5.5). For this, IUCo had to make sure that what mattered to the organization's performance was explicitly reported (score: 4.7) to everybody in the organization (score: 4.0). Also, IUCo's processes had to be continuously simplified (score: 5.0) and aligned (score: 5.0). This meant that IUCo had to continue with strategic performance management and start with process management. During the four-day workshop a start was made with improving the HPO factors. Management chose for updating the strategic objectives, critical success factors (CSFs) and key performance indicators (KPIs) because it was felt that with clear strategic objectives and measurements people at IUCo would better understand what was expected from them. The reformulation of the strategic objectives was accompanied by a discussion about the performance-driven behavior that IUCo's management and employees had to show to achieve the strategic objectives successfully.

Results of the 2009 HPO workshop

In February 2009, IUCo's management invited the author again to come to Iringa and review the progress made by IUCO on its transition to becoming an HPO. During the review meeting, the new HPO status of IUCo, results achieved so far on the strategic objectives, and possible recommendation for further improvements were discussed. The HPO Questionnaire was again distributed and filled in, interviews were conducted, and a workshop was held with almost 100 IUCo managers, academics and employees. The middle curve in Figure 4.1 depicts the HPO status of IUCo as of February 2009. The HPO score curves for both years have the same shape, meaning that IUCo's organization and culture had not changed dramatically in eighteen months time (as could be expected). However, the HPO status of 2009 showed a distinct improvement compared to the 2007 status, meaning that IUCo had improved its performance in the mean time.

IUCo's performance in the 2007-2009 period

When the HPO status of an organization improves, its financial and non-financial results should also have become better. At IUCo this certainly was the case. The organization had become financially stable and experienced a substantial increase in student enrollment. Many new students and new faculty were transferring from other universities to IUCo, and IUCo alumni were hired more than ever before to teach at other universities or to work in government. IUCo's staff were doing more research and had an increased number of academic publications. Furthermore, IUCo had been chosen to participate in a Tanzanian-wide quality

HPO FACTOR 2 – OPENNESS & ACTION ORIENTATION

assurance pilot. And most importantly, students were increasingly proud to be studying at IUCo. When looking in more detail at IUCo's ten strategic objectives as defined in 2007, the organization had moved forward on these too:

1. *Rank (in quality reputation) among the top 10 of peer East African universities by the year 2011/2012* – Management had taken two actions to achieve this objective. They had reviewed the quality of programmes offered by IUCo and made a plan for further development of academic staff.

2. *Achieve national and international recognition and awareness by the year 2011/2012* – IUCo staff were asked to join accreditation committees, and IUCo alumni had started teaching at other universities. Internationally, IUCo had made links to several universities worldwide, and international researchers now came to IUCo to do joint research.

3. *Recruit and retain more students, especially female* – The enrollment of students had increased from 2,526 in 2008 to 2,720 in 2009. The rate of student retention was also good and not many students were dropping out.

4. *Raise the education quality experience to match the increasing education cost* – IUCo was adding more programs, some of which were the first to be offered in Tanzania.

5. *Be within at least 80% of the nationally recommended facility specifications by 2011/2012* – A huge extension of the library, including a digital centre, was built so it became the research centre for the Southern region of Tanzania. Also, more lecture theatres were planned to be built to facilitate the increased student enrollment.

6. *Attain 80% of client satisfaction by the end of 2011/2012* – In regard to students there was no specific information on this at the time. In regard to academic staff, its compensation had

been increased and a management development program was in place.

7. *Register at least 80% in provision of students' welfare* – More and better student accommodation and dormitories were planned and being built.

8. *Attain a budget of at least 20% non-fee of the total income by the year 2011/2012* – IUCo was still completely dependent on student tuition fees so this objective was not reached. IUCo was looking for alternatives, such as participating in projects which would generate additional income by setting up a Consultancy Bureau.

9. *Design and carry out at least 15 community sensitive researches by 2011/2012 and be actively involved in at least two substantial ongoing community based programmes at any one time by the year 2011/2012* – Many programmes were established which involved the community. For instance, IT students helped businesses with activities such as advertising, IT workshops were conducted at youth centers, and the Law faculty was giving legal advice to people.

10. *Design an appropriate organizational structure and schedule all IUCo meetings* – A new organizational structure had been developed and proposed by IUCo's management, and was waiting for approval of the Tumaini board of directors to be put in place.

It could be concluded that IUCo was gaining a growing reputation as a quality educational institution. At the same time, IUCo was not yet an HPO but the organization was well on its way and was committed to further improvements in the future.

HPO FACTOR 2 – OPENNESS & ACTION ORIENTATION

Palestine Polytechnics University (Palestine Territories): working on HPO in difficult circumstances

KEY MESSAGE

Even in difficult environments there is a strong desire for, and there are possibilities of, achieving excellence and creating HPOs.

Higher education has developed very quickly in Palestine over the past three decades but at the same time it has been facing severe challenges. [59] These were caused by the increasing number of high school graduates who had to be accommodated with classes and teachers, efficiency and quality issues related to the development of courses, and financing problems resulting from the aftermath of the troubles in the area. In response to these challenges, the Palestinian Ministry of Higher Education and Scientific Research developed a higher education strategy which proposed a different financing strategy for the education sector. In developing the strategy, the reality was acknowledged that the level of financial support for Palestinian higher education was not likely in the foreseeable future to be sufficient to ensure financial sustainability of the complete education system. Therefore, major financial reforms were proposed, which meant that financing the educational institutions was to become incentive-based rather than regulatory, with a strong emphasis on increasing the quality of the educational institutions. This was to be achieved by introducing competitive funding of selected projects (new courses, new research studies) with the requirement that the quality of the management of the 'winning' educational institutions had to be improved as well.

One of the educational institutions which was affected by the new strategy was the Palestine Polytechnic University (PPU), one of the leading polytechnic universities in Palestine. PPU was based in the Hebron district on the West Bank, 30 kilometers south of Jerusalem, Israel. It was founded in 1978 by the University Graduates Union and officially recognized by the Palestinian Ministry of Higher Education. The mission of PPU was to improve the quality of vocational and technical engineering education. This had to be achieved by providing students with practical knowledge to help them acquire an up-to-date experience directly related to their disciplines. There were over 5,000 students enrolled in PPU's four colleges: the College of Engineering and Technology, the College of Applied Science, the College of Administrative Science and Informatics, and the College of Applied Professions. PPU dedicated specific attention and commitment to enhancing its relationship with the local community, by identifying potential community priorities and needs and then developing programs to meet these priorities and needs.

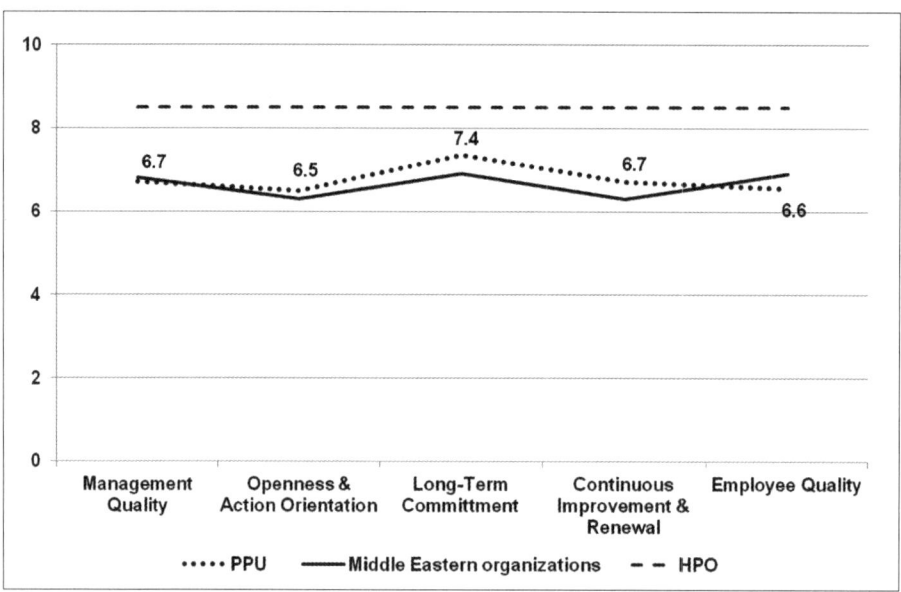

Figure 4.2: HPO status of Palestine Polytechnic University, compared with Middle Eastern organizations

HPO FACTOR 2 – OPENNESS & ACTION ORIENTATION

In order to be able to satisfy the requirements of the new educational strategy, PPU's management decided to start working dedicatedly on improving the quality of the organization. For this, they decided to conduct an HPO Diagnosis. The HPO Center was invited to conduct an HPO workshop at PPU's premises in Hebron. During the workshop, management and staff filled in the HPO Questionnaire. The resulting HPO status of PPU, and the comparison with the HPO status of other Middle Eastern organizations in the database of the HPO Center, is depicted in Figure 4.2.

With an average HPO score of 6.8, PPU is an average scoring organization that performs more or less the same as the other Middle Eastern organizations in the HPO database (average score: 6.6). The strengths of PPU could clearly be found in the HPO factor Long-Term Orientation. This was caused by the strong focus of PPU on delivering quality to its students, giving them a better chance on a good (professional) life, and the strong ties with the local community (the stakeholders). Also, many people tended to stay a long time with the organization as they found PPU's management to really care about their well-being and professional development. From the HPO scores and subsequent discussion during the workshop, two main issues for PPU emerged that had to be addressed in order to transform the university in an HPO. The first issue was that PPU's performance management process had to be improved as not everything that mattered to PPU's performance was adequately communicated to everybody in the organization. The second issue was that the performance-driven behavior of PPU's people had to be strengthened as the decision-making and action-taking processes took too long and people were not resilient and flexible enough to deal swiftly with changing circumstances, resulting in an organization that was not as performance-driven as it could be. Management decided to first improve PPU's strategy and mission, by converting these into SMART strategic objectives,[60] critical success factors (CSFs) and key performance indicators (KPIs). After this, the culture of PPU was discussed and new performance driven values were developed which had to promote performance-driven behavior in PPU. We will focus our discussion on the second issue. As several of the workshop participants said, PPU's culture could be described by the saying "When I am right nobody remembers, when I am wrong nobody forgets." The participants agreed that this had to change to "When I am right everybody remembers, when I am wrong everybody forgets." So it was decided that the first step in changing PPU's culture into a performance-driven one was to introduce performance-driven values. The following eight values were agreed upon:

1. Respect time arrangements.
2. Conduct regular dialogues and sharing of knowledge meetings, both along horizontal (colleagues) and vertical (following the hierarchy) lines.
3. Give clear responsibilities to staff.
4. Feel responsible and accountable for your results.
5. Be firm with executing accountability, and deal with non-performers.
6. Live according to PPU's reputation as a high performance university.
7. Give more non-financial incentives, such as complements to show appreciation.
8. Give fair treatment to peers.

These performance-driven values were to be the rules according to which PPU's management and staff had to live up to in order to be able to together transform PPU into a high performance university.

Chapter 5

HPO factor 3 – Long-Term Orientation: *stakeholder thinking trumps shareholder management*

LONG-TERM
ORIENTATION

Chapter preview

In the HPO, long-term continuity of the organization always has priority over achieving short-term profit. This long-term thinking of the HPO extends to all its stakeholders: customers, suppliers, employees, government, interest groups, society ... everyone who has a relation with the organization should be positively affected by it.

This chapter discusses the five characteristics of the HPO factor Long-Term Orientation. A definition is given for each characteristic followed by a description of the behaviors of HPO managers and employees that is typical of the characteristic. In addition, a number of 'ideas to get started' are listed to improve the characteristic discussed. This HPO factor is further illustrated with two short discourses, one on the myth of economic growth and the other on the relationship between corporate social responsibility and the HPO Framework.

5.1   Stakeholder orientation

Stakeholder orientation is defined as 'the aim to benefit all parties that are affected by the future success or failure of an organization.' People in an HPO find shareholder thinking too limited and therefore make sure they maintain good and long-term relationships with all stakeholders, creating win-win relationships.[61] They understand the needs of key stakeholders by staying in close contact with them, and they continuously align stakeholder needs with the organization's needs. They are generous to society by demonstrating significant financial commitment to local economies and environments by regularly investing in these. They develop a good corporate reputation by focusing on corporate social responsibility (CSR), making this a real living activity.

> ❝One of our strengths is the way we treat everybody who has dealings with us, be it clients, suppliers, or our neighbours in this area. We regularly take stock of our stakeholders and think about the way we interact with them: what do we want to achieve with them, which way do we need to go with them, how can we improve our cooperation. We like to involve our stakeholders in what we are doing, ask their opinion, solicit their ideas. We don't do this in a quick and dirty way, we really take our time to interact with them. What helps is that many of our people, including management, live in the area so they are immersed in the local community and thus well-informed about possible sentiments toward Tata Steel. This attitude of ours developed in the 1960s and 1970s when Hoogovens was the largest employer in this area, which comes with a huge responsibility as management

HPO FACTOR 3 – LONG-TERM ORIENTATION

realised that many families were dependant on the company for their livelihood. We must have done something right because our people are not job hoppers and tend to stay long, and we have good relationships with people representatives organized in, for instance, the works councils. Investing in your stakeholders is not only a moral obligation but also makes perfect economic sense: it is a very good, pleasant and therefore productive environment here!"

Jan Maas, TATA Steel

IDEAS TO GET STARTED TO FOSTER A STAKEHOLDER ORIENTATION

You can do the following to foster a stakeholder orientation in your organization:

- Create an organization with a coherent identity and a common purpose.
- Develop a long-term perspective that justifies short-term financial sacrifices in order to achieve that common purpose and to endure over time.
- Articulate a purpose broader than making money, thereby letting people think about new sources for innovation.
- Create public-private partnerships, in which societal interests come together with business interests.
- Give people room to express personal values in their everyday work.
- Apply co-creation with stakeholders, by inviting them to participate in the dialogue around new products and services of the organization.

> "A good manager at Unilever has both a to-do list and a to-be list. In business we are focused on hard-nosed achieving targets and creating shareholders value so we tend to be led by to-do lists. We focus on what we need to do and forget what we want to be. But in business you also have a corporate social responsibility which is value driven and this provides you with a to-be list. So it is a combination of what you want to achieve and why you want to achieve it, and you have to manage both well. It is easy to manage on results, but it is much more difficult to manage on values because you first have to answer difficult questions like: Who do we want to be as a company? What do we stand for? What is our point on the horizon, what do we want to achieve for society? At the same time you have to achieve your targets, you have business goals to achieve. Many people say that shareholder value and corporate social responsibility are mutually exclusive but they are not, not when you deliberately manage them together simultaneously. That's why you need two lists, one 'to-do' for business and one 'to-be' for social responsibility."
>
> Lennard Boogaard, Unilever

The myth of economic growth

Chief executive officers can place their organizations, and themselves, in severe difficulties by promising the stock market that their companies will grow 15 percent in turnover a year. [62] In itself it is not so surprising that chief executive officers make these forecasts time after time. After all, a yearly growth of 15 percent means profits can double every five years, which will make these chief executive officers the favorite of analysts and shareholders. They will be ranked among the most-admired business leaders, a temptation only few are able to resist. Unfortunately, the reality is rather more complex. Research shows that a growth rate of 15 percent is unattainable for most companies and can therefore be considered an illusion. This was the outcome of a study which calculated the average growth rate in earnings per share for a cross section of Fortune 500 companies, over the last four decades, as depicted in Figure 5.1.

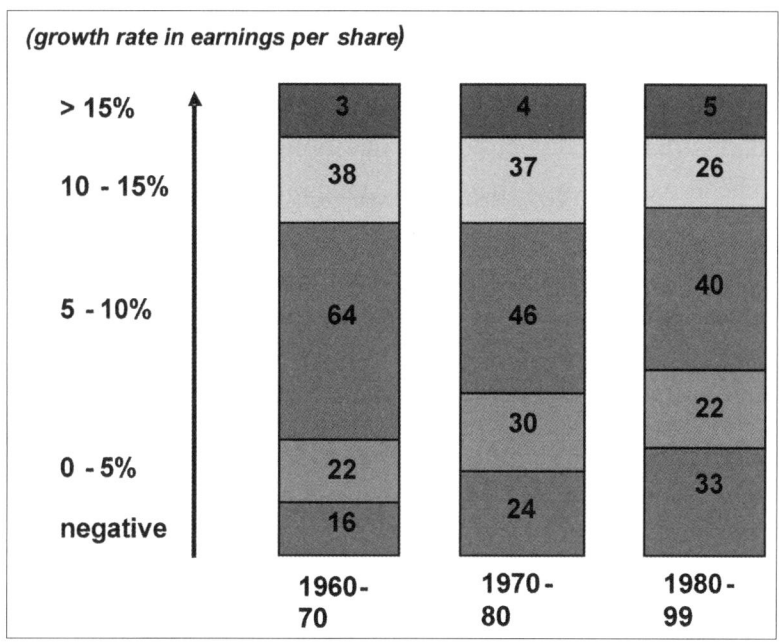

Figure 5.1: Average growth rate in earnings per share for a cross section of Fortune 500 companies

The results were astonishing: only a maximum of five companies (of the 126 examined over the period 1980-1999) obtained an average growth rate of 15 percent or more. At the same time, there were 33 companies with a negative growth rate. Companies which repeatedly fail to realize forecasted growth are likely to practice rollercoaster management (Figure 5.2).

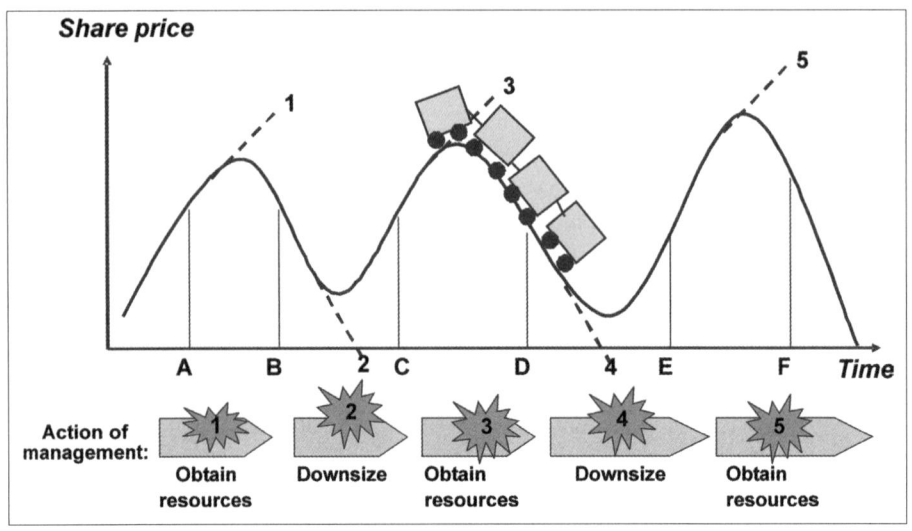

Figure 5.2: Rollercoaster management

Once a company has announced its growth expectations, management has to obtain and employ the resources needed to process the expected volume of trade (situation 1 in Figure 5.2). The stock market rewards this vigor of management with a rising share price. However, when turnover growth and profits lag behind expectations, the stock market responds by selling of shares: the share price goes down. On top of this, the organization now has a resource surplus which it has to get rid of: dismissals are the result (situation 2). In the next stage, new management makes new promises. Again, the stock market rewards this vigor and the share price rises (situation 3), and so on and on. Needless to say, this kind of management creates havoc in an organization. The urge to grow fast does not necessarily produce a good strategy. A study shows that of the 100 largest American companies at the beginning of the 20th century, only 16 made it to the end of the century.[63] It turned out that company size was not indicative for the chance of survival of a company. Another study shows that fast growth does not necessarily yield higher profits or shareholder value.[64] On the contrary, fast growth can in fact have an opposite effect. When the results of almost 3,000 organizations in the period 1993 to 1998 were examined, it turned out that companies with a moderate but steady growth of turnover and assets had the highest return on investment and EVA! A one-sided focus on fast growth can make a chief executive officer lose sight of a company's main goal: continuity. In addition to achieving a certain margin and return for all stakeholders, a chief executive officer has to guarantee the survival of the company. It is therefore important that management changes its strategic orientation from 'growth and shareholder value now, continuity tomorrow' to 'profitable and sustainable growth today'.

5.2 Customer orientation

Customer orientation is defined as 'the attitude of an organization toward the persons who buy goods or services.' People in an HPO display a great customer orientation by being as it were 'obsessed' with the customer. They learn what the customers want and understand their values by having direct contact with them. They build excellent relationships with the customers by engaging them and being responsive to their questions, concerns and needs. They focus on increasing customer loyalty by making customer satisfaction a central goal and then identifying the key factors that are critical for superior customer satisfaction. Subsequently, they regularly obtain feedback for evaluating customers' satisfaction. In the meantime, they create high standards for dealing with the customers and practice these. They put this into practice by delivering products and services that consistently meet customers' expectations, and by anticipating clients' unarticulated needs.

> ❝We have the rule at Schuberg Philis that we do everything in co-creation with the customer so there needs to be lots of contact. If you don't have much contact with a customer, then you should get worried about your job because that is just not acceptable.

Particularly because our customers value the contact with highly-skilled specialists who are really interested in their business. Our people thus get their satisfaction from a job well done, from a customer who is fully satisfied, and from working in a team with peers. Many of them say that at their former employers they were kind of sitting on an island, that there were no kindred spirits who wanted to jointly do the best they could. Now they have this and it stimulates them to get the most out of themselves. As a result, we don't have a huge turnover, about 2 to 3 percent while the industry norm is between 15 and 25 percent, but we have a very high customer satisfaction."

Pim Berger & Ilja Heitlager, Schuberg Philis

"What makes Handelsbanken different from many of our peers in the banking market is that we are a highly decentralised organization. We say that our branches *are* the bank. That means that most decisions are taken in the branches, all customers 'belong' to a specific branch, customer responsibility is placed with the branches, the branches decide everything in relation to the customer. They decide where the branch should be located, how many people should work there, the salaries for the employees, the local strategy. There are very few things they cannot decide on. The effect is that compared to our competitors the customer gets a significantly better service, our costs are lower and our return on equity is higher. More satisfied customers create more business, because they will give you new business and they will refer friends and family and business colleagues and so on to your bank. And that means that you will grow automatically. So all the branches focus very much on having satisfied customers."

Mikael Sørensen, Svenska Handelsbanken

IDEAS TO GET STARTED TO FOSTER A CUSTOMER ORIENTATION

Customers are more inclined to 'punish' bad service than to reward excellent service: they buy from the company because it sells quality products, they leave the company because of bad service. What customers are looking for is a satisfactory solution to their problems, which means getting a swift and complete solution without having to make an unnecessary large effort. Therefore you have to make sure that your customers do not experience the following: [65]

- having to explain their problem time after time to the organization's representatives

- having to switch service channels (for instance, from web to phone) because the answer cannot be found

- being transferred around the organization's departments looking for an answer while nobody at the organization seems to feel responsible for solving their problem

- forced to contact the organization several times before their problem is addressed adequately

- feeling they have to do too much effort to get their issue resolved.

You therefore have to focus on reducing the effort customers are making, by doing the following:

- Prevent the need for follow-up calls from the customer to the organization's call center, so focus on the 'first time fix'.

- Listen well to the customer's problem, and focus on complete problem solving and not on speed of dispatching.

- Structurally improve customer service by not only resolving current issues but also heading off new issues.
- Train employees to deal with the emotional side of interaction with disgruntled customers.
- Minimize the need for customers to switch service channels by making self-service options as simple as possible.
- Use feedback from unhappy and struggling customers to reduce the customer's efforts when complaining.
- Empower the front line employees to deliver a low-effort experience, by putting the quality of interaction with the customer above the speed of interaction.

❝Our vision has not changed since we started in 2000, our principles are still valid. While the organization has grown tremendously, we still want to get a rating of at least 8 out of 10, preferably higher, for customer satisfaction at every customer, and we have many customers that have been with us since the beginning. Some customers have left in mutual agreement because they were not big enough for the size that Schuberg Philis was growing to and maybe their business model did no longer match with ours. To some potential customers we say 'no' because we don't see a match in the way we would cooperate during a long-term relationship. For instance, if these potential customers would say that they don't necessarily need a 100 percent uptime and that 98 percent will also do for them, we cannot do business with them because that goes completely against our philosophy of doing business: 100 percent is 100 percent! Short cuts will create fingerpointing and feeling less responsible. We will always place quality before growth since we are sure that sustainable growth comes from satisfied customers. We get our satisfaction out of customer contacts, cooperating in achieving their business

HPO FACTOR 3 – LONG-TERM ORIENTATION

objectives, what we learn from them and from each other, from the way we grow, and it is nice that we can do this while earning a decent living. Our ideal is that people at the end of their career will say they had the best time of their working life at Schuberg Philis because they were able to get the most out of themselves. 🙸

Pim Berger & Ilja Heitlager, Schuberg Philis

🙶It really has been about quality and not quantity. We could have done more acquisitions but we do not exist just to get bigger and bigger. That is because we have this vision of being a community bank at any size, and that is hard to do. People should have the feeling that they are not a number. Sure, a big bank has all the bells and whistles, you know like the best this and the best that in terms of transactions. We are trying to achieve both, to have all the bells and whistles of a bigger bank and at the same time conveying the sense of knowing the clients, of having a relationship, of using our facilities for things outside of banking. If we can achieve that, even at 20 or 40 billion, it would be huge.🙸

Lani Hayward, Umpqua Bank

Creating HPO interactions with customers

Research has shown that the interaction between employee and customer is the most important determinant of the customer's perception of service quality. Exceptional service during employee-customer interaction drives customer satisfaction and customer loyalty and thereby organizational profitability. It is therefore paramount that the employees of the organization behave in such a way toward customers that they are fully satisfied and also become loyal to the organization. Recent research has identified the factors that are important for employees to be able to create HPO interactions with customers:[66]

- *High-quality employees* – The organization has to make sure it has intelligent, capable, knowledgeable, professional people with passion for their job.

- *High-quality service* – The high-quality employees have to provide high-quality service to customers, which is prompt, quick, accurate, reliable, complete, and done right the first time.

- *Understanding the customer* – Customers need to feel that they are understood by the employees who therefore should be understanding, caring, interested, and warm personalities who want to give customers personal and careful attention.

- *Understanding the customer's needs* – The employees should show they understand the needs of customers by being interested in, listening to, thinking about and understanding what the customers ask and then trying to meet and even anticipate their demands, so they feel they are valued as customers.

- *Responsiveness* – The employees should be responsive to customers by being readily available when needed, taking their time to service customers, giving them their full attention, being responsive and not dismissive to questions and requests of customers, and thus being fully engaged with customers.

- *Courtesy* – Employees are courteous during their dealings with customers by being respectful, helpful, attentive, patient, friendly and polite. This attitude should also show physically in smiling, cheerful and enthusiastic employees, who have a sincere facial expression while talking to customers in a relaxed manner.

- *Trustworthiness* – Employees have to convey a trustworthy posture by always giving their honest and reliable opinion, being sincere, natural and genuine toward customers and making them feel comfortable and safe in their dealings with the organization.

5.3 Longevity

Longevity is defined as 'long stay with the organization.' HPO managers typically stay with the organization for a long time. In this way, they become very knowledgeable about the industry and the customers and about the organizational mechanism and the employees. This makes it possible for them to put in new ideas very effectively and thereby continuously add value. HPO managers exercise careful stewardship of the organization and focus on the long-term survival of the organization. They avoid 'fad surfing' and do not strive for short-term gains, but are interested in techniques that can help their organization to become and stay sustainable. They are also good at balancing organizational interest with self-interest, and they teach colleagues and employees how to put the needs of the organization first. HPO managers create long-term relationships with people in the organization by staying themselves for a long time and enticing others to stay long.[67]

> **"**Our turnover rates are very low at senior levels. Of course, that is not necessarily healthy because you do need new blood in the organization. You have got to be careful about becoming too clubby, too insular. But the good thing is, it is about loyalty, people tend to stay a long time with SABMiller. The loyalty to the organization is very high. We bring people in who then become very loyal to the organization. And it is not because of the salary because those are average, with long-term incentives for higher management. So people can be headhunted for higher salaries but they stay anyway. There is something about the culture here that binds people and makes them loyal to the organization. Hopefully it is the degree of trust that we give to people. Maybe it is the levels of responsibility that we give to people, or the fact that we do care about individuals and their families. Over time, these things all come together and bring that loyalty.**"**
>
> *Alan Clark, SAB Miller Europe*

IDEAS TO GET STARTED TO GET PEOPLE TO STAY A LONG TIME

These are some practices you can apply to entice your people to stay longer at the organization:

- Install long apprenticeships. This way people know what kind of organization they are dealing with and they can make up their minds about whether they want to work there for a long time.
- Provide people with challenging tasks to work on. This will keep them on their toes, and will keep them interested in their work.
- Give people more responsibility and the freedom to act and to do their jobs as they see fit. This will allow them to develop themselves and their managerial capabilities.
- Permit taking risks and making mistakes, without fear of negative consequences. Thus people know they can develop themselves without anxiety.
- Provide people with the opportunity to build a professional reputation. They can build a name for themselves and be proud of themselves and of the professionalism of their organization.
- Give people the opportunity to develop diverse competencies that are highly marketable. This will give them the feeling of having options (which often results in people staying because they don't feel they are locked in by the organization).
- Practice long-term job planning for people. Because of this, people will know you care about their future within the organization.

> "Our people generally work a long time at Tata Steel and have in that time gained much knowledge, experience and skills. You start work here and either after six months you leave because you don't like it at all or you stay here almost forever. If you have a feel for the product, the steel, and you like the culture and atmosphere of the company, you have found your home. We have a lot of internal career opportunities. But, to be eligible for promotion you need a lot of knowledge of your function, whether you are in the operation or in services departments, you have to be a pro at what you are doing. We need to keep the knowledge and experience in the company, craftsmanship is very important to us. And not only in regard to functions which directly have to do with the steel, it also concerns client management, account management or maintenance etc. We need to be able to do these things ourselves to get the right quality and, when we do hire outside contractors, to be able to manage them well. Many companies have made the mistake to outsource too much so they became completely dependant on outsiders. We didn't fall in that trap, we know what our core competencies are and we keep these in-house, even when outsourcing was the hot trend and there was a lot of pressure exerted on us to also go with that flow."
>
> Jan Maas, TATA Steel

5.4 Promotion from within

'Promotion from within' is defined as 'the raising of a person who already works in the organization to a higher rank.' In the business world there has been a tendency to bring in outside managers to lead the organization because boards expect that these outsiders will bring some fresh air into the organization. However, a majority of the outside chief executive officers deliver disappointing results and they are asked to leave after a short while. Externally recruited chief executive officers thus have on average shorter tenures than homegrown chief executive officers.[68] In contrast, several studies show that organizations with home-grown chief executive officers far outperform organizations that hire new chief executive officers from the outside. HPOs ensure that managerial positions opening up can be filled from the inside by encouraging people to become and behave as (future) leaders. They carefully choose new hires from their management potential, which entails that they have the purposefulness, energy, stamina, and ability to inspire others. HPO managers create leadership development opportunities through job rotation and professional enrichment programs, and identify talented high potentials and emerging leaders and put them in critical business opportunities, to test their competence as leader.

> "Top management has always put a lot of time and effort in the development of people. There is a Monday morning meeting in which top management sits down with the vice president of Human Resources and the management development officers of the divisions. They talk about people, their potential, their next steps, possible additional training and education they might need. They do this for the future management of KLM, but they also talk about the management trainees who are our potential for the future. They follow these trainees during their two-year program and make sure they get what they need to develop rapidly. KLM has not often cut down on its trainee programs, as management trainees are the new blood for the organization. What we did do in the past during tough years, was to announce vacancy stops for new trainees. We regretted this very much because it is a short term saving which will bite you in the tail a few years down the line, when positions open up and you don't have the right talent to fill these. The trainee programs now always provide us with a supply of fresh and smart new people so we try not to economize on them."
>
> *Arend de Jong, Air France KLM*

> "It is very clear to our people what our goals are and what needs to be achieved. We have a tight control on that. But we give room to people to grow and to explore their creativity to constantly seek new and better roads to reach they are aiming for. Development of

HPO FACTOR 3 – LONG-TERM ORIENTATION

people is key at Microsoft. We consciously intervene to maximize growth for our people. As an example, we developed tools to foster self-awareness. One of them maps how current roles fit to people's dreams. How do my competencies match my ambitions? This way we provide a mirror for assessing the most suitable next step in their career. Everyone is invited to use the tool whenever they want. This self assessment is not part of the formal appraisal and it can be discussed with a manager any time. Our aim is to develop well-rounded people. We want them to understand and oversee more than just their own area of expertise. For that we use job rotation, and also ask them to participate in community projects. We use scenario-thinking to develop people. My experience is that people often think too linear. Talents in sales often think their next step should be sales manager, then sales director and so on. But maybe someone needs to learn more about marketing or about different business models, or has to learn to give employees more room to excel. We give feedback to people about where they can build up their competencies and show them other possibilities to move to positions. Everyone moves about every two years. Where and how is decided in an open dialogue between manager and employee."

Theo Rinsema, Microsoft Netherlands

IDEAS TO GET STARTED WITH GROWING NEW MANAGEMENT FROM WITHIN

To be able to fill managerial positions from within, you can do the following:

- Develop clear 'fit criteria' which makes it possible to evaluate whether candidates fit the organizational culture and requirements of the opening position.

- Set up long-term succession planning for the next generation of leaders.
- Discuss candidates for the top positions regularly with the board.
- Set up a senior management program which includes talent from middle management and employees, so there is a large enough pool of suitable candidates for opening positions.
- Set up a mentorship program in which senior managers mentor middle managers, and middle managers mentor employees.
- Establish a nominating committee so the organization is not dependent only on the choice of the current chief executive officer (but do involve the current chief executive officer in the succession process).
- Stress that it is a daily activity of current leaders to challenge, mentor, coach and strengthen future leaders.
- Evaluate managers and hold them accountable for the strength of the talent pool they actively build.
- Train yourself and other selectors to eliminate bias in the selection process, since bias creates a liking for some people over other, potentially better candidates.
- Make sure you yourself prepare your own successor.

❝Good managers develop their employees. We prefer to recruit internally in the bank, because our culture is so special. It is always easier to have somebody who knows the culture already to take up a new job than to take somebody from outside and teach him or her how it works. And to be able to do that, we need a pool of talent to recruit from. So it can be that branches that are not necessarily at the top of the league in Handelsbanken – they are not doing bad, but they are not at the top either – are very good at developing people and are sending people all the time to new positions in the bank. They are seen in our organization as very successful branches."

Mikael Sørensen, Svenska Handelsbanken

"All our chief executive officers have been self-made executives who started at the lower levels of the company and worked their way up. They are real company persons who made it because of their talent. They are very aware of their humble beginnings and will therefore not become too big for their boots. They are not vain and you will not see them among the rich and famous on the television. As one of our chief executive officers once said in an interview: "I'm very proud and humble that I am lucky enough to be allowed to end my career as president of the KLM." Did you know that in our existence of 92 years we have now our eighth chief executive officer? This means our people stay a really long, long time. The promotion from within is an important element for us, that we are able to inspire people in such a way that they don't feel that they have to stay at the company, maybe for financial or career reasons, but because they want to, because they feel a great loyalty toward the company and because they feel they can and are allowed to grow continuously, throughout their whole career."

Arend de Jong, Air France KLM

5.5   A secure workplace

A secure workplace is defined as 'a stable workplace untroubled by danger and fear.' HPO managers create a secure workplace by giving people a sense of psychological safety. They work on retaining employees and do not lay off people until it cannot be avoided. They create an open atmosphere in which employees can voice criticisms and concerns, put forward ideas, are heard by management, and have the freedom to act and to do their jobs as they see fit. HPO managers strive for a low employee turnover by creating an organization that looks after its employees. In return they expect employees to perform well and help achieve the organizational goals. HPO managers also work on increasing the self-confidence of people as confident people rely less on rules and procedures, with the constant fear of breaking these, and more on their own judgment. Confident people feel more secure in their job and their activities, dare to speak up and in general behave more like high performance individuals.[70] HPO managers make sure people know that failure to achieve the agreed upon targets will not get them fired, instead they will get trained in identified areas of weakness or will be moved in the organization to places where their skills are more appropriate.

> ## *IDEAS TO GET STARTED TO CREATE A SECURE WORKPLACE*
>
> In order to keep a secure workplace, it is important that you are able to recognize the signs of fear in the workplace. Fear is often created by the negative behaviors of managers, such as:
>
> - looking out for what is good for themselves, instead of taking care of their employees
> - practicing macho management and command-and-control management
> - canceling consensus-building conversations with employees
> - preventing lateral communications between employees without them being present
> - shunning or oustering persons who speak their mind
> - surrounding themselves with yes-men and yes-women because it's more pleasant to hear the 'right' answer than the truth
> - putting more emphasis on performance indicators than on humans

HPO FACTOR 3 – LONG-TERM ORIENTATION

- letting rules and procedures govern the workplace instead of common sense

- creating a shift in attention from 'How can we do the right thing for our customers and employees?' to 'How can we keep our stature, our jobs, and the status quo intact, at any cost?'

In response to negative managerial behavior, employees also start to show behavior which is counter-productive, such as:

- worrying less about the quality of the work they deliver than about how they are perceived by their managers

- constantly talking about who's rising and who's falling in the organizational hierarchy

- constantly worrying about whether it is safe to tell something to someone

- stealing one another's ideas

- hoarding information to get or consolidate power.

> "We don't have a culture of hire and fire. We try to develop and accommodate our staff, coach them and bring them to a new position. Also in situations ensuing from an economic crisis, we try to improve productivity, move people from one job to another but try to keep the family together as much as possible. This is our culture of safety for our employees, it has been this way for a long time, and we like and appreciate it that way."
>
> *Arend de Jong, Air France KLM*

The relationship between Corporate Social Responsibility and the HPO Framework

Corporate social responsibility (CSR) is a form of corporate conscience which functions as a built-in, self-regulating mechanism whereby an organization monitors and ensures its active compliance with the spirit of the law, ethical standards, and international norms.[69] The goal of CSR is to embrace responsibility for the organization's actions and encourage a positive impact through its activities on the environment, consumers, employees, communities, stakeholders and society. The literature strongly indicates that a good application of the CSR concept supports an organization to achieve high performance. Consequently, an organization that applies CSR more fully should achieve better organizational results than an organization which uses CSR less in it business dealings. Thus there has to be a relation between the CSR concept and the HPO Framework. CSR aspects are an integral part of the HPO Framework, specifically of the HPO factors Long-Term Orientation and Management Quality. The factor Long-Term Orientation deals with the stakeholders of the organization and in that respect it is not surprising that the influence of CSR is biggest in this factor. In addition to the external nature of this CSR influence, CSR also has an internal impact, in this case on the HPO factors Management Quality and Employee Quality. Thus, relations can be found between CSR and the following seven HPO characteristics:

▸ *Management of the organization is trusted by organizational members* – This is possible in an environment where management is ethical, creates and maintains individual relationships with people at all levels, has belief and trust in others, shows people respect and exhibits fairness in the way people are treated.

HPO FACTOR 3 – LONG-TERM ORIENTATION

- *Management of the organization has integrity* – It is important that management is honest and sincere so as to lead by example. The demonstration of commitment, enthusiasm and respect in accordance with ethical standards is strongly encouraged in order to support the ethical level of the organization. The display of public commitments needs to be honored so as to enhance an internal environment of credibility and instill more motivation in the organizational members.

- *Management of the organization is a role model for organizational members* – This is related to creating clear, strong and meaningful core values which are put in practice, showing decisiveness and acting boldly if needed, in particular, with fundamental social responsibilities linked to employees. These elements increase the visibility of the management leadership and will encourage organizational members to follow the leader.

- *The organization maintains good and long-term relationships with all stakeholders* – Organizations are not only managed in the interests of their shareholders but also in those of a range of stakeholders that have a legitimate interest in the corporation. CSR responsible behavior of organizations toward stakeholders is a rational strategy to minimize conflicts and optimize synergies in the complex network of relationships with the stakeholders.

- *The organization is aimed at servicing the customers as best as possible* – CSR shows first and foremost in a fair pricing of the product and service delivered to customers but also in taking interest in the customer beyond the product/service exchange. At the same time, consumers are becoming more interested in buying products from socially responsible companies.

- *The organization is a secure workplace for organizational members* – In terms of labor issues, when subscribing to the CSR concept the organization is committed to providing high-quality working conditions while improving employees' productivity and reducing potential liabilities and operational costs. All employees should feel safe, fulfilled and motivated in their workplace and firms should actively work to create such an environment. Employees' safety, health and working environment are therefore fundamental corporate responsibilities.

- *The organization grows through partnerships with suppliers and/or customers* – Through globalization of the economy, organizations are increasingly involved in a network of international chains of suppliers and customers. It has therefore become important for an organization to establish alliances and partnerships within the value chain and to be part of a value creating network. Partnerships force participating organizations to conduct business responsibly not only individually but also in the complete chain.

KEY POINTS CHAPTER 5

- The HPO values the long-term continuity of the organization above achieving short-term profit. Therefore stakeholder management is more important to the HPO than the limited focus on shareholder value.

- The characteristics of HPO factor 'Long-Term Orientation' are: stakeholder orientation, customer orientation, longevity, promotion from within, and a secure workplace.

- One of the most important groups of stakeholders of the HPO are its customers, as servicing the customers as best as possible is seen as the reason for being of the organization.

- The HPO safeguards its continuity by focusing on customer loyalty, management loyalty and employee loyalty, and building lasting relations with all parties that have dealings with the organization.

Two mining multinationals (Peru): using the HPO Framework for corporate social responsibility purposes

KEY MESSAGE

Paying dedicated attention to practicing corporate social responsibility will influence the HPO status of the organization positively, which in turn will result in better performance. Practicing CSR will pay off!

The importance of Peru in world mining goes back to the 16th century, when Spanish colonial rulers first started exploiting Peruvian mines. [71] Peru is currently the world's number 2 producer of silver; number 3 producer of lead, zinc and tin; number 5 in copper; and number 8 in gold. Mining has represented a major part of Peru's exports for over 350 years and still plays a central role in the Peruvian economy as the main provider of foreign exchange funds. Unfortunately, the mining sector has been and still is responsible for major environmental problems and in the past years there have been many conflicts in Peru between mining companies and the surrounding communities. This case study examines two mining companies in Peru to evaluate whether the mining company that paid more attention to the characteristics in the HPO Framework than the other performed the best. The two mining companies in question were Minera Yanacocha, the world's most profitable gold mine and Latin America's largest gold mine, based in the northern highlands of Cajamarca; and Antamina, ranked second in the mining exports of Peru and located in the central highlands of Ancash.

The HPO Questionnaire was distributed among the management of both mining companies. With the received data the HPO Center calculated the scores for the seven HPO characteristics which are related to corporate social responsibility (CSR): management is trusted by organizational members; management has integrity; management is a role model for organizational members; the organization maintains good and long-term relationships with all stakeholders; the organization is aimed at servicing the customers as best as possible; the organization is a secure workplace for organizational members; and the organization grows through partnerships with suppliers and/or customers.

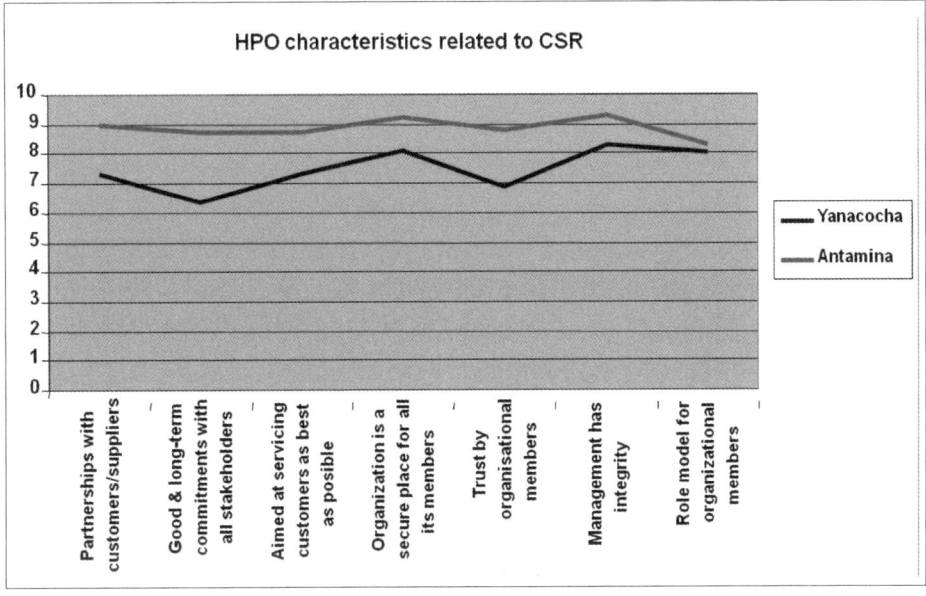

Figure 5.3: Scores for the HPO characteristics related to CSR, for Minera Yanacocha and Antamina

Figure 5.3 shows that the scores on the seven HPO characteristics are higher for Antamina than for Minera Yanacocha. This result is consistent with the situation at both mining companies. Minera Yanacocha was at the time of the research still struggling with the aftereffects of the local communities' protest against a mercury spill which took place in 2000. Also, Minera Yanacocha started to implement CSR programs after that crisis arose and was thus lagging behind, although management said it was making conscious efforts to improve stakeholder management. A different situation was present at Antamina, whose management stated that "being a new mine, Antamina has been able to apply modern approaches to community relations from the outset." Antamina has obtained national recognitions linked to the CSR field, among which the Social Responsibility Prize, awarded by SASE and Universidad del Pacífico (in the years 1999, 2000, 2001 and 2002), and the 2006 and 2007 Sustainable Development prize, awarded by the National Society for Mining, Oil and Energy. The HPO Framework predicted a correlation between the HPO status of an organization and its financial performance, thus Antamina's financial results were expected to be better than those of Minera Yanacocha. When we looked at the financial performance over 2005 and 2006, Antamina's net profits of US$862 (2005) and US$1,698 million (2006) were indeed better than those of Minera Yanacocha being US$535 (2005) and US$568 million (2006). While Minera Yanacocha indicated that its performance was equal to its competitors during the past few years, Antamina clearly stated that it performed better than all its main competitors. This case study therefore shows that paying dedicated attention to CSR will pay off!

HPO FACTOR 3 – LONG-TERM ORIENTATION

Archway Marketing (USA): flipping the organizational pyramid to become HPO

KEY MESSAGE

An organization can take drastic measures to prepare the HPO transition – such as flipping its organizational pyramid – but in the end, the people will make the difference whether the transition will succeed. It is therefore of paramount importance to build a culture of engagement and attention for the people in the organization.

Less than an hour by car from Minneapolis, Minnesota, lies Rogers, a town that at first glance looks like any other small Midwestern town. But, as is often the case, appearances can be deceptive. Businesswise, Rogers is a real hotspot, home to a variety of large and interesting companies. One of these is Archway Marketing Services, Inc. (Archway), a company that provides consolidation, kitting, fulfilment and transportation of sales and marketing materials for Fortune 500 companies including leading big box retailers, quick-service food chains, and automotive giants. This means that all 'not-for-sale' items such as promotion displays, point of sale signage, brochures and samples are transported from Archway's warehouses to its clients' retail locations and field sales offices. For a medium-sized client, this easily amounts to 6,000 different items. It is therefore not surprising that companies outsource their marketing logistics to a specialist like Archway, whose efficient business practices save its clients considerable amounts of money.

But Archway does more. This organization not only profiles itself as a logistics provider, but also as a marketing fulfillment service provider. Archway partners with its clients on their strategic marketing and promotion policy and the logistics consequences of that strategy. A new promotional campaign, for instance, must be supported by all kinds of materials that must in turn be present in all retail locations across the country at the same time. In the beginning of this century, what is now known as Archway had gone through significant change. Ownership had changed multiple times, business divisions were divested and stripped away with the intent of focusing solely on marketing fulfillment without the distraction of the other service offerings. Due to the amount of change, the company was experiencing difficulties sustaining its turnover and profitability and there was a growing discontent with the way management at that time was leading the organization. New ownership brought new leadership. In 2004, a complete new management team was appointed whose focus was to stabilize the business and introduce a new business model focused on client satisfaction and accelerated growth.

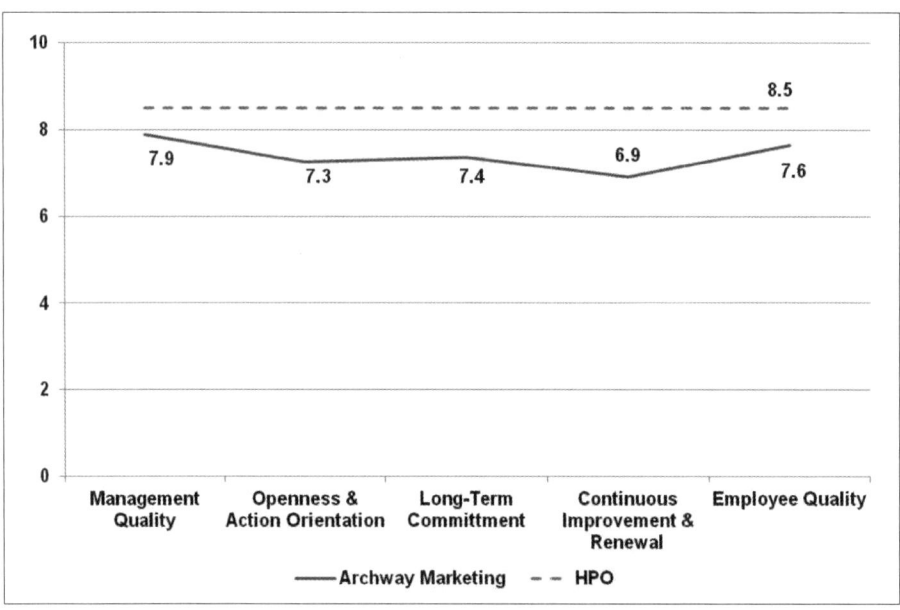

Figure 5.4: HPO status of Archway Marketing

The HPO Diagnosis at Archway

The HPO Diagnosis at Archway began, as usual, by collecting data using the HPO Questionnaire followed by interviews which

HPO FACTOR 3 – LONG-TERM ORIENTATION

were conducted by the HPO Center at Archway's headquarters in Rogers.

As shown in Figure 5.4, the average HPO score for Archway was 7.4, meaning that Archway qualified as an average scoring company, but with great potential. The latter can be seen from the relative high scores for the HPO factors Management Quality and Employee Quality. These high scores indicate that the people of Archway had the potential to bring their company to the HPO status if they would dedicatedly work on improving the other three HPO factors. The interviews conducted at Archway concentrated on two questions: What had Archway done to improve so significantly in the past five years? and In which areas had Archway to improve to become a full HPO?

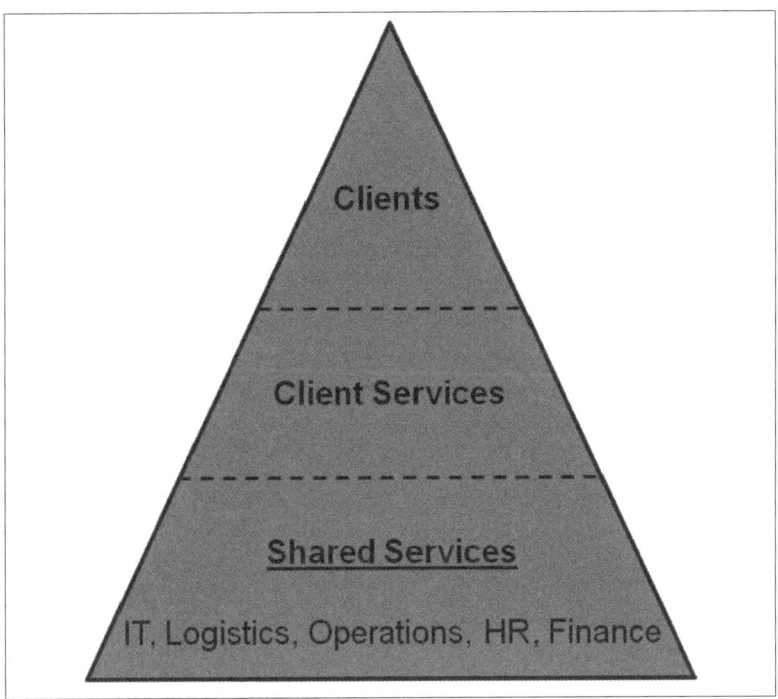

Figure 5.5: Archway's reverse organizational pyramid

The sharp rise in performance of recent years was explained by three success factors. The first success factor was the introduction of a new service model. In this model, the reverse organizational pyramid, there was a strong focus on long-term partnering with clients. To facilitate the client focus, the organizational pyramid has been reorganized so that the client was at the top, the Client Services group in the middle (whose only focus was clients), and the Shared Services group as the foundation. This group combined all departments (IT, Logistics, Operations, HR, Finance) that enabled the Client Services group to serve clients as efficiently as possible. The Shared Services group did this by partnering with the Client Services group to execute on client desires and make strategic recommendations to improve client business processes as effectively and as quickly as possible (Figure 5.5). It was clear to everyone in the company that both groups were on equal footing and had to act like partners to be successful, which meant there was no internal competition about 'who was more important than who' for the success of Archway.

The client focus was also expressed in quarterly meetings in which the client filled out a 'Performance Review Scorecard' for Archway. This card contained the performance indicators that Archway was continually monitoring to service its clients. Interestingly, the Client Services group, which was responsible for the client, first evaluated Archway in relation to these indicators. In other words, not only were the absolute scores given by the client discussed, but also the difference between the client scores and Archway's own scores. This took place every quarter as part of the ongoing dialogue between Archway and the client. Having these discussions allowed Archway to adjust on the fly throughout the year to continue to exceed client expectations. There were also quarterly business meetings between the Client Services group and the Shared Services group, using key performance indicators, to evaluate the services of both groups and to look for ways to improve these services to clients. In all these meetings, senior management was present to emphasize the message to the organization that the client comes first.

The second success factor was Archway's culture of engagement and attention to people. Archway had developed a strong culture that was based on a set of consistent values and clear rules of engagement, and backed this up with strong attention for the development of Archway's people. Archway's Value Statement was:

- The Best Team Wins: We are passionate about our people!

- Client Service is Our Business: We win when our clients win.

- Continuous Improvement is Our Way of Life: We are never satisfied.

Archway knew that if it did not have the right people in the right jobs it could not be successful in servicing clients. Over the last five years, the company had been diligent about reviewing job descriptions, assessing talent and looking towards the future to make sure they set up for long-term success. During this time the company had put talents in the right roles as well as brought in fresh talent from outside the company to fill critical talent gaps. Mike Moroz, Archway's President explained: "Our culture is very important to us, but as we grow we know we need to continue to evolve our culture and expand our talent pool to meet the challenges of a large company that we haven't had to face in the past." A key to the success of this evolution was communication. "Every year we survey our team and every year we hear they want more communication. The good news is that they are engaged and want to know everything that is going on. We are focused on creating new vehicles to communicate with our diverse population," Mike Moroz continued. Archway had to rely on multiple forms of communication to reach its entire employee base. The company therefore leveraged a number of tools including teach-out decks, where management cascaded information during face to face meetings with teams; town halls where the President and General Managers of divisions hosted live meetings to address everyone at once in person on a quarterly basis; printed company newsletters; a company intranet; and social media sites including Facebook, LinkedIn and Twitter.

The third success factor was Archway's absolute focus on continuously increasing the quality in everything that the company did. There were continuous discussions about improvements, formally during quality meetings and informally during conversations between people. There was a continuous search for best practices, either in the organization or from outside (which was one of the reasons Archway's management wanted to do the HPO Diagnosis), doing benchmarking, and creating an atmosphere of allowing mistakes when trying new ideas. Finally there was a drive to employ strategic performance management, as this technique provided clarity on goals and results could easily be tracked with key performance indicators. The result, as chief operating officer Bob Adkinson described, was "a company which is much more professional than the competitors in the industry, which sets us apart for the clients. The not-invented-here syndrome is dead in our company, it doesn't exist here. We have no trouble going outside to get new knowledge, whatever it takes to improve."

Improvement suggestions for Archway

Archway had doubled in size between 2008 and 2011 and planned to double in size again in the coming years in order to serve and continue to serve the largest companies in the United States and Canada. The concern was how the organization could achieve this without compromising its strong culture and client focus. The question, therefore, was whether Archway was ready for the next phase in its development, in which the organization had to obtain a higher maturity level, create a big company mentality if

HPO FACTOR 3 – LONG-TERM ORIENTATION

necessary, deal with more demanding large clients and deal as well with more complexity, all the while maintaining the same great culture (Figure 5.6).

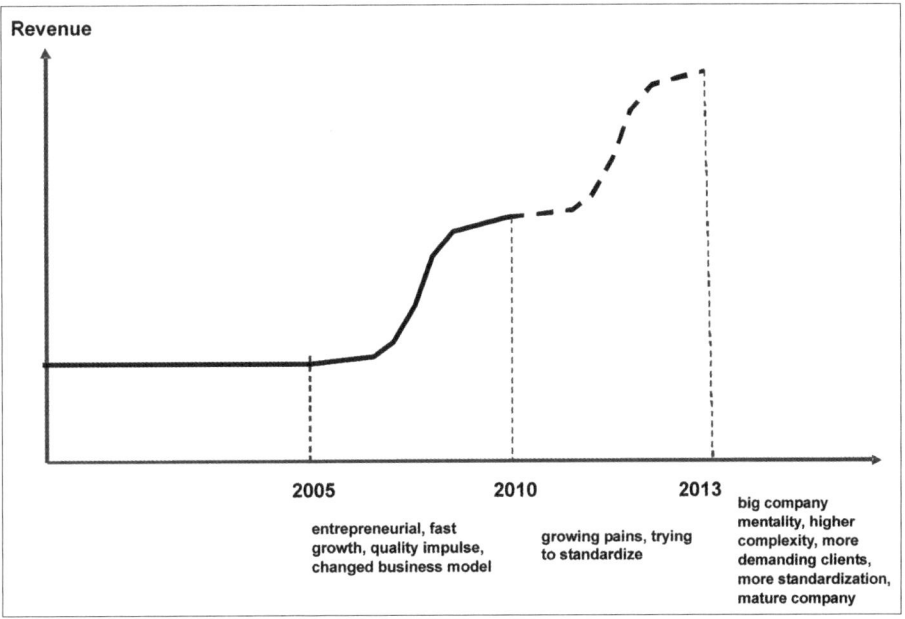

Figure 5.6: The development of Archway through time

The HPO Diagnosis revealed a number of improvement suggestions which Archway could follow up in order to make the transition to a full HPO. Archway has taken these suggestions to heart and immediately following the HPO Diagnosis began addressing them. The first improvement suggestion was to provide more clarity on how goals and targets had to be achieved. Although it was clear to everyone what the goals and the targets for the future were, the how was not. There were questions such as What should the organizational design be?, Which types of employees and leaders were needed?, and What type of clients did Archway want to service? The leadership team of Archway therefore had to make a conscious effort to put its thoughts down on paper and start discussing these with the teams and the locations, to make people familiar with what was in store for the future and to get input from them for refining and improving the plans. At the time this book went to press, Archway had already begun to do this as part of its strategic planning process. They established criteria for success as a way to communicate the vision to the company and as a benchmark for making decisions on projects, investments in the company, talent, business development and other critical areas.

The second improvement suggestion was to strengthen the process improvement process. Despite the strong focus on continuous improvement, there was still not enough consistency in process execution due to the acquisitions Archway had made. There was not yet a uniform practice that was consistently deployed enterprise wide, creating some lingering inefficiencies. As some interviewees commented: "Too much reinventing the wheel, not enough standardization" and "Too many initiatives are seen as flavor of the month and don't get executed … without consequences." The main thing to do here was to pay more attention to better define initiatives and then prioritize these with an appropriate resource allocation. One recent change Archway had made to pick up on this improvement suggestion was to redesign the role of the vice president of operations, to focus on process standardization across all locations as well as to own at a global level the continuous improvement initiatives to drive communication and idea sharing across the company.

The third improvement suggestion was to prevent the further development of silos in Archway. In spite of the reverse organizational pyramid, there existed a danger that further growth of the company would result in the Client Services group no longer working for Archway and for each other, but more for themselves and their own clients. Creating the Client Services and Shared Services groups initially got rid of the silos on paper but almost naturally the client teams in Client Services, the departments in

Shared Services, and the locations ran the risk of operating as silos. An interviewee shed light on the reason why: "I don't have enough exposure to other locations and teams so we don´t do as well as we should in sharing ideas and best practices." An effort had to be made to bring people together by means of job rotation, staffing improvement projects with people from different teams and locations, and stressing in the Archway Leaders Academy that an individual could only be successful in Archway if the whole company was successful. An action taken to address this was the hosting of Archway Universities, where leaders from the Client Services and Shared Services groups came together to discuss topics and brainstorm on issues to help eliminate reinventing of the wheel. These sessions allowed people at different locations to build their internal networks so they could keep abreast of what was going on across the company.[72]

Chapter 6
HPO factor 4 – Continuous Improvement & Renewal: *keep improving ... and be truly innovative*

CONTINUOUS
IMPROVEMENT
& RENEWAL

Chapter preview

People in an HPO feel a moral obligation to always strive for the best results and to get the best out of themselves, their colleagues and the organization. To achieve the best they can, they continuously improve their current products, services, processes and core competencies – to become better at what the organization is already doing – and at the same time continuously renew what they are best at – to develop and be truly innovative.

This chapter discusses the eight characteristics of the HPO factor Continuous Improvement & Renewal. A definition is given for each characteristic followed by a description of the behaviors of HPO managers and employees that is typical of the characteristic. In addition, a number of 'ideas to get started' are listed to improve the characteristic discussed. This HPO factor is further illustrated with a short discourse on the role and importance of strategy in the HPO.

6.1 A unique strategy

A unique strategy is defined as 'a plan of action in business of which there is only one.' In many sectors it is difficult to develop a strategy that is truly different from competitors' as many of them basically sell the same type of products and services. However, the manner in which these are sold and the attitude toward customers can be hugely different. Thus, the management of HPOs finds uniqueness both in content and execution of the organizational strategy. They consciously ponder and then answer the question: "Why should people come to our organization and not go to the competitor, what makes us different?" They then build this strategy gradually and consequently, thereby creating widespread opportunities and breakthroughs. They are consciously developing many new options and alternatives to compensate for dying strategies. Strategic plans generally tend to become elaborate, detailed plans which are difficult to comprehend. In contrast, HPOs make sure the description of the organization's uniqueness fits on the first page of the strategic plan so people are directly focused on the distinguishing factors of the organization and can also easily understand these. In non-profit and governmental sectors the tasks (i.e. the content) which organizations have to perform are often prescribed by law. However, the manner in which the tasks are to be performed is left free. This gives these organizations the opportunity to distinguish themselves from similar organizations in the way they approach their tasks and service their customers and constituency.

> ❝The content of our strategy is not so different from that of competitors. Bank products are bulk commodities, they look more or less the same in all banks. If one bank creates a new product it is not difficult for the competitors to copy that product quite fast. The difference is in strategy execution. We say that 10 percent is

about content and 90 percent is about execution of the strategy. That is why we are structured differently and why we behave so differently from the average competitor. We also say 'walk the talk'. We want our managers to be a good example for everybody, a visible example, and not just sit in their offices making strategies that everybody else should follow. No, they should be the first ones to show employees how the strategy should be executed. And that in itself is also different from other banks. **"**

Mikael Sørensen, Svenska Handelsbanken

IDEAS TO GET STARTED TO CREATE A UNIQUE STRATEGY

The following things you can do to establish the conditions favorable for creating a unique strategy. [73]

- Redefine the industry you are operating within so that the minds of your people are broadened and more possibilities emerge. For instance, Southwest Airlines says it is not in the airline business but in the freedom business, and Umpqua Bank states it is not in banking but in retailing.

- Let your people think consciously about and then articulate what makes working at the organization a unique experience, and what makes the organization stand out from the competition.

- Hire people from outside the industry, to get fresh ideas. Practice branchmarking, by looking outside your own sector into other industries where you can get new ideas and become inspired. Also realize that you don't always have to be the first with an idea: you don't always have to be original as long as you are different in your own industry.

- Don't think about the competition because you will get distracted by what they are doing and that might also influence your own line of thought. Just think about and stay focused on the customer. Do your own thing.

- Develop your own language and symbols which express the uniqueness of the organization to the people and to the customers (if you think differently about your business, then you also talk differently about the business).

- Keep spending time on teaching how management and employees can live up to the uniqueness of the organization.

❝Our strategy in regard to products and markets is not that different from the other steel companies. If you put a new product on the market, within a short period of time others will have similar products, and most of us have the same clients. Our difference is in the execution of the strategy. We have put tremendous effort these past years in improving our processes and we still do that, it is continuous improvement what is so important to us. Every year we will and need to produce more and have less problems. One of my service managers recently expressed it quite nicely. He said: "I have to be careful now. We just got very good satisfaction scores from our internal clients and that might mean we are not critical enough. So if they are now satisfied with us we might not be enough of a nuisance, I have to investigate this." I like this attitude, it shows that you always need to be on the look-out for things that can be improved, don't become complacent. And this relentless focus on finding new ways to execute our strategy makes us different.❞

Jan Maas, TATA Steel

HPO FACTOR 4 – CONTINUOUS IMPROVEMENT & RENEWAL

> "Our uniqueness is in the execution, we are always looking for better ways and especially new ways to do things. We think the term 'smart leadership' is pre-eminently applicable to us. KLM people do not get excited by being followers in the sector, they really want to be leaders and distinguish themselves from the other airlines. Yes, we make mistakes because of this, that is bound to happen if you are the first with things. But that is compensated by the immense energy you get by an energetic and enthusiastic group of leaders."
>
> *Arend de Jong, Air France KLM*

Strategy only matters a bit

One of the most important tools of every organization is the strategy development process. A well-formulated strategy indicates the manner in which an organization plans to anticipate changes in its environment and the consequences these changes will have on the quality, price and delivery times of the products and services of the company. For many years now, developing and executing a strategy well has been accepted as a main source of competitive advantage for organizations. However, do we know for sure that the strategy is in practice as important for an organization to become and stay successful for a long period of time as we think it is? And what then should be the content of that strategy? To obtain answers to these questions we once more turn to the results of the research into the characteristics of HPOs.[74]

In the 290 studies reviewed in Phase 1 of the HPO research, 13 potential HPO characteristics with respect to strategy were identified. For these 13 characteristics the weighted importance was calculated and it became apparent that the following six characteristics surpassed the threshold of a weighted importance of 9 percent:

(1) The strategy consists of a strong vision that excites and challenges.

(2) The strategy balances the long-term with the short-term focus.

(3) The strategy contains clear, ambitious, measurable and achievable goals.

(4) The strategy creates clarity and a common understanding of the organization's direction.

(5) The strategy sets the company clearly apart from other organizations.

(6) The strategy aligns objectives and goals with the demands of the external environment and builds robust, resilient and adaptive plans.

During the empirical study only one of these six characteristics showed a significant correlation with competitive performance: *the strategy sets the company clearly apart from other organizations*. This result means that the organizational strategy plays a relatively limited role in supporting an organization to become and stay an HPO. It does not, however, mean that the strategy process is not important for an organization. It is important, but as a hygiene factor: every organization needs a strategy but having a strategy in itself does not necessarily mean the organization will be(come) an HPO. After all, competitors also have a strategy. What makes the difference is a strategy that is unique, in the sense that it makes the organization stand out from other organizations. The implication for management is clear: it is no longer enough to have 'just' a well-crafted strategy which is known to everybody in the organization. The emphasis during the strategy development process should be on identifying the elements that make the organization stand out from its competitors, and then on devising ways to exploit the unique traits of the organization in order to achieve sustainable competitive advantage.

6.2 Process improvement, process simplification and process alignment

Process improvement is defined as 'the act of making internal business operations better.' Process simplification is defined as 'the act of making internal business operations easier.' Process alignment is defined as 'the act of bringing internal business operations in line with each other.' People in an HPO are continuously looking for ways to improve and simplify all the organization's processes, to improve the organization's ability to respond to events efficiently and effectively. They eliminate unnecessary procedures, work, and all forms of excess and waste, and standardize the remaining work. They fight information overload, use just-in-time processes, and right-size and reengineer processes to improve speed. They align all the processes seamlessly and without bottlenecks and hick-ups. They achieve continuous process optimization by connecting the entire value chain and applying value chain efficiency models. They do this by applying a strong systems perspective, thinking lean about every aspect of work, and becoming adept at rapidly designing and installing new ways of working.

> *Every person in the bank feels a responsibility to improve a process. So if we have a person in our payment department who can see that there is something wrong in the way we make cross-border payments, then he or she feels a responsibility to bring that up. We encourage people to make decisions so they are more prone to start improving. By encouraging people and even say that it can be justified to make a wrong decision as long as you learn from it, then you actually increase the likeliness that they will work to improve the processes without fear of failure.*
>
> *Mikael Sørensen, Svenska Handelsbanken*

IDEAS TO GET STARTED WITH IMPROVING BUSINESS PROCESSES

Studying the data in the HPO database reveals that for organizations worldwide the average scores for process improvement, process simplification and process alignment are 7.0, 5.6 and 4.8 respectively (on a scale of 1 to 10). This can be explained by the fact that organizations generally have no shortage of ideas and often energetically take up many improvement ideas – starting up process improvement is therefore not the problem. It is a complete different matter when we look at whether the process improvements have actually been followed through, and if so, did these result in simpler and more aligned processes. The data indicated that this is often not the case. People are good at starting but not so good at finishing process improvements. This is what you can do to make process improvement work:

- Focus, focus, focus! Select a limited number of improvement initiatives for implementation and make clear how important these are in relation to the day-to-day business.

- Make sure that nobody can start an improvement initiative without first submitting a plan with clear accountability setting, due dates and deliverables.

- Only start something new when the previous, agreed-upon improvement initiatives have been finalized, within time and budget.

- Conduct continuous discussions in the organization about the improvement initiatives, so everybody knows they are important and at the same time knows the status of the initiatives.

- Hire a dedicated person, a chief improvement officer, who is in charge of systematic development and improvement of all processes.

HPO FACTOR 4 – CONTINUOUS IMPROVEMENT & RENEWAL

- Introduce quality assurance procedures for the improvement initiatives and make these topics of regular discussion.

- Implement a planning tool to keep track of the improvement initiatives.

- Make sure improvement initiatives are not seen as flavor of the month which, if they don´t get executed properly, will not yield consequences. Process improvement is serious business!

❝We realized early on that all processes have to work well together to get a successful flight. The passengers generally only notice a safe and on-time flight. But everything before and after the flight, such as planning of the flight schedule, sales of tickets, check-in, crew planning, maintenance, are connected and have to merge seamlessly to result in this good flight. So we have process managers who are in charge of a certain process. For instance, the process manager for the process of the timetable and flight schedule gets all disciplines involved sitting around one table to jointly make the decisions to get an optimal timetable. No one discipline is more important than the others at this table, we are all in it together to achieve the best possible outcome. People come prepared to these meetings, with figures and business cases so they can have discussions in an evidence-based manner. The meetings take place every two weeks so people from different disciplines see each other regularly and can keep communicating.❞

Arend de Jong, Air France KLM

> "At Microsoft we embrace continuous improvement. It is our mission to help organizations to improve their processes, therefore we also need to have a strong focus on this ourselves. But, most of the time, process optimization is in fact for most people a dissatisfier. Every process that supports the organization to achieve good results is often perceived as a neutral fact in the organization, while if a process is not delivering it is immediately considered a negative factor. Therefore the basis for continuous improvement in an organization is in the reason why you do things. I strongly believe that if people know what the company stands for, why we do what we do, improvements will follow naturally. You have to load it, so people get positive vibes from it. As long as you approach continuous improvement as a process to resolve negativity, for example when you need to improve in order to decrease costs or gain productivity, it is not something that will inspire people. If you take the lead from an inspirational goal and it is clear to people what your unique vision entails, you provide the context to improve. I never get tired explaining what we stand for and how continuous improvement supports that."
>
> *Theo Rinsema, Microsoft Netherlands*

6.3 Performance management

Performance management is defined as 'the process in which steering of the organization takes place through the systematic definition of mission, strategy and objectives of the organization, making these measurable through critical success factors and key performance indicators, in order to be able to take corrective actions to keep the organization on track.'[75] Performance management consists of two HPO characteristics, performance reporting and organization-wide reporting. People in an HPO make sure that what matters to the organization is measured by developing a model of the business that links overall goals to specific items the organization needs to control and therefore needs to measure with critical success factors and key performance indicators. Then they rigorously measure progress on the critical success factors, consequently monitor goal fulfillment and honestly confront the facts to analyze why goals were not reached. Facts and measurement are found more important than intuition and opinion, and people tend to focus on what is really going on rather than just on appearances. Thus, people in the HPO focus on results and output, not on input. For this, they design measures that are objective, timely, understandable and easy to calculate. Then, they make sure that the financial and non-financial information needed to drive improvement is reported to everyone in the organization, so people can use this data to improve their operations.

> **"**It is interesting that in such a turbulent environment as the airline industry a tight performance management process is very important. Because of that tight process there is no chaos as everybody knows what to expect and what they have to do. Within the boundaries of the performance management process, lots of creativity and flexibility is possible but there are boundaries which can never be crossed, under no circumstances, like 'never compromise on safety' and 'be punctual, reliable, considerate and friendly.'**"**
>
> *Arend de Jong, Air France KLM*

IDEAS TO GET STARTED TO IMPROVE PERFORMANCE MANAGEMENT

Because performance management consists of two parts – the performance management system and the people who are using it – you need to address both to improve:

- Integrate the planning and reporting processes in such a way that data have to be entered only once in the performance management system (PMS) for it to be used in all the strategic, budgeting, forecasting and reporting processes. Integrating the processes makes it also possible for the results of higher organizational level performance management processes to be used as input at lower organizational level processes.

- Keep the PMS simple by basing it on a limited number of critical success factors and key performance indicators and by making sure that strategic plans and budgets are only made for these.

- Regularly check whether information, critical success factors, key performance indicators and plans in the PMS are still relevant for the organization. If not, remove them to prevent information overload.

- Make sure the reports and IT systems used in the performance management process are easy to understand and to operate. Use as much standardization as possible, without ignoring relevant local differences.

- Align the human resources tools with the PMS so that people are trained in, evaluated on and rewarded for the items that are important to the organization (the critical success factors and key performance indicators).

- Apply exception reporting, which means that only unexpected negative or positive results are discussed and acted upon.

- Train and coach the people in the use of the PMS. Make sure they understand what performance management, critical success factors and key performance indicators are and how these can be used to evaluate and improve their performance. Train them in holding discussions about lagging performance without looking for guilty parties but instead looking for ways to remedy disappointing results.

> "We are very disciplined in performance management. We conduct monthly review meetings with the same group of people, including the vice president of the division and the chief financial officer, to talk about the results of the month and the forecast until the end of the year. There is a discussion on the financial results and financial developments, but also on the non-financials such as quality, claims, punctuality and everything else that is of interest that month. What we see is that because we conduct these meetings at the highest organizational level always, rain or shine, the lower levels do the same. So at department level and team level they also conduct these meetings with iron discipline and in the same manner, so there is a tremendous feeling of accountability throughout the company. This performance culture is very attractive to our people as there is a low employee turnover, has been for years, and we have been in the top of attractive employers for years."
>
> *Arend de Jong, Air France KLM*

6.4 Innovation of products, services, processes, and innovation of core competencies

Innovation is defined as 'bringing in new methods and ideas.' People in an HPO are continuously innovating products, services, processes and core competencies thus constantly creating new sources of competitive advantage for the organization. They rapidly develop new products, services and processes to respond to market changes. To be able to do this, they encourage creativity through cultivating an environment of learning, openness to change, challenging of old methods, an attitude of continuously seeking improvement, and an obsession with innovation. People in an HPO foster generating and experimenting with new ideas and then excel at implementing these. They continuously innovate current core activities while simultaneously developing new activities, and look for both incremental and disruptive innovations. They know what the unique core competencies of the organization are, master these and then develop and renew these. They stick to what the company does best, keep core competencies inside the organization and outsource non-core competencies.

IDEAS TO GET STARTED WITH INNOVATION

The three most important sources of innovative ideas are employees, business partners and customers, in that order. It is therefore important to create the conditions under which these three stakeholders can be as innovative as possible. This is what you need to do: [76]

- *Create space for entrepreneurship in the organization*: make sure there is room for taking risks and making mistakes, create excitement for trying new things, make room for learning, actively encourage employees to come up with ideas, let people step outside well-worn organizational pathways, encourage trying unusual and 'crazy' approaches, ask people to do things they have never done before, welcome uncertainty and luck.

- *Create space for creativity*: make sure there is diversity among your employees, cherish mavericks, see customers and partners as part of your business and involve them too, make use of open source social media to involve stakeholders in generating new ideas, create an attitude of 'it can *always* be improved', don't stop at 'very good' but keep improving.

- *Create a customer-centric orientation*: don't just listen to your customers but really understand them, their needs and wishes, their situations, their points of view, and then think about how you can address these.

- *Create organizational room for innovation:* clear away organizational barriers (such as rules, procedures, formal approvals, cost allocations) that prevent creating the aforementioned spaces, make resources for innovation available, and actively reward innovative ideas.

HPO FACTOR 4 – CONTINUOUS IMPROVEMENT & RENEWAL

> - *Create room for trying out things:* don't launch a new idea on a grandiose scale but first pilot them and learn from problems and mistakes, then try again and again.

❝We always use pilot projects. A pilot project for us is like an experimental garden. We have a good idea which is not fully grown yet, so we plant it in a controlled environment where you can manage the growth process and can learn from what happens. We evaluate the growth results and if we are happy we roll out the idea throughout the company. So we try something on a small scale and if it works we upscale. Instead of taking a giant step which brings with it a lot of risk, we take small steps in a manageable and reversible way. We take this approach with most new ideas, small or large. Especially in the latter case we need to do it this way because if you want to change something, for instance, in the configuration of the airplanes, than it will take us at least two years before all aircraft have been modified. You cannot afford flops there. So taking small steps and after proven success start a big roll-out is in our genes. A lot of people are involved in these pilots. They do this in addition to their daily work because we don't like separate improvement projects as these have a habit of growing in size and then getting away from you. So we incorporate the improvement projects as much as possible in the daily work and the person that comes with the idea is also in charge of the pilot and its subsequent implementation. This gives more work pressure but most of our people don't mind this as they are so curious about new things and like to be innovative.❞

Arend de Jong, Air France KLM

KEY POINTS CHAPTER 6

- If there is something that distinguishes HPOs from non-HPOs it is their strong focus on continuous improvement.

- People in an HPO always strive for better, not because they have to but because they want to and because they feel they should get the best out of themselves and their colleagues for the stakeholders.

- The underlying eight characteristics of the HPO factor Continuous Improvement & Renewal are: a unique strategy, process improvement, process simplification, process alignment, performance reporting, organization-wide reporting, innovation of products, services, processes, and innovation of core competencies.

- HPOs find uniqueness both in content and execution of the organizational strategy. So these organizations really do things differently.

- Managers of HPOs are not afraid to face the brutal facts. They put an emphasis on performance management: not only measuring performance but also acting on information received, without excuses or hesitation.

- Everybody in an HPO receives the information they need to improve and renew.

Amanco Plastigama (Ecuador): emphasizing corporate social responsibility as part of HPO

KEY MESSAGE

Also in developing countries and upcoming economies it is possible to create and maintain HPOs for years. Interestingly, organizations in such countries often put a lot of emphasis on corporate social responsibility by explicitly undertaking activities that benefit society.

Amanco Plastigama is one of the leading companies in the plastics sector, based in Ecuador and with offices all over South and Central America. The company, established in 1960, has approximately 500 employees. Its main activity is to deliver solutions for the transportation of fluids, both in private and public construction and agriculture, for water supply and pipeline infrastructure, and sanitary facilities. Amanco Plastigama is well-known and recognized for the high standard of quality of its operations, throughout Ecuador and many countries in Latin America. Currently, the company is part of Mexichem, a multinational with activities in over 50 countries. The mission of Amanco Plastigama is to produce and commercialize complete, innovative and world class solutions for the transportation and control of fluids. The company employs the 'triple result', which means that the fulfillment of the mission must be accomplished within a framework of ethical values, eco-efficiency and social responsibility. Amanco Plastigama's mission therefore has been translated in the following strategic objectives: to promote a healthy and safe environment; to safeguard the welfare of the professional staff and employees; and to respect the law and basic norms of social responsibility.

Amanco Plastigama is a very successful company. At the time of the HPO Diagnosis its market share in Latin America was 56 percent, while its main competitors Tigre and Esquivel had respectively 29 and 15 percent. On the Ecuadorian market, the company had an undefeatable sales market share of 65 percent for more than ten years, where its closest competitor Rival only had 17 percent. The company had also been in the Top 10 of Great Places to Work in Ecuador for several years in a row. To examine what the foundations of Amanco Plastigama's success were, the HPO Diagnosis was conducted at the company. The HPO Questionnaire was filled in by managers and employees, and interviews were conducted on site in Guayaquil. Figure 6.1 shows that Amanco Plastigama clearly was an HPO as its average score was 8.5 and the company scored significantly higher than the other Latin American organizations that were present in the HPO

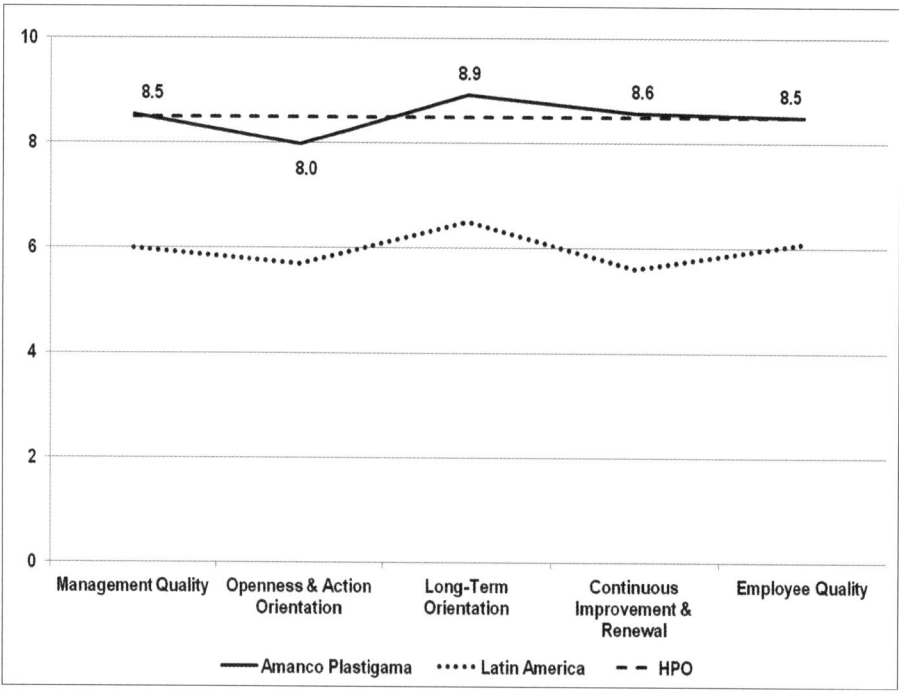

Figure 6.1: HPO status of Amanco Plastigama, compared with Latin American organizations

HPO FACTOR 4 – CONTINUOUS IMPROVEMENT & RENEWAL

database of the HPO Center. In the remainder of this case study we will focus on the strong points of Amanco Plastigama.

The most obvious strong point was the HPO factor Long-Term Orientation which scored an 8.9. The strength of the company manifested itself in the excellent relationships that Amanco Plastigama maintained with its stakeholders. Internally, the company strived for long-term employment and internal promotions for its employees and it took great pains to create a safe and secure workplace. The latter was looked at in three ways: emotionally safe by conducting stress measurement of employees and offering counseling; physically safe by conducting health checks by doctors and offering physical therapy; and working safety by having a fire brigade on site. The company also took care of the families of its employees by organizing regular sports, theater and other family activities and by making its park available in the weekends for families to enjoy. In addition, the company provided spouses with microcredit, so they could set up their own small businesses, generating additional income for the families. Finally, there was a variable reward system according to the achievement of strategic goals. Thus, Amanco Plastigama made sure that if the company was doing well, its workers and employees were also doing well. The satisfaction that all these provisions had created among the workforce was apparent in the fact there had not been labor conflicts for many years. An interesting activity Amanco Plastigama undertook was providing training in its products to third parties. As the company had such a big market share in Ecuador for many years, Amanco Plastigama had become a household name for almost everything to do with sanitary facilities. It often occurred that a plumber, while installing or repairing sanitary facilities in a house, made a mess of it. He then would blame Amanco Plastigama for faulty products, even when the plumber did not use products of the company. To prevent this from happening, Amanco Plastigama conducted free training sessions for plumbers in constructing high-quality sanitary facilities. To participate in this training, plumbers did not necessarily had to use Amanco Plastigama's products, they could use the competitor's ones. This did not matter to Amanco Plastigama because, as the company's managing director said, the company satisfied several goals at the same time when increasing the quality of the plumbing sector in Ecuador: it did not get blamed for sanitary construction problems anymore and society profited from better sanitary facilities. Amanco Plastigama also maintained good long-term relations with customers and suppliers. As the Finance Director explained, "We always try to make win-win business relations. Every time we sign a contract, we have a 100 percent respect for that contract, we don't compromise on them. That is why many of our customers have been with us for thirty years or more. We also strive for long-term relations with our partnerships. For instance, 70 percent of our raw material is resins, and our supplier from Colombia has been with us for 20 years."

As to the HPO factor Management Quality, the activity which attracted most attention was the attitude of management toward employees, suppliers, customers and society. This attitude could be described with one word: respect. As the managing director illustrated: "When I go down to the factory floor there is always a lot of noise. Also, the hall is quite big. So if I need to talk to somebody who is working on the other side of the hall, I could call out to him with a loud voice to make him come to me. In Amanco Plastigama this is seen as a sign of disrespect: the raising of one's voice and yelling at somebody disturbs everybody working in the hall. This kind of behavior is just not allowed here. So I will walk through the hall and go over to him. After all, I was looking for him so I need to go to him." To this, he added: "We respect all of our people as individual human beings. Because we think it is good business to respect them and to guarantee a good work climate: their performance will always be better if they feel respected by the management and colleagues. We are convinced that the man who works at the machine every day is an expert at his job. He is the first to know how to solve problems in his machinery because

HPO FACTOR 4 – CONTINUOUS IMPROVEMENT & RENEWAL

he has the expertise and knowledge. They feel proud of talking with us because they feel we respect them."

As to the HPO factor Openness & Action Orientation, Amanco Plastigama spent at least 70 hours of training per person per year, which included a lot of knowledge sharing. There were monthly feedback and evaluation sessions with managers and employees. For the yearly evaluation, employees filled in a self-evaluation which was compared to the evaluation the managers made and then discussed. People could also learn from mistakes because these were emphatically allowed. Amanco Plastigama made a clear differentiation between mistakes and irresponsibilities, these last were not tolerated. In contrast, mistakes were allowed and there were different stages before somebody got penalized. When there was a mistake, the company trained the person who made the mistake so he or she would not do it again. Lastly, management tried to maintain an open culture, as the managing director said: "We keep our people constantly informed, and not just on the financial aspects of the company but on everything which might be important to them. We believe that people who are well informed are more trustable and comfortable with the company."

As to the HPO factor Continuous Improvement & Renewal, Amanco Plastigama conducted periodical lunches during which new ideas and inventions were rewarded. These lunches had a motivational purpose as these new ideas and inventions were shared with everybody and everyone could add their own suggestions to them. This activity seemed almost trivial but the effect was profound, as one of the interviewees stressed: "Innovation is clearly one of our strengths which makes us different from competitors and through the lunches we keep being focused on it. We continuously keep implementing new technologies to serve the market and our customers in a better way. The competitors are always trying to copy what we are doing. In this way we will always hold the first position in the industry."

As to the HPO factor Employee Quality, Amanco Plastigama had formulated several values, which could be seen as commitment pledges to the employees and which governed the relationship between managers and employees: have mutual respect, focus on team work, continuously develop professionalism of people, guarantee safe and secure workplace conditions, and show passion and enthusiasm. Amanco Plastigama explicitly stated that the key success factor of the company was its people. That is, high-quality management as well as high-quality and motivated employees were seen as the real sustainable competitive advantage of the organization. And when the people had an attitude of commitment for the long term, interest in continuous improvement as well as an action-orientated behavior, the company could pursue the highest levels of competitiveness and profitability.

Two diamond companies (Europe): strengthening the value chain through HPO

KEY MESSAGE

The HPO Framework can be used to evaluate the quality of the cooperation between an organization and its supplier. In order to create a high performance partnership, it is essential that both organizations in a collaborative relation have similarly high HPO scores and that they work together to increase the quality of their collaborative processes.

The diamond industry consists of many parties which are involved in exploration and mining, trading of rough diamonds, diamond cutting and polishing, polished diamond trading, jewelry design, manufacturing, wholesaling, and finally retailing.[77] Figure 6.2 presents an overview of the links in the diamond industry value chain. Mining companies mine and sell rough diamonds to dealers or directly to intermediate companies. Dealers sell the diamonds to intermediate companies, and the latter cut and polish the diamonds (either by themselves or via outsourcing) for sale to jewelers.

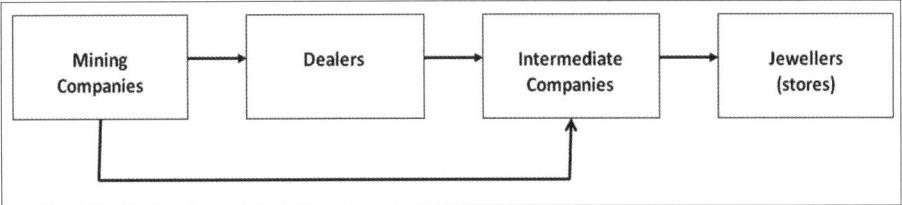

Figure 6.2: Diamond industry value chain

In the diamond industry value chain, about US$74 billion is added in value per year, of which US$13 billion in mining and US$61 billion in dealing and retailing. In recent years, many activities have been undertaken to make this industry more corporate socially responsible and ban, for instance, the blood diamonds. The potential for rough diamonds is considered good in the long run, as there is a developing shortage of rough diamonds and at the same time an increasing consumer demand in emerging markets such as India and China. Two-thirds of the production of diamonds is located in the African continent. The demand for diamonds is driven by economic growth, consumer confidence and fashion. There is a huge seasonal impact because of the North American market, where about half of the world's diamonds is sold: the majority of diamonds sales take place between Thanksgiving and Valentine's Day. In order to achieve a satisfactory margin, the parties in the diamond industry value chain have to cooperate closely. To see whether the HPO Framework could help these parties cooperate better, it was applied at two diamond companies.

The first company, Intermediate Amsterdam, was founded in Amsterdam, The Netherlands, in the 17th century as a family-owned business specializing in polishing diamonds. Its expertise had been passed on for generations and since the beginning of the 20th century Intermediate Amsterdam was considered one of the most renowned diamond polishers in the world. Intermediate Amsterdam could be characterized as a long-term oriented and results-oriented company, because profitable continuity of the business was regarded as very important by its management. Intermediate Amsterdam targeted the upper segment of the market and sold polished diamonds and design jewelry to jewelry stores throughout the world. The company purchased diamonds either directly from mining companies which produced rough diamonds and, on request, polished diamonds; or through dealers on the open market in Antwerp, Belgium, the center of the diamond trading industry. Company number two, Dealer Antwerp, a small diamond dealer based in Antwerp, acted as a go-between for Intermediate Amsterdam and the mining companies and occasionally other dealers. Dealer Antwerp was informed about what kind of stones Intermediate Amsterdam was interested in and offered suppliers the opportunity to present their diamonds to Intermediate Amsterdam at the dealer's office. After that, Intermediate Amsterdam decided to buy or not to buy and Dealer Antwerp received a commission for its function as intermediate party. There was a high degree of trust between Intermediate Amsterdam and the dealer due to their long-standing relationship. People of both companies filled in the HPO Questionnaire (see Table 6.1) after which several interviews were conducted at both companies.

Intermediate Amsterdam scored higher than Dealer Antwerp but the difference was not that great, which meant that the organizations were a good match for each other. The HPO factor that scored highest for both companies was Long-Term Orientation. Intermediate Amsterdam used Dealer Antwerp as an intermediate party for purchasing diamonds, and this was not without reason.

HPO Factors	Intermediate Amsterdam	Dealer Antwerp
Management Quality	8.4	8.3
Openness & Action-Orientation	7.8	8.0
Long-Term Orientation	9.3	9.3
Continuous Improvement & Renewal	7.5	6.4
Employee Quality	8.0	7.3
Average	*8.2*	*7.9*

Table 6.1: HPO scores of Intermediate Amsterdam and Dealer Antwerp

Dealer Antwerp had been working in the diamond industry for over 30 years and was very familiar with the open market in Antwerp. Consequently, Dealer Antwerp was able to do business with a lot of diamond suppliers and put Intermediate Amsterdam in contact with the best suppliers in the market. In addition, Dealer Antwerp was a flexible organization. This meant that when Intermediate Amsterdam wanted to purchase new diamonds on short notice, Dealer Antwerp would take care of this immediately. The HPO factor with the most room for improvement, again for both organizations, was Continuous Improvement & Renewal. Intermediate Amsterdam had to improve the processing and registration of assets and invoices. When Intermediate Amsterdam bought diamonds, these then first had to be transferred from Antwerp to Amsterdam over a distance of some 160 kilometers for inspection and polishing, then they were sent back to Antwerp for certification, and finally the diamonds were returned to Intermediate Amsterdam in Amsterdam for further distribution to its clients. This was an inefficient process and Intermediate Amsterdam was aware of this but had not yet acted on it. As soon as these processes were optimized, the processes of Dealer Antwerp would also be positively influenced as this organization had to be less involved as a go-between in the various transfers. Dealer Antwerp could become more HPO by improving the quality of its employees so they could better execute the activities required for a smooth collaboration, and also better handle selling the new jewelry line that Intermediate Amsterdam was on the verge of introducing in the market. It was also clear that for both companies their management should become more involved in the continuous improvement efforts. It was also remarked that if Dealer Antwerp did not keep up with Intermediate Amsterdam and the difference in HPO scores between the two parties would increase, this would potentially damage the collaboration between the two parties. This could eventually lead to termination of the collaboration, and Intermediate Amsterdam would be forced to look for a supplier that matched its increasing HPO score. Actively simplifying, improving, and aligning processes and a complementary work force would help both organizations in raising their HPO status.

Temping Agency (Europe): looking internally for best ideas

KEY MESSAGE

Matching the average HPO scores for the units in an organization with their financial results provides a quick way to identify the best and worst operating units. This in turn gives the opportunity to internally look for *best ideas*: what did the best operating units do to become so good and can this be transferred to the other, less well operating units?

The core activities of Temping Agency Nearby (TAN) consisted of dispatching and detaching temporary workers, recruitment and selection of personnel, and obtaining temporary work assignments.[78] The mission of TAN was to be an attractive employer and a strong player in the temping sector. TAN´s culture was characterized by employees who were committed and professional. The main performance indicators for TAN were market share, client satisfaction, employee satisfaction, temporary worker satisfaction, and fulfillment rate (i.e. have all the requests from the clients for temporary workers been fulfilled?). TAN was organized into three regional business units (BUs), each of which consisted of multiple operational units with several branch offices. Because of the lengthy recession in the Dutch economy TAN eventually started to suffer from a decline in revenue and profitability and at the same time competition between the temping agencies increased substantially, causing a downward pressure on prices. As a result, all players in the temping market fought hard to stabilize and preferably increase their turnover and market share. Some of TAN's operational units were doing very well at that time while others could not keep up with the pace of the market, and certainly not with that of major competitors in the battle for a top 3 position in market share. TAN's management was wondering why basically similarly organized operational units responded so differently to changes in the market. Which factors had caused some to perform well and others not? In consultation with the HPO Center, TAN's management therefore decided to perform an HPO Diagnosis in BU West, one of the more successful business units and consisting of five operational units, to identify the determining factors of high performance. The outcome of the research was going to be used by TAN to improve the performances of the less successful units. The HPO status of BU West was determined by means of the HPO Questionnaire, Table 6.2 shows these scores and the subsequent ranking of the units.

WHAT MAKES A HIGH PERFORMANCE ORGANIZATION

HPO factor unit	West 1	West 2	West 3	West 4	West 5
Management Quality	6.9	7.3	7.5	7.0	7.3
Openness & Action Orientation	7.1	7.4	7.4	6.7	7.4
Long-Term Orientation	7.3	7.6	7.8	7.1	7.6
Continuous Improvement & Renewal	6.6	6.9	7.3	6.4	7.0
Employee Quality	6.7	7.0	7.4	6.8	7.2
Average	6.9	7.2	7.5	6.8	7.3
Ranking	4	3	1	5	2

Table 6.2: HPO scores and ranking of the five operational units of BU West

The HPO scores given in Table 6.2 were related to the financial performances of the operational units. For this, the turnover data of the past five years were collected (Table 6.3).

Year/Unit	West 1	West 2	West 3	West 4	West 5
1	2,660,480	2,223,255	3,177,056	2,425,639	2,613,796
rank	2	5	1	4	3
2	2,689,614	2,351,494	2,999,057	2,495,728	2,300,409
rank	2	4	1	3	5
3	2,708,945	2,294,959	3,376,300	2,728,522	2,469,788
rank	3	5	1	2	4
4	3,545,548	3,323,997	4,589,721	2,990,772	3,590,173
rank	3	4	1	5	2
5	3,888,001	3,492,560	5,054,749	3,367,900	3,791,476
rank	2	4	1	5	3

Table 6.3: Turnover per FTE (in €) and competitive rank of the five operational units of BU West

The turnover ranking of Table 6.3 was matched with the HPO ranking of Table 6.2. A summary of the matching results is given in Table 6.4. The matching yielded a clear HPO leader, which had both the highest HPO scores and the highest turnover ranking: operational unit West 3. In addition, the match indicated a clear HPO laggard, which had both the lowest HPO score and the lowest

HPO FACTOR 4 – CONTINUOUS IMPROVEMENT & RENEWAL

turnover ranking: operational unit West 4. Therefore the HPO Center looked closer into these two units.

	HPO Ranking	Oper. unit	Financial ranking in year:					
			5	4	3	2	1	
highest	1	3	*West 3*	*West 3*	*West 3*	*West 3*	*West 3*	highest
	2	5	West 1	West 5	*West 4*	West 1	West 1	
	3	2	West 5	West 1	West 1	*West 4*	West 5	
	4	1	West 2	West 2	West 5	West 2	*West 4*	
lowest	5	4	*West 4*	*West 4*	West 2	West 5	West 2	lowest

Table 6.4: Matching of the HPO ranking with the financial performance rankings for the West units

Operational unit West 3, the leader in performance, operated in a region of the country where only a few large companies were based. As all temping agencies operated in the same market, West 3 had to work hard to obtain new clients. Because of this, West 3 had developed a culture of constant fighting for clients, developing new market approaches, being innovative in services and being customer oriented because management and employees knew this attitude was needed to survive and thrive in this highly competitive market. It came as no surprise that West 3 was the first unit to embrace the HPO Diagnosis and its results. Operational unit West 4 had performed quite well up to year 3. In that period an interim operational manager was present who dealt with many of the problems created by his predecessor. At the end of year 3 a new operational manager was appointed who was familiar with the industry but only had experience with business-to-business and also had difficulty adjusting to the different demands of working with both businesses (the clients) and individuals (the temporary workers). Because of this, the operational manager did not develop many initiatives and was in general rather inactive and as a result both turnover and growth versus the market suffered. To delve even deeper into the causes behind the deviation in HPO scores between unit 3 and unit 4, the operational managers of these units were interviewed by the HPO Center about the HPO characteristics which differed most. The following short quotes from the operational managers provide some insight into how they dealt with particular HPO characteristics at their units.

Unique strategy

"I always say it is the person that makes the organization unique. TAN has a three-part strategy which states that we specialize in a limited number of industries, we strive for the lowest integral cost for the client, and we do our work in the typical TAN manner, which is energetic, with determination and purposeful. I am sure the last part is the most important. Competitors also do the first two parts so it is in the third part, our way of working, that we make the difference, which makes us unique. So I spend a lot of my time with people to talk about their attitude and method of working, to make sure they operate in line with TAN's method of working. I coach people on this and I will speak to them when they do not behave accordingly. As a result, people in the market place look upon us as go-getters, much more pro-active than our competitors." *(Operational manager of West 3)*

"You just have to say you are the best! That is not so much our organizational strategy but that doesn't really matter. You always have to show to clients that you're eager, that's how you distinguish yourself. The other thing I do is to give all my people key performance indicators that reflect market developments. I tell them that they have to improve on these indicators, no matter what the strategy of headquarters or of competitors is. So they go to their clients and say 'I have a target of 40 percent market penetration.' Why do we say this? Because the client than knows we are eager to become a big player in providing temporary workers for them. So they should be more inclined to hire you as their temp agency and that will increase your market share." *(Operational manager of West 4)*

Process improvement

"We regularly look at the processes with fresh eyes. For instance, we recently changed the lay-out of the branch office to make it more welcoming to people who walk in to register as a temporary worker. We now have a central desk where a hostess receives the visitors and directs them to the right person within TAN. This is also much more efficient for us, as people now go directly to the right person who can help them. So I try to encourage people thinking about continuous improvement and I reward them for it." *(Operational manager of West 3)*

"I try to stimulate and motivate the employees to continuously improve the way they are doing things. But I found I have to check up on them if they actually made any improvements otherwise nothing happens. They always come up with the excuse that they don't have time for improvement but then I discuss this with them and tell them continuous improvement is part of their tasks. But then again, if the BU manager tells me to participate in certain improvement projects, I often catch myself thinking of excuses as I give operational issues priority." *(Operational manager of West 4)*

Chapter 7

HPO factor 5 – Employee Quality: *without good employees the HPO can never be achieved*

EMPLOYEE
QUALITY

Chapter preview

To become an HPO it is a precondition to hire and retain employees that have an incurable curiosity, want to be challenged, need to have responsibility and at the same time ask to be held accountable, and want to perform better ... everywhere and anytime. These high performance employees perform better than the average employee, and because of that contribute more to the effectiveness of the organization.[79] With this type of employees, an organization can transform into a true HPO.

This chapter discusses the four characteristics of the HPO factor Employee Quality. A definition is given for each characteristic followed by a description of the behaviors of HPO managers and employees that is typical of the characteristic. In addition, a number of 'ideas to get started' are listed to improve the characteristic discussed. This HPO factor is further illustrated with a short discourse on recent research into the high performance employee.

7.1 Inspiration

Inspiration is defined as 'the act of making a person enthusiastic to do something.' HPO employees want to be inspired by their managers to continuously perform better and achieve extraordinary results. They want to be kept on their toes and be challenged. They continuously want to develop themselves, to achieve the best they can, and because of this contribute to the success of the organization. As employees of an HPO are quite extraordinary, it requires focused attention of managers to keep these people interested in working at the organization. HPO managers therefore consciously inspire their employees by giving them interesting work, challenging tasks and increased responsibilities; and stressing that they should be proud of their own achievements and those of the organization. They stimulate self-confidence, an entrepreneurial attitude, firmness, a can-do attitude, and a winning mindset in employees. HPO managers raise the performance of their people and themselves by setting high standards and stretch goals. They let people feel they are part of a bigger picture and inspire them to achieve greatness as part of the organization. They possess a crusading enthusiasm and take time to win people over.

> ❝I walk the talk because that talk is what attracted new employees to the bank. When I had job interviews with people before they started at the bank and I told them how we work, then that was what interested them in the bank. So it is important that when they come in, it actually works this way. And this congruency inspires them.❞
>
> *Mikael Sørensen, Svenska Handelsbanken*

HPO FACTOR 5 – EMPLOYEE QUALITY

❝A good manager is challenging, for yourself and your people. Not in an aggressive sense, but somebody who is questioning, who is probing, who is trying to understand, who is trying to get behind the thinking of employees and colleagues. The main way we judge people in terms of career advancement is if they are doing the job for the challenge of the job. Whether they want to be in command of the job, want to master it, want to do better, want to perform within this role, and see career advancement as a consequence of doing that well. We are suspicious of people who are seen to be doing a job because they believe it is going to take them higher up the corporate ladder, that is a negative mark for us. It is the self-motivation and self-challenging, the intrinsic locus of control that are important themes in our organization.❞

Alan Clark, SAB Miller Europe

IDEAS TO GET STARTED TO INSPIRE EMPLOYEES

There are two main ways how you can inspire your employees: by changing your own behavior into being more inspirational and by creating conditions for your employees which will increase their motivation. For both ways ideas are given underneath. [80]

Become an inspiring person yourself by doing the following:

- Be passionate about the goals of the organization, show emotion, and generate enthusiasm for these in your employees.
- Connect with your employees by showing real interest in them and finding out what motivates and inspires them, and actively looking for their ideas and opinions.

- Be somewhat unconventional and take personal risks, by doing things differently and operating outside 'normal' organizational boundaries and outside your comfort zone, and letting your employees do the same.
- Make sure inspirational moments are succeeded by follow-on actions, so your employees see that you act upon your inspiration.
- Be engaging and a team person, and regularly express to your employees it is all about 'we' and not about 'I'.
- Become a 'story-teller' who is able to package messages in an appealing form that captivates your employees.

Create motivational conditions for your employees, by doing the following:

- Paint your employees an attractive picture of the future of the organization and their place in it and provide the rationale why certain goals have to be pursued.
- Give your employees interesting and meaningful work that challenges and vitalizes them. This work should require them to do things differently, with more risk and uncertainty, which gets them out of their comfort zone.
- Set stretch goals for your employees and give them more responsibilities and freedom to schedule their own work, while including the possibility of setbacks that they will have to overcome.
- Provide your employees with the possibility to get into contact with the beneficiaries of their work, i.e. the customers, so they can see the results of their work.

HPO FACTOR 5 – EMPLOYEE QUALITY

❝I believe 90 to 99 percent of all employees in an organization mean well by what they do for the company. It is the task of a manager to use all that potential to become an HPO. As a manager you focus on equipping your employees to do the right things. Only when people really understand and internalize what the organization aims for, will they use their energy and focus to contribute to that mission. Therefore you need to provide people freedom to act, a context where they can be creative, and create trust. And if you get teams to cooperate based on this, you are up to something great. It is not the task of the manager to take responsibility to become high performing, it is the task of the manager to inspire employees to take that journey. It is the way you use the energy of all those talented individuals. The journey is not about process optimization anymore, that task has become just one of the hurdles to take on the journey ahead. It is all about giving meaning. That is key.❞

Theo Rinsema, Microsoft Netherlands

❝We each have our own way of inspiring our people. I am participating with my people in the creation of new ideas, encouraging them to find ways to develop new ideas for the company. I remind my people of the culture by demonstrating it or by showing an example. And then celebrate when we do well. I get inspired by hiring people that inspire me. With these people I try to create a sense of entrepreneurship. That comes by letting ideas flow, gathering these and doing something about them that makes sense. I don't know if you have seen our signs that read 'Welcome to the world's greatest bank'? This was created by an associate without prior approval and now it's our vision statement. I think that encouraging associates to have a little bit of rebel-like response is good. It breeds new ideas and drives curiosity. There are fine lines and some may cross them, but you're not going to be reprimanded for trying new things and improving the customer experience. You will not lose your job in Umpqua because of something like that."

Lani Hayward, Umpqua Bank

7.2   Resilience and flexibility

Resilience is defined as 'the ability to recover easily and quickly from setbacks' and flexibility is defined as 'the ability to be adaptable, versatile and variable.' HPO employees have the attitude of "We will get to Rome, one way or the other." HPO employees just don't give up and keep on trying new things until the goal has been reached. They are very willing to learn new skills and obtain new knowledge. Therefore they continuously develop themselves by attending courses and classes, by taking on new jobs and responsibilities in the organization, and by being willing participants in job rotation schemes. Managers in an HPO take great care to continuously strengthen the resilience and flexibility of employees by applying the master–apprentice principle, according to which younger people can learn from older, more experienced people. They provide on-the job training to teach employees how to embrace and accept change as an essential part of doing business and make sure people can cope with uncertainty. They recruit people who have shown great resilience and flexibility in their previous jobs.

"We select new people on their flexibility. During an interview with potential recruits I spend much time talking about what they have gone through in life and how they dealt with that. I rather have somebody who has been a bit damaged in life, who had setbacks and overcame these, than somebody who was born with a golden spoon in his mouth and who has sailed through life without a hiccup. With that person I am not sure whether and how he will hold up in adverse times. When people are working at Unilever we don't have special flexibility training as such, but we do devote time during regular development sessions on questions as 'How do you deal with things that come at you?' "

Lennard Boogaard, Unilever

> ## IDEAS TO GET STARTED TO INCREASE RESILIENCE AND FLEXIBILITY
>
> There are several techniques you can apply to increase the resilience of your people: [81]
>
> - Foster an optimistic atmosphere in the organization, as people with an optimistic mindset are better able to deal with setbacks by viewing these as temporary and opportunities for improvement.
> - Apply appreciative inquiry, as questions framed in a positive way focus on positive aspects of issues.
> - Practice strategic resilience, by actively looking for future threats for the organization and then turning these into opportunities.
> - Stress regularly that change is a fact of life and should be welcomed as it offers new opportunities and chances of success.
>
> There are also several techniques you can apply to increase the flexibility of your people:
>
> - Introduce rolling forecasts that look six quarters ahead, to identify possible future performance issues. This makes it possible for people to anticipate issues and proactively deal with these.

- Introduce scenario planning that captures the possible futures of the organization. This promotes a forward-looking attitude in people and lets them think about future possibilities and threats, which they can proactively deal with.

- Introduce relative and dynamic targets which are set against the competition and economic circumstances. This increases flexibility because people are not limited by fixed targets which make reacting adequately to developments difficult.

- Train employees for agility by looking at incidents which happened in the past in the organization, drawing lessons from these and discussing alternatives for ways to act next time such incidents occur.

- Apply regular job rotation. This way people frequently have to adapt to changing (job) circumstances.

- Experiment regularly, so people learn how to deal with ambiguity, uncertainty and failed experiments and look for alternative ways to get things working.

❝In the IT industry there are few constants, with new business models and players emerging every year. Moving with, and leading change or tweaking our business is an integral part of the organization and what we do. What may be a good market approach this year might have to be completely different next year. We hire and develop for adaptability and flexibility, so even as our workforce is now a few years older than 10 years ago, that basic trait is still there. This increases the speed of implementing change. Last year I agreed to transfer a part of our division's business to another business unit. We spent a few months thinking through the decision, but once taken, the handover was completed for more than 80 percent within two weeks! There was little need for my involvement after the decision was made, as people switched quickly to the new realities and made it happen. 99

Rik van der Kooi, Microsoft USA

66 What you see in our bank is that the one who really makes a career is the generalist. But you can only become a generalist if you are flexible and work in different areas, you have to try a lot of things in your career. So we move people regularly around the organization so they can have many new experiences. In this manner we help people to become flexible. 99

Mikael Sørensen, Svenska Handelsbanken

7.3 A diverse and complementary workforce

A diverse and complementary workforce is defined as 'the people who are employed by an organization who differ from one another in many ways and because of that collectively have all the strengths the organization needs.' Such a workforce is important because the different experiences, perspectives and mindsets generated by diversity lead to new ideas and increase the problem-solving capacity and strength of the organization. Managers in an HPO assemble a diverse and complementary management team and workforce to make sure that the team possesses all the skills, experiences and creativity needed to face the challenges of the organization and solve its problems. They hire people with different abilities, backgrounds, personalities, experiences and complementary skills.[82] They get these different people by using different approaches to recruiting, identifying and developing talents.

IDEAS TO GET STARTED TO CREATE DIVERSITY

To create diversity in the organization you need to assemble a group of people who are different in age, gender, ethnicity, education, country origin, work-life history and so on. Balancing the men-women ration alone is not enough. This is what you can do: [83]

- Educate your people on the benefits of diversity and require from them affirmative action plans which should increase the cognitive diversity in their teams in the next few years. Measure the impact of these plans, review progress regularly and hold people accountable for their diversity results.

- Make diversity management part of the organization's strategic plan. Then measure the degree of diversity in the organizational units and organizational levels, and identify the areas of the biggest imbalance. Take action to rectify the imbalance as quickly as possible. If needed, create special positions and special training programs to neutralize the imbalance.

- Hire new people not on the belief that the best team consists of the best individual people but on the knowledge that the best team consists of people who are both capable and diverse. So look for diversity in training, experience and identity. Make sure you and your colleagues are in different networks which makes it then possible to find the required diversity.

- Introduce job and location rotation programs which allow people to get new and different experiences.

- Make sure every new recruit has a long-term career plan so diverse talents will move up to higher management levels. Identify role models of talents with different backgrounds and make sure they are visible to the organization and new recruits.

> • Minimize conflicts between diverse people by recruiting people who want to cooperate with people who are different from them; supporting newcomers; not stopping arguments but refereeing these; and encouraging dissidents to speak up.

7.4 Partnership

Partnership is defined as 'a relationship in which two or more people or organizations work together as partners to achieve common goals.' HPO managers and employees create partnerships and join value creating networks in order to grow themselves and the organization. They stimulate cross-organizational collaboration by making teamwork and collaboration top priorities of management and teamwork and cooperation with suppliers, customers and partners standard throughout the enterprise. They strive to create high performance partnerships (HPP) that consist of organizations that are HPOs and that have world-class collaborative processes.[84] For this, they embrace the vision of virtual integration with these parties in the value chain, and therefore redesign and streamline inter-enterprise processes. People in an HPO consciously and consistently look for opportunities to partner with external parties as they know they can learn a lot from others.

> ❝ Working together with partners is crucial at Microsoft. To create value for our customers we have to work together intensely. We are actively looking to cooperate with all kinds of organizations that can help us create value for customers in unexpected ways. But you do not own these partners so the relation has to be like an ecosystem, which only functions when all partners benefit. Microsoft helps its partners to attract the best talent, which helps our clients and in the end also helps us. More and more we collaborate with parties that are not part of our business model to create more value for our clients. These are, for example, companies that specialize in a specific area of expertise like change management. We try to

include more of these organizations so we can support our clients in building better organizations. This way of working is a learning process. Sometimes it works, sometimes the click with other parties is just not there, so we are learning every day how to build and maintain the right kind of relations."

Theo Rinsema, Microsoft Netherlands

IDEAS TO GET STARTED WITH THE HIGH PERFORMANCE PARTNERSHIP

Research by the HPO Center into the factors that make a high performance partnership – a collaboration between two parties that is of world-class quality and brings high mutual benefits – shows that there are three factors you need to work on, together with your partner, to create an HPP:

- Openness in the partnership. There needs to be regular dialogue between the two partners to inform each other about significant occurrences and developments, share ideas and align processes in both organizations; this will create a strong personal relationship between the two partners. Decisions regarding the partnerships always have to be taken mutually and both partners have to do their utmost to fulfill their promises to each other.

- Equality of the partnership. Each partner should be as strong as the other partner in the partnership, in the sense of equal power and equal say in decision-making, and should be as dependent on the success of the partnership as the other partner. The organizational cultures of both partners should match as

> much as possible to prevent misunderstanding. Changes in the planning of activities or demands regarding the partnership should be communicated timely.
> - Conflict management in the partnership. Conflicts in the partnership should be averted as much as possible, by preventing conflicting goals of the partners for the partnership, actively managing differences between people of both partners, and working on increasing trust between people of both partners.

❝Being an HPO is not only about having top notch units but also about having a top notch value chain. The complete process has to be high quality, both the units and the transfer points have to be high performing. So you need to get people willing to look over their fence at the neighbours and then help that neighbour so that the company benefits from synergy and excellent cooperation and can thus deliver. We therefore look for the competency to be able to cooperate when we consider people for a certain job or promotion: do they fit in with the group of key-players in the value chain? Can they move around the network of key-players, is there enough sensitivity to deal with people from other companies, do they have the right antenna to find people to improve the process chain? So what we are looking for is no longer people who can only manage their unit well, that is a precondition. We are looking for people who can get results using the networks in the value chain.❞

Jan Maas, TATA Steel

KEY POINTS CHAPTER 7

- To become and stay an HPO it is a precondition to hire and retain high performance employees. These employees have a higher performance than the average employee as a result of which they contribute more to the effectiveness of the organization.

- The underlying characteristics of the HPO factor Employee Quality are: inspiration, resilience and flexibility, a diverse and complementary workforce, and partnership.

- High performance employees want to be challenged, get much responsibility, and be held accountable for their result. They want to work with people who are and think differently from them, both inside and outside the organization, so they can learn from them.

- There is a strong relationship between the characteristics of HPO factors Employee Quality and Management Quality: as employees want to be inspired to do great deeds, managers must be inspirational; and as employees want to have responsibility and be accountable, managers cannot hesitate to hold them accountable.

Atrion Networking Corporation (USA): being HPO in inconspicuous surroundings

KEY MESSAGE

Many organizations score relatively low on the HPO factor Continuous Improvement & Renewal. And, as this case study shows, even HPOs have difficulty with this factor. However, HPOs acknowledge this issue and will take immediate and strong action to work on strengthening this HPO factor.

Warwick, Rhode Island, is not the world's most beautiful place. The building of Atrion Networking Corporation looks inconspicuous on the outside: the building's only two windows are at the front in the reception area and there's nothing else but plain walls. Not exactly where you'd expect to find an HPO ... but looks can be deceiving. Established in 1987, Atrion operates at the cutting edge of information technology and business. The company specializes in the fusion of business and technology. Through building relationships with and focusing on its clients' business goals, Atrion accelerates business productivity and satisfaction with full-scale customized technology solutions, including consultation, project management, manufacturer-certified training, carrier services, telephony, software and application services, equipment procurement, local and wide area networks, managed services and digital, and interactive and mobile media design. Atrion focuses on IT as a core business utility, driving strategic business productivity and client satisfaction. The personal and professional workshops given by the company and the industry publications and published articles written by Atrion's staff exemplify the passion and commitment of Atrion to its clients and the industry. As a result, the company has been growing steadily and was named the 2010 and 2011 Best Place to Work by Providence Business News, and in 2009 a Fast 50 Company to Watch and Fastest Growing Private Company. We were curious how this company had achieved this.

The HPO Diagnosis at Atrion

As is customary in the HPO Diagnosis, the HPO Questionnaire was distributed among the people in the company and, after the HPO Center processed the data (see Figure 7.1), interviews were held with managers and employees during a week at Atrion's premises in Warwick. This week was concluded by a presentation of the HPO Diagnosis results to representatives of Atrion's management.

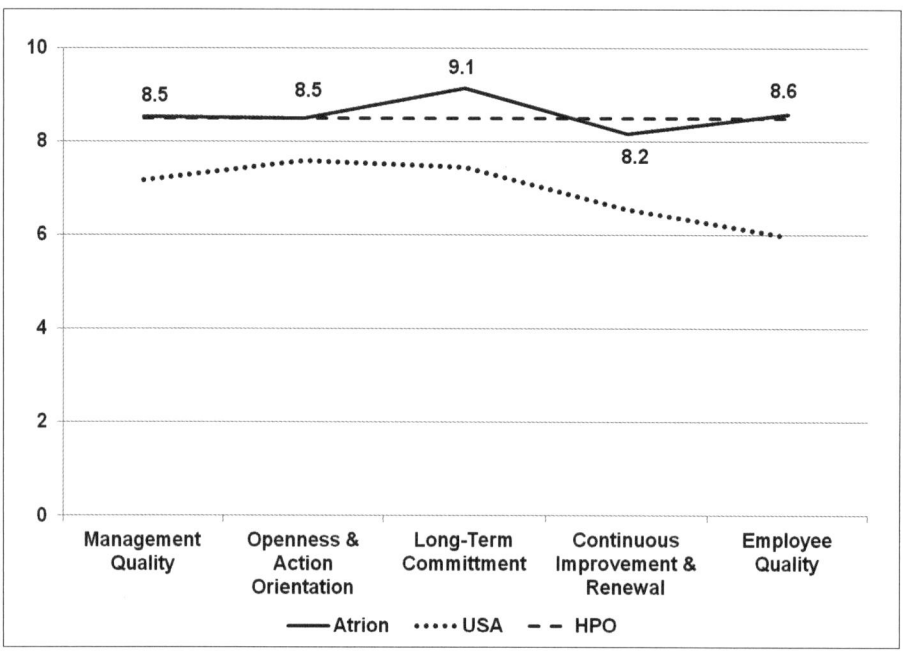

Figure 7.1: HPO status of Atrion Networking Corporation, compared with US organizations

The average HPO score for Atrion was 8.6, considerably higher than the average HPO score of the 20 US companies in the database of the HPO Center at that time, meaning that Atrion qualified as an HPO. The interviews conducted at Atrion concentrated on two questions: What made Atrion great? and In which areas could Atrion improve so it would not only remain an HPO but actually increase its HPO status?

HPO FACTOR 5 – EMPLOYEE QUALITY

What made Atrion great was found in five success factors. The first success factor was Atrion's service model which strongly focused on long-term partnering with clients. Tim Hebert, Atrion's chief executive officer, stated: "We believe that the term client implies that we have a responsibility to protect individuals that choose to do business with Atrion. When we talk about client focus and client relationship, it comes down to the core values of the company. Therefore we say: if you are having doubts about a choice, your values will be your compass and you will always choose in the best interest of the client. If the client is successful, it follows that Atrion will be too." This strong client focus meant that there were companies that had been clients of Atrion since 1987. Michelle Pope, chief operating officer, said: "We feel strongly about relationship building and partnering. Our clients feel more and more that we are an extension of themselves, we are their employee in the way we behave, we are only not situated in their building."

The second success factor was Atrion's strong people focus. The company made a conscious effort to grow people from within. This started from the hiring process in which people with ambition to develop themselves were hired. Then all people were trained to become well-rounded and leaders. Tim Hebert explained: "We have a rigorous hiring process that focuses extensively on the content of the character of the individual that we wish to employ. We look for and examine attitude, ambition to grow and learn, and core values." Interestingly, everybody, whether in a managerial position or not, received leadership training. There was also a lot of coaching-on-the-job and formal development programs and people got much freedom to shape their own career.

Thirdly, Atrion had developed a strong culture based on a value set which included empathy, honor, integrity, trust and especially openness. According to Michelle Pope: "You cannot have an open-door policy if the managers are not engaged, sitting bent down over their desks in their offices. Therefore Atrion does not have offices, even the office of our chief executive officer is an open space where everybody can walk in. You will never see managers walking down the hallway without saying "Hi"' to the persons they pass and without engaging them in conversation, even if that is brief. People feel we are really interested in them, and in turn they are really interested in us."

Fourthly, Atrion had a strong emphasis on the quality of the services it provided, as Melissa Delprete, director of Marketing, put it: "We have an absolute focus on quality, not on cash." Managers and employees constantly talked about how and where they could improve. This continuous improvement called for a rigorous focus on strategic performance management in which Atrion's critical success factors and performance indicators were charted and passed on to everyone in the organization. Also, the organization recognized and rewarded good performance with small bonuses, honorable mentions and prizes such as a parking space right in front of the entrance for the month's best employee (who is chosen by fellow employees).

Fifthly, Atrion strived to be recognized as a thought leader in the industry: "We want to be the Harvard University of our industry." It was notable that Atrion was not satisfied with itself being an HPO in the sector. Instead Atrion is an organization that worked specifically on raising the whole sector to a higher quality plane. The company did this by offering its leadership courses free of charge to clients and suppliers – who welcomed this with open arms – and by developing 'thought leader' concepts in order to get players in the sector thinking and improving so that everyone's clients were given a better service.

Improvement suggestions for Atrion

The HPO Center formulated four attention points during the HPO Diagnosis that, if addressed adequately, would help Atrion

HPO FACTOR 5 – EMPLOYEE QUALITY

become an even better organization. The first attention point was to create a vision of the future Atrion which would be known by everybody in the company. The chief executive officer had a clear image of the future Atrion and how it could be achieved, but that vision was not yet being shared with and embraced by the other managers and employees. The second attention point was related to the first and was to create more engagement for the next growth phase of Atrion. Atrion's chief executive officer did spend time on strategic discussions with the managers but did not check whether the strategic message was subsequently cascaded to lower levels. However, as the managers of Atrion were very hands-on and operationally focused, they had difficulties in really involving employees in strategic process improvement and innovation and cross-functional collaboration. Therefore the managers had to spend more time on tailoring strategic messages to their business units. The third attention point was to create more uniformity in the quality of execution. This quality, although good, could be even higher if several issues would be addressed. An example was that the management of process improvements was not good enough: often structural solutions were implemented to solve behavioral problems, such as implementing an IT system for collecting ideas while the real problem was that people did not want to share ideas cross-functionally. The fourth attention point was to develop a level of professionalism that would suit the next growth phase of Atrion. At the time of the HPO Diagnosis, there was still too much emphasis on a fire-fighting mentality as if Atrion was still a start-up and consequently people were too reactive to problems and not enough proactive to prevent problems. Lastly, Atrion waited too long to deal with non-performers.

Sometime later we caught up with Tim Hebert who told us what Atrion had done with the attention points: "In regard to the first two attention points, we implemented a new monthly full-day strategy session for all senior leaders. This meeting is called

COMPASS, and consists of three components: Strategic Education, Harvard Business Review Case Study work, and a Vision Strategy and Execution discussion. This meeting has been in effect since April 2011 and we are seeing great results. We then launched a monthly half-day strategy session for team leaders and leaders. At the same time, we have begun a rigorous process of developing mid-level leaders and we have hired some seasoned mid-level leaders. This upgrading of leadership skill at this level is giving our senior levels more time to be strategic. We are six months into this and we are already seeing great and improved results. For the third attention point, about the uniform quality, we have started to embrace the LEAN methodology within our organization. The first six months of 2011 were focused on a more grassroots approach. Selecting small but important systems to work, we are engaging more of the frontline workers with less oversight from senior managers. The working teams now consist of cross-functional stakeholders. And on the fourth attention point, at the time of the HPO Diagnosis 90 percent of all changes were driven and produced by our senior leaders, there was little involvement from the rest of the stakeholders and therefore limited buy-in. As I said, we are now implementing the LEAN methodology within Atrion that consists of cross-functional stakeholders that work on the continuous improvement process. Now, change involves less leadership involvement on a day-to-day basis while the staff is owning the entire process. They are empowered to make continuous improvement on a daily basis which speeds up the change process considerably. Finally, looking at the non-performer issue, we are in the process of reviewing all roles and positions within Atrion. This review has highlighted that we have several people performing functions that have outgrown them. We are also in the process of implementing a stronger culture of accountability. And also, Atrion has recently moved into a new, much nicer building so feel free to come back and visit us!"

South American College of Higher Education (South America): balancing growth with stability

KEY MESSAGE

It is possible for a fast expanding organization to succumb to its success. This happens when there is a main focus on getting more clients and more turnover during the growth without paying enough attention to strengthening the organization itself so that it can manage the growth. As this case study shows, the HPO Diagnosis gives insight into this tension between growth and stability, thus providing suggestions for how to balance these two in a way that the organization can keep on growing in a profitable manner.

The South American College of Higher Education (SACHE) is a college which offers vocational education in business economics, management, accountancy, business law, human resource management, and logistics.[85] Currently SACHE facilitates more than 1,000 full-time and part-time students, 60 full-time and part-time instructors and 15 staff members, and achieves a turnover of close to US$2 million. The college seeks active cooperation with local and foreign colleges and universities and the business community to make sure that its graduates can seamlessly start a follow-up study at the university or quickly find a job on the job market. Despite the success of SACHE in the past years, the recently appointed management team wanted to evaluate the status of the organization as there were signals that the college was experiencing growth pains. For the evaluation, the HPO Center was asked to conduct an HPO Diagnosis. The HPO Questionnaire was filled in by the management team, staff members and instructors and, after processing the data, the HPO Center conducted several interviews on the premises of SACHE in South America. Figure 7.2 depicts the HPO status of SACHE.

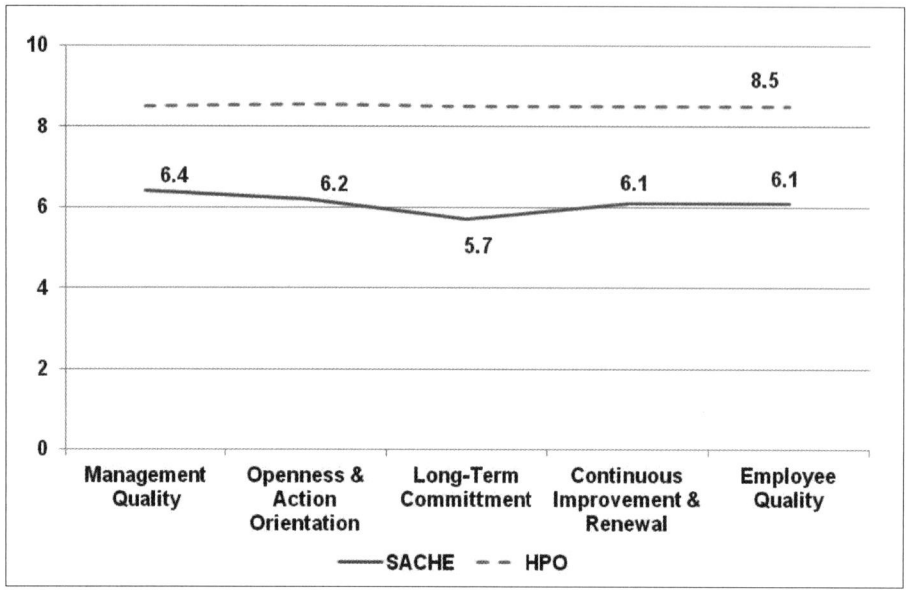

Figure 7.2: HPO status of SACHE

The average HPO score for SACHE was a 6.1, indicating that the college was not a high performance college yet. SACHE had some clear strengths such as the close ties to the business community and the cooperation agreements with foreign colleges, the strong image which attracted more and more students and better qualified instructors, an enthusiastic and committed staff and a new, 'fresh' management team with high ambitions. At the same time, the problem of SACHE was that most effort of management and staff in the past years had gone into the facilitation of the growth in students, in the sense of securing better teaching facilities and teaching material and adding more courses. This had left little time for developing the internal organization of SACHE, which started to show cracks. Staff became less satisfied, some quality problems started to appear, and managers started to leave the college. Figure 7.3 depicts the development of SACHE through time.

During the start-up and growth stages SACHE had grown rapidly in students and instructors. The interviewees felt that if an HPO

HPO FACTOR 5 – EMPLOYEE QUALITY

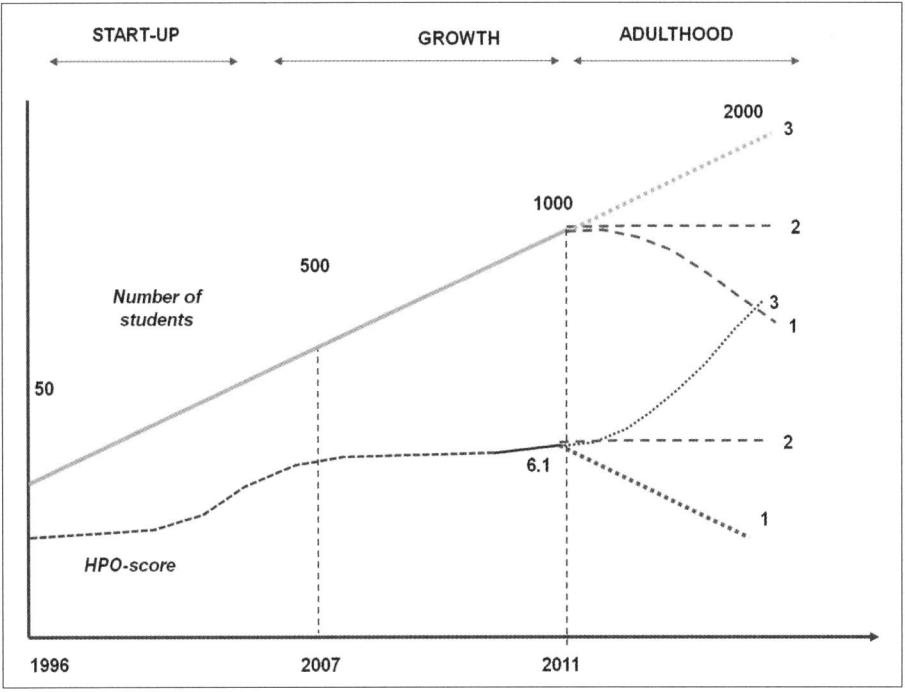

Figure 7.3: The development of SACHE through time, including three possible future development routes

Diagnosis had been conducted during this period, it would have shown an increase in HPO score in the start-up phase as the organization had to improve some of its entrepreneurial and somewhat opportunistic management processes. However, during the growth stage little attention was paid to the internal processes, so the interviewees felt that the average HPO score of 6.1 was probably accurate for the complete stage. During the feedback session with SACHE's management, the HPO Center suggested that the college was now at a crossroads, with three possible routes. If nothing would be done about the internal organizational processes, SACHE would succumb. The organization would no longer be able to cope with the growth in students and instructors, the quality would inevitably suffer and the college would go into a decline (Route 1 in Figure 7.3). The college could also opt for the approach of trying to keep the holes plugged and do the bare necessities to keep the organization floating. This was basically what the college had been doing out of sheer necessity. The expectation was that the growth of the college would level out quickly but that it would be viable for quite a while (Route 2). The third route was to start paying dedicated attention to improving the internal organization, by addressing the attention points derived from the HPO Diagnosis. This would strengthen the organization to not only cope with the growth but even facilitate it (Route 3). The management team opted for Route 3 and decided to address the attention points which were formulated by the HPO Center for four of the HPO factors. These are described underneath. A short quote from the interviews is given which best illustrates the attention point discussed.

1. *Management Quality: 'Management has only one role ... the role model.'* A management team with the aura of an HPO management team had to be created. This could be achieved by the management team giving people more insight into the ins and outs of the management team's activities and the reasons why certain decisions were taken – without necessarily starting long discussions with staff – and what the alternatives were which had been considered. In addition, standardization in the way people were treated by management had to be created, and the coaching role of management had to be strengthened and maintained. Also, management should train itself in becoming more emphatic and in better listening. This all would increase trust in the management team.

2. *Openness and Action-Orientation: 'You can work till you drop ... but you don't mind as long as your heart is beating for the cause.'* The quote illustrates how committed many of SACHE's people were, and this commitment could be increased even more by

involving staff and instructors expressly in the ins and outs of the college. One way to do this was by giving more financial and non-financial information about SACHE's results, and creating common values and rules of conducts so people had something on which to orientate themselves. In addition, the communication function had to be professionalized so that new recruits would get an introduction program to immediately know what was expected from them and how the college operated; and the staff would be timely informed on important developments.

3. *Continuous Improvement & Renewal: 'Control is not a hostile act.'* The management of improvements had to be improved itself by making sure the PDCA cycle (plan-do-check-act) for one improvement activity would always be finalized before the next improvement activity was approved by management and started. During improvement activities staff from multiple departments and the instructors had to be expressly involved, so that cross-functional fertilization could take place and everybody would work for the greater good of SACHE. In addition, a real improvement attitude had to be created by welcoming interventions, not taking criticism personally and stressing that everything could always be improved ... for the good of the students.

4. *Quality of Employees: 'Practice what you teach.'* The strengthening of the staff and instructors professionalism had to be addressed by creating clearer job descriptions and responsibilities, strengthening the HRM department, and developing personal education plans. In addition, a real professional attitude had to be created by not allowing complaining without suggesting solutions, being proactive, giving feedback but also being able to receive it, and being self-starters.

After the HPO workshop the management prioritized the attention points and discussed these with staff and instructors. Then they asked people for their commitment and participation for going ahead with addressing the attention points and turning SACHE into a high performance college. An action agenda was made and controlled by the management team. Finally, a second HPO Diagnosis was announced which had to take place 18 months later, to evaluate progress.

Nabil Bank (Nepal): achieving the sector's top position

KEY MESSAGE

Improving the average HPO score will go in small steps on a year to year basis, probably somewhere between 0.3 and 0.5 point a year. This is because improving all five HPO factors is a difficult task. However, even with a modest increase in the average HPO score, an organization will improve its performance considerably and will work on achieving a top position in its industry.

Nabil Bank Limited, the first foreign joint venture bank of Nepal, started operations in July 1984.[86] Nabil was incorporated with the objective of extending international standard modern banking services to various sectors of society. Nabil currently provides a full range of commercial banking services with 505 employees working in 19 bank branches across Nepal. The bank provides a range of services for consumers, retail, SME and corporate banking and is banker to a multitude of large corporations, international aid agencies, NGOs and embassies. It is the largest private bank in Nepal in terms of branch and ATM network. Operations of the bank including day-to-day operations and risk management are managed by a qualified and experienced management team. The mission of the bank is to be the 'Bank of first choice' to all its stakeholders. Therefore, the organization has customer satisfaction as the focal objective while doing business and also stresses the introduction of innovative products. Nabil Bank has the reputation of being one of the best banks in Nepal and in South Asia. It is the second largest bank of Nepal and has shown continuous growth over the last decade while being one of the most profitable banks (see Table 7.1).

Return on Assets (%)	Fiscal Year					Absolute ranking	Average ranking
	2004/05	2005/06	2006/07	2007/08	2008/09		
Nabil Bank	3.06	3.23	2.72	2.32	2.55	1	1
Standard Chartered Bank	2.46	2.56	2.42	2.46	2.53	2	2
Nepal Investment Bank	1.42	1.61	1.79	1.77	1.68	4	3
Himalayan Bank	1.11	1.55	1.47	1.70	1.80	3	4

Non-performing loans (%)	Fiscal Year					Absolute ranking	Average ranking
	2004/05	2005/06	2006/07	2007/08	2008/09		
Nabil Bank	1.32	1.38	1.12	0.74	0.80	3	1
Standard Chartered Bank	2.69	2.13	1.83	0.92	0.66	2	2
Nepal Investment Bank	2.69	2.07	2.37	1.12	0.58	1	3
Himalayan Bank	7.44	6.60	3.61	2.36	2.16	4	4

Table 7.1: Financial data of Nabil Bank versus its three main Nepalese competitors

At the beginning of 2007 the first HPO Diagnosis was performed at Nabil Bank. The second HPO Diagnosis followed at the end of 2008, 18 months after the first diagnosis. Both times, managers and employees filled in the HPO Questionnaire and the average HPO score was calculated. Figure 7.4 shows the scores for each of the five HPO factors, for both years. As can be seen from Figure 7.4, the curve shapes of 2007 and 2008 are almost identical, which indicates that we are dealing with the same organization. It can also be noticed that the 2008 average score (7.1) is higher than the 2007 average score (6.8).

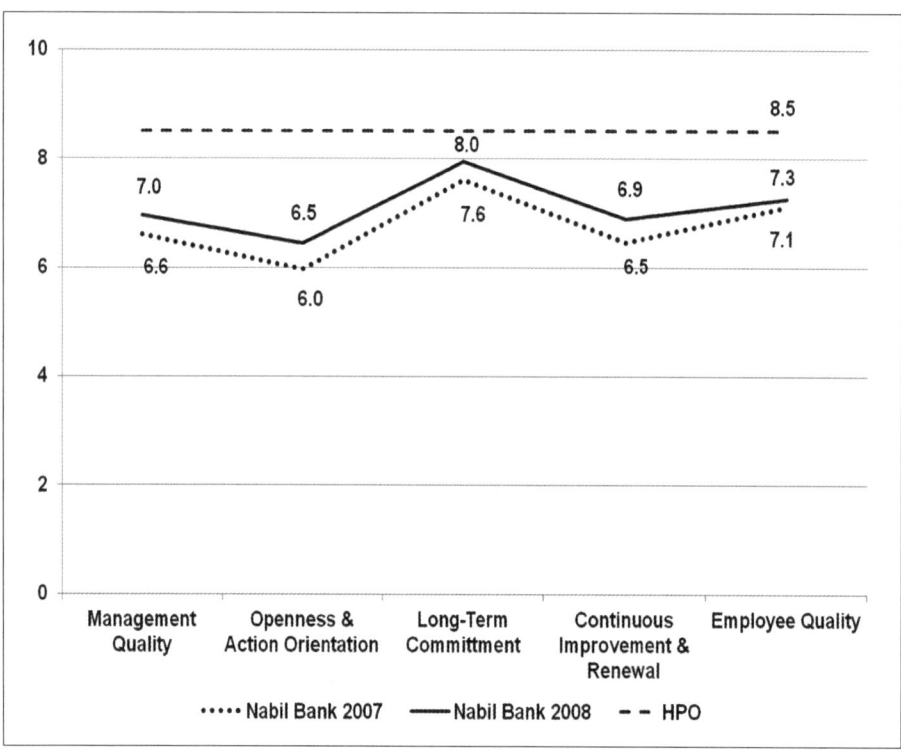

Figure 7.4: HPO status of Nabil Bank in 2007 and 2008

The interviews, conducted by the HPO Center on Nabil Bank's premises in Kathmandu, focused on the main positive differences

HPO FACTOR 5 – EMPLOYEE QUALITY

in scores between the two diagnoses.[87] Looking at HPO factor Openness & Action Orientation, in 2007 management realized that it had to improve the dialogue between managers and employees. Therefore weekly supervisory meetings and monthly department meetings were introduced which increased the frequency of information exchange. However, the dialogue between management and employees still had to be improved as the interviews showed these meetings were more appreciated by managers than by employees. As for the HPO factor Long-Term Orientation, it was interesting to see how much attention Nabil Bank paid to improving its relationships with stakeholders, and specifically the community. While other Nepalese banks had a strategy which was focusing on a few big branches in cities, Nabil Bank opened more and more branches in villages during 2007 and 2008, which was more convenient for local customers. In addition, Nabil Bank employed local people from tribes in the rural area for these branches. These people were first trained in the Kathmandu head office to get familiar with the organizational culture of Nabil Bank, and after that they were employed at the branches. A large increase in score could be found for the HPO factor Continuous Improvement & Renewal. This was caused by the implementation of a new performance management system which improved the information flows and management reporting considerably.

Chapter 8

The HPO transition process: *make it happen*

Now that the five factors of high performance are clear, the HPO transition can begin. Just as implementing the HPO Framework does not follow a prescribed course (telling an organization exactly what to do), implementing the HPO transition process does not either. In fact, each organization makes the transition in its own way, according to its own insights. However, the HPO Center has observed several commonalities in the different approaches which provide some 'free' guidelines for starting the transition. These commonalities have been categorized in four phases.[88] (1) In the introduction phase, the need for becoming an HPO is discussed with everyone in the organization, the way the organization as HPO could look like is visualized, and an HPO Diagnosis is performed. (2) In the preparation phase, the transition strategy is determined, and a team is assembled of people who will act as pioneers in the transition. (3) During the execution phase, the transition strategy is put into practice. It is decided which transition activities will be performed in which order. (4) Finally, in the perseverance & arrival phase, the organization checks whether it has improved on its previous HPO scores and organizational results, and identifies additional and, if necessary, new attention points. This phase is repeated until the organization reaches the desired HPO status, which is then, of course, celebrated.

In this chapter, the four phases are described in four sections. Ideas to get people excited about HPO are given for each phase. The HPO Center got these ideas from managers who came up with them during transition activities that were executed at their organizational units. The ideas have been marked as either 'necessary' or 'inspirational'. Necessary ideas are considered essential for a successful execution of the phase; inspirational ideas provide additional stimuli that help execute the phase. This chapter also includes a section on the main reasons for performing an HPO Diagnosis.

8.1 Introduction phase

The HPO transition process starts with creating awareness of the need for HPO in the organization and getting management and employee buy-in. This may be accomplished by doing, for instance, the following activities:

- *Convey the need for HPO to everyone in the organization by defining and articulating a succinct and compelling reason for the transition.* This reason is based on a sense of urgency or a desire or aspiration. The most obvious reason is the 'burning platform' caused by severe problems or a compelling event, for example a change in strategy or a change in the execution of the current strategy because of dramatically changed circumstances. However, even in a seemingly calm situation urgencies and chances for improvement can and will exist. The reasons for change are brought about by showing how other organizations (preferably competitors) have made successful transitions; using benchmark figures to show the comparative performance of the organization; showing the negative difference in performance that exists between the organization and its main competitors; talking about current bottlenecks and failed projects and what the costs of these are to the organization; discussing how the urge to be the best requires the transition; and by indicating the organization is not ready (enough) for the increasing dynamics of the economy and the environment. However, you do not have to focus only on the negative things. A positive way to create awareness is to appeal to the ambition and pride of people in the organization to work for the best organization in the sector. Aspiration, the desire to want to become a better organization, is a great motivational force and the concept of HPO will certainly cater to this desire. An added benefit is that an appealing picture forms a vision, a dream, which can push people farther along than they ever thought they could go. The gap between performance in the current state and performance in the desired HPO state is quantified by applying the HPO Diagnosis, to show the potential and opportunity that exist within the organization.

- *Paint an appealing picture of the future of the organization as HPO.* A positive and inspiring picture of HPO is created by managers and employees together, which makes people enthusiastic and creates something they can believe in. The HPO picture contains the purpose of the change and the reasons why it is worth undertaking, and describes the positive differences between the current and the desired state. Emotional arguments are used in creating and conveying an appealing picture of HPO, by describing strong negative consequences when the change fails, using words with an emotional and positive connotation, and metaphors. The picture is made appealing by using alluring names, images, pictures, slogans, music, colors and humor, to create a good feeling about HPO. Active language is used to convey the dynamics of the change. When presenting the picture, emotions are shown to carry across warmth and sincere commitment. Fears about the change are reduced by emphasizing the opportunities HPO brings. People can almost 'smell' and 'touch' HPO. They can start the transition with an image of the end goal in their minds.

- *Translate the transition to HPO to each organizational level.* The consequences of what HPO means is made tangible by managers and employees in each unit of the organization, by discussing in a positive way the practical implications for the structure, processes and people of those units. It is made clear what is and what is not going to change and agreed is that good things will not be tempered with (such as existing social security arrangements). The role that organizational levels and individuals can play in the HPO transition is discussed. A clear strategy, with short term and long term objectives, for the transition is set so that it can be steadfastly guided. People can picture what HPO will bring for them, how they will personally benefit from it – 'what's in it for me' – and how they can contribute to it. They might not necessarily understand all the ins and outs of HPO and its implications, but they can certainly believe in it.

- *Make the HPO transition the most important priority for the complete organization for the coming years.* Priorities for the transition activities are set, based on the outcome of the HPO Diagnosis, and resources are made available for these. Running and proposed projects are evaluated on their contribution to the HPO transition. Projects that have added value to HPO are incorporated, other projects are not commenced or continued, to free up the organization's time and resources. Enough resources are made available on a continuous basis to source the transition to HPO.

- *Appoint one or more sponsors for the HPO transition.* The sponsor – one of the senior executives – supervises the HPO transition and takes responsibility for its success. This person has to be acceptable to the organization based on experience, seniority, credibility, likeability and objectivity. The sponsor must make sure to spend enough time on HPO so that the organization sees the promoter, and therefore the top management team, is taking HPO seriously. Because the transition takes a lot of the organization's effort, active and visible support by top management, and budget made available for the transition, it is essential to convey the importance of HPO to the organization. The sponsor regularly communicates progress and results to the organization. For instance, this can be done by regularly scheduling meetings to discuss the HPO results. Top management visibly drives the transition, and helps people to make this transition by creating the conditions which make it possible for them to make the change and excel. Also appoint an 'HPO Challenger', someone who challenges each project on its contribution to HPO. If a project, or even an activity, does not help the transition to HPO, the HPO Challenger will flag this and make sure the organization will not continue with it.

- *Conduct the HPO Diagnosis.* The HPO Diagnosis will not only give the current HPO status of the organization, but will make people aware of the current strengths and weaknesses of the organization and of the need for a transition to HPO.

IDEAS TO GET PEOPLE EXCITED ABOUT HPO, DURING THE INTRODUCTION PHASE

Necessary activities
- Conduct an awareness workshop: discuss the results of the HPO Diagnosis at every organizational unit, with all employees present.

Inspirational activities
- Make an HPO video: put together a video – preferably by the employees themselves – on the awareness workshop, and distribute it over the organization.

Reasons for starting an HPO Diagnosis

The main reason for starting an HPO Diagnosis is management's strong wish for the organization to excel. In addition, there are quite a few other reasons for starting the diagnosis. Here is a list of some of these reasons as given by the clients of the HPO Center:

1. *"We want to know where our organization stands."* A diagnosis of the current strengths and weaknesses of the organization, in comparison with the peer group and – even more importantly – with the absolute scale of HPO gives insight into where the organization currently stands in the competitive field.

2. *"We have a great need to improve."* Improving is good, but randomly starting improvement actions is not. The diagnosis pinpoints the organizational areas where improvement is needed.

3. *"We are performing quite well, but we can't afford to become slack."* The organization uses the HPO Diagnosis as motivation for its people to keep improving, because – as the diagnosis will show – there are always areas which can be improved, even in organizations which are already doing quite well.

4. *"We want to evaluate our strategic plan."* The goal of the strategic plan is to improve the organization so it can excel and beat the competition. The diagnosis gives direction to the strategic plan in the sense that it highlights the areas in which the organization has to strengthen itself.

5. *"We are already undertaking many improvement efforts but are these right ones?"* Organizations often undertake many improvement efforts and implement a plethora of improvement techniques – such as total quality management, six sigma, the balanced scorecard – but they are not sure whether they are implementing the right improvements and are using the most effective techniques. The diagnosis shows the areas where improvement is needed and subsequently indicates whether

the improvement techniques used by the organization are adequate or if maybe other or additional techniques are needed.

6. *"We want to rally our organizational units and our people behind one common course."* Becoming an HPO is a great cause to rally behind as it involves every organizational member partaking in realizing a better future. The diagnosis makes people aware of how that better future could and should look like and what is needed to get there.

7. *"We want to improve our management but we are not sure what is really necessary for them to learn."* Most organizations have management development courses but the contents is often of the shelf and quite generic. The HPO Diagnosis shows how the managers of the organization score on the HPO factor Management Quality. Thus information becomes available as to which HPO characteristics these managers have to strengthen themselves, and management development courses can be tailored accordingly.

8. *"We need to professionalize the organization."* This is often said in relation to the dealings the organization has with its customers and suppliers. The HPO Diagnosis shows how the organization scores on the HPO factor Long-Term Orientation. Information comes available whether the organization is good enough in its dealings with stakeholders – and especially customers and suppliers – and specific training courses can be set up for strengthening the HPO characteristics in question.

THE HPO TRANSITION PROCESS

❝ATLAS is a hugely complex program that, for a host of reasons, got off to a poor start in 2005. In the first two and a half years ATLAS delivered 42 applications and 10,000 user access devices to 17,000 users, so clearly the delivery had been difficult. Each partner in the consortium was doing what he thought was right, which caused a lot of friction. There were 129 continuous improvement programs all full of good intent but with no clear target framework. So when I took charge I had to instil vigour and discipline. I needed to have a framework to guide us in every continuous improvement effort, every piece of work we delivered, and every bit of cultural change. I looked around and found the HPO Framework. What I liked about it was that it didn't feel like management speak or the latest greatest idea that somebody had. It is an analytical fact-based methodology, derived from analyses of companies globally and looking at the characteristics you need to have at the heart of your business if you want to be high performing. What I also liked is that a huge component of the framework is about getting people in the right place in their own heads, how they should work with each other, how they should believe in the company. The HPO Framework helps with the three touch points you need to get your organization moving: you need to understand where you are, where you want to get to, and how you are going to get there.❞

Huw Owen, HP D&S

❝I was looking for something to help us achieve several things. Firstly, making the organization better, not immediately better than the competition, but as a first step, making its better than it was. Secondly, I was looking for something that could affect employees, something that would inspire them. When we got acquainted with the HPO Framework it touched me, it made me

251

want to become an HPO. Thirdly, it had to be something which could give us confidence that we would become better on purpose with a sense of direction, not by accident. And fourthly, it hinted of something grand, something which could create a change on a large scale. I found all four in the HPO Framework, that is why we use it."

Martine Ferment, Ziggo

8.2   Preparation phase

The preparation phase is about creating the right conditions. It starts with assembling the right team of people willing and capable of making the HPO transition. This can be done as follows:

- *Identify the core competencies, with accompanying patterns of behavior, which are required to get to and stay HPO.* These competencies do not only relate to skills and intelligence but also to mentality and attitude. Select people inside the organization as HPO Coaches (see also section 8.6), based on the match between their characteristics and these competencies. These HPO Coaches function as ambassadors of the HPO framework and are kept informed at all times on the status of the transition, its difficulties and its progress. The coaches appeal to the pride of people in their work and stimulate a mentality and a drive to increase the quality of processes, products and services. They create a feeling of unity and a winning spirit among the organizational members: "We are all going for it!" Make sure the HPO Coaches form a cross-functional team consisting of people with different backgrounds, genders, cultures, ages, experiences and organizational functions, to get a good mix of ideas, flexibility of thought and different opinions. Appoint a transition manager to manage the day-to-day activities. This transition manager is preferably an expert in change management and excellence and knows how to deal with the pitfalls and opportunities of this type of transition. Make sure the transition manager has access to people from the marketing (for the communication side) and human resources (for the people side) departments.

- *Apply, for the transition itself, preferably a combination of the experience-based approach and the readiness-based approach.* The transition approach has to be

THE HPO TRANSITION PROCESS

chosen based on the organization's experience with change processes and the level of acceptance that exists in the organization for HPO. It is what management knows about managing what has to be done and how far others are open to it that decides the mix between the experience-based and the readiness-based approach. In the experience-based approach, management knows enough to assess correctly what the aims of the HPO transition are, specifies accurately what has to be done to get to HPO, and resources these activities in the right manner. This creates acceptance for HPO from all concerned. In the readiness-based approach, the climate in the organization for going to HPO is receptive but real experience with this type of transition is lacking. Management moves forward by making sure there are no structural obstacles (for instance, departmental structures and authority structures) that prevent people from working on HPO activities. Management also ensures focused priority for the HPO transition so that other issues do not intrude too much and managerial attention is held by the process. This way, the organization chooses for the 'go-ahead and learn by doing' way. Because HPO is new for many organizations, the readiness-based approach is the most obvious choice. However, by identifying people in the organization that have previous experience with similar types of change processes (for example at previous employers) and giving these people a leading role during the transition (as HPO Coach), a combination with the experience-based approach can be made. This is the best choice: the experience-based approach provides stability for the transition while the readiness-based approach makes the organization open to new experiences and learning.

- *Make a flexible and adaptive transition plan which is not too elaborate.* As all projects and activities which do not contribute to the HPO transition should have been flagged by the HPO Challenger, they should not be in the transition plan, which will save a lot of time. The plan should be all about focus. Set transition goals and a timeline for these, to build momentum and to show progress from day one. Do not schedule giant leaps but small steps – preferably with a maximum time span of three months – to keep the transition activities manageable and adaptive to changing circumstances. Take your time to get to HPO, build in some slack so unexpected setbacks or delays can be dealt with without having to change the complete schedule, but do not falter in getting to the end result which is beyond discussion. Take current HPO-like activities into account and use these as starting point for the plan. Do not only deal with changes in the current organization (with its current processes) but also anticipate (fundamental) changes in the environment which may affect the HPO transition. Involve people in deciding how to get to HPO, give them a say in the setup of the transition plan and in the starting time for the transition. Mobilize in this way the collective knowledge of the organization and increase its brainpower and thereby the self-confidence. Obtain ideas of employees to increase the quality of the transition plan and to gain their support for the transition plan. Give everybody in the organization a role in the transition.

- *Continuously train the organization in HPO.* Introduce 'change-eager management' training sessions to help people make the HPO transition. In these sessions people start to understand what HPO means for their activities, performance and behavior. They start speaking the same language and adhere to the same performance-driven values. Set up a strategy to deal with 'the noise' in the organization: the political games that are played, the egos that come into play during a transition. Celebrate the start of the HPO transition by celebrating the past before departing from it ('look at what we have achieved') and then introduce stimulating content ('and now we are going to become even better').

- *Establish and execute a tailored communication strategy, to create shared expectations and report progress.* Tailor the communication to the type of the organization: use words, images and symbols which are aligned with the organization's current culture and which resonate with people. Convey the message that HPO is definitely coming and that it is not just a 'flavor of the month' activity, and emphasize that HPO will make the organization the frontrunner in its sector. Stress that the transition to HPO is a joint voyage of discovery. Make sure the communication isn't one-way but a real dialogue: two-ways followed by action. Set up a dedicated intranet site with a forum where employees can actively discuss HPO with executives.

- *Establish 'the tone at the top.'* In every transition, the role model of management is crucial for its success. By guarding the 'tone at the top' there is always alignment between the pronouncements, statements and declarations of top management and its actual deeds and behavior. When management walks its talk, does what it says, shows the organization that HPO is really important by paying continuous attention to it, and also gets 'dirty hands' by involving itself in some of the day-to-day transition activities, then the organization will follow suit. Define a key set of transition principles at the outset. These principles stipulate, for example, that management always treats people in the organization with respect and in a fair and honest way during the transition to the new situation; that people can raise objections to and criticize certain parts of HPO or to the transition route towards it; that management will sympathize with people's needs; that management will always hold each other and employees accountable in a constructive way for results; and that everybody will persevere on the road to HPO.

IDEAS TO GET PEOPLE EXCITED ABOUT HPO, DURING THE PREPARATION PHASE

Necessary activities

- Conduct a call to action workshop: put the HPO transition plan for the organizational unit together with all employees.

- Execute a tailored transition plan: decide that each organizational unit can execute its transition plan in its own tempo, so no standardized approach for the complete organization.

Inspirational activities

- Make HPO videos, this time on the call to action and Go HPO (see section 8.3) workshops, and distribute these over the organization.

- Send out HPO news: send out periodic HPO news bulletins, originating from the management team, containing information on the progress of the transition and inspirational stories of employees about what they experienced during the transition.

- Make a customized HPO App with content, activities, videos, for sharing best ideas.

- Create an HPO intranet: make a specific site where everything concerning HPO can be found and where employees can post questions and ideas on which management reacts.

- Celebrate HPO inspiration moments: discuss during team meeting inspirational moments which people had during the transition, for example, with customers who experienced service on HPO level.

8.3 Execution phase

The execution phase is about improving the HPO factors. It starts with choosing which attention points have to be performed and when. The HPO Diagnosis provides the most urgent attention points (probably three to five) which have to be addressed to make the HPO transition.

- *Choose the sequence of attention points to be addressed.* Although all attention points are important, you have to stay practical and keep the transition manageable, thus you have to choose a certain order in which you are going to address these points. Do this based on the life cycle of the organization (what needs to be 'rejuvenated' now), the current situation of the organization (what needs to be 'fixed' right away), HPO-like projects that are currently going on (where can you piggyback on), the size of the organization (multi-process and multi-business will require a different order and approach than single process and single unit), and the culture of the organization (the amount of change an organization can handle stipulates the speed of the process).

- *Just start.* Start before everything is perfectly thought out and before everybody completely understands everything about the HPO transition. If you wait until every last detail of the transition plan is in place, chances are you will never start the transition at all. Experience is the best teacher, so the sooner you start the transition the more you will learn. Starting on time has the advantage that the tempo of transition, if needed, can be set a bit slower. Rather have a steady pace which brings you to the finishing line than a quick dash and collapse before that line. During the transition there will be plenty of time to change and adapt activities and maybe even the transition plan and approach, if needed. But you need to get going, remember that you cannot steer a car that stands still.

- *Start creating a culture of dialogue and co-operation.* During the transition, individuals and groups have, and take, the opportunity to question, challenge, interpret and ultimately clarify the goals of the different activities that need to be performed to get to HPO. They regularly engage in a dialogue to monitor behavior and ensure it is aligned with the goals of the HPO transition. Take the lead to instigate the dialogue and to guard the transition principles, and at the same time be receptive to employees addressing your behavior. Conduct regular discussions, for example, during management team meetings, in which progress of the transition is openly discussed, including possible setbacks and suggestions for adapting the transition approach.

- *Regularly discuss the progress of the HPO transition.* This means discussing the current rate of transition, degree of organizational stability, interference of the transition with daily routine operations, time spent on the initiative, and possible damage of excessive change. Take appropriate follow-up action to either slow down or speed up the process. Balance continued delivery of service with transition activities, making sure that delivery of regular services is not disrupted by the transition activities. Clients need to be serviced no matter what internal changes are going on, so the organization has to stay externally oriented. Acknowledge the different activities in the transition by celebrating that the organization completed a transition activity successfully. Then review the way forward and the required team competencies for the next activity. After completing an activity, make sure it is maintained and its quality is guarded while the other activities are executed.

IDEAS TO GET PEOPLE EXCITED ABOUT HPO, DURING THE EXECUTION PHASE

Necessary activities

- Conduct a Go HPO workshop: have an official meeting with all employees in which the transition plan for the organizational unit is ratified and work on the HPO attention points is started.

- Conduct review/preview sessions: have meetings with employees in which the progress on the attention points and the changes in the past quarter are discussed, developments for the coming quarter are identified, and the transition plan – if needed – is adapted.

- Appoint HPO Coaches and conduct an HPO Coaches expert program (see section 8.6).

- Offer HPO learning impulses: organize special sessions for managers and employees – with possible outside experts – during which they can go deeply into the HPO attention points to obtain the knowledge they need to address the points adequately at their unit.

Inspirational activities

- Conduct HPO lunches: organize two-monthly lunch meetings in which management visits the organizational unit to lunch with employees, and to discuss the HPO transition with them.

- Give out HPO logs: give employees log books or HPO Apps which they can use to note down their experiences during the HPO transition. This information can be used for other inspirational activities (such as HPO videos).

8.4 Perseverance & Arrival phase

The perseverance & arrival phase concentrates on setting new goals. To be able to do this the organization regularly (once every 18 to 24 months) checks whether it has improved its scores on the HPO factors and its organizational results by conducting an HPO Diagnosis. This diagnosis is executed by the HPO Coaches, who are supported by the HPO Center. From each diagnosis additional and/or new attention points for the transition are identified and then addressed. When the desired HPO status is reached, the organization takes time out to celebrate its achievements, to recuperate, and to enjoy its success. After the celebration, management takes stock and sets its sight on new objectives. In the spirit of continuous improvement, the new goals and targets are higher and more difficult than the old ones. To reflect the achieved HPO state, a new or updated evaluation and reward system is installed that is aligned with the changed culture and new organizational goals. Finally, the organization goes into its next developmental phase in which it starts to think about improving the value chain in which it operates, for instance by working on creating high performance partnerships (see section 7.4).

IDEAS TO GET PEOPLE EXCITED ABOUT HPO, DURING THE PERSEVERANCE & ARRIVAL PHASE

Necessary activities

- Conduct HPO behavioral sessions: organize sessions in which managers and employees discuss the desired HPO behavior in the organization.

- Offer HPO learning impulses: short learning sessions on HPO characteristics which provide new motivation and energy to the participants.

- Organize HPO intake sessions: conduct training sessions for new managers and employees about the HPO Framework, results of the HPO Diagnosis and the progress of the HPO transition.

> **Inspirational activities**
>
> - Hold an HPO employee day: organize a yearly day for employees around an HPO theme.
> - Assemble an HPO report: give employees periodically insight into the status of the organization in relation with the HPO transition.
> - Use an HPO scoreboard: hang a scoreboard on the wall, with the HPO scores, the HPO attention points and the progress made on these.
> - Continue with the HPO lunches and the HPO log.

8.5 Four phases overview

Table 8.1 gives a descriptive overview of the four phases. For each phase, the focus of the phase is given (i.e. the main goal to be achieved in the phase); the expected consequences for resources, organizational structure, the people and the processes; and the time needed on average for the phase. Again, the activities mentioned in this table are all optional and other activities can be added depending on the situation and views of the organization.

	Introduction Phase	Preparation Phase	Execution Phase	Perseverance & Arrival Phase
Focus on	Creating awareness and buy-in	Creating the right conditions	Improving the HPO factors	Setting new goals for the HPO factors
Resource consequences	* Choose priorities among current projects * Make sufficient resources available	* Assemble the right (cross-functional & skilled) team	* Divide resources over the HPO attention points	* Look for resources for additional/new improvements on the HPO factors

THE HPO TRANSITION PROCESS

	Introduction Phase	Preparation Phase	Execution Phase	Perseverance & Arrival Phase
Organizational consequences	* Describe what HPO looks like at each organizational level	* Make a transition plan for all organizational levels	* Work on the HPO attention points, in the whole organization	* Set new goals for organizational excellence and high performance
People consequences	* Appoint sponsor from top management * Seek sponsors in the organization	* Train the organization * Establish 'tone at the top'	* Train the organization * Apply a mix of coaching and resolution * Measure tempo of change	* Set new goals for people excellence and high performance
Process consequences	* Paint an appealing picture of the desired HPO status	* Set up a communication strategy	* Create a process for communication & dialogue	* Set new goals for process excellence and high performance * Update evaluation & reward system
Throughput time	1 – 3 months	4 – 6 months	7 months – 3 years	3+ years

Table 8.1: Overview of the four transition phases

> ❝It was a pleasant surprise how easy it was to explain the HPO Framework to employees, and the readiness with which they accepted the concept of our organization as HPO. It also turned out not so difficult to start the transition and improvement projects and to have fun while doing this. HPO really touches people and they want to be part of it. There was some resistance and skepticism about whether these changes would actually materialize and also some hesitations about embarking on a two-year program in view of the rapidly changing business environment in the

telecom industry. So we had to work on the credibility of the HPO initiative, emphasizing that it was for real and that people needed to participate and contribute actively for a long time. With the CEO showing public commitment to HPO, people started believing that we were really serious about HPO."

Martine Ferment, Ziggo

"It will take three to four years to transform to HPO. After one year, a company will be operating like a more joined business. In two years then, it will be a lot better again and then in three to four years it will be institutionalised: everybody has a clear view of the business' vision and strategy and they feel they own these, they understand their contribution to the strategy, and know what they can expect from the business in return for their contribution. Not just money, it is about getting recognition and respect from colleagues, having a voice in the business, their clients seeing that they work in a high performing business. Everybody gets who they are, where they are, where they are going, and how they are going to get there, on every level in the organization. Everybody's objectives, incentives, rewards, and recognition are absolutely linked in to the outputs required to breathe life into the HPO story. Then, throughout the whole of the organization, whoever you are, you believe that you are a role model that needs to reflect and convey and be an ambassador for the HPO story. You live it, you breathe it, it is part of your culture. People will own HPO, they will feel an integral part of HPO."

Huw Owen, HP D&S

8.6   HPO Coaches

To help people in an organization make the HPO transition you can appoint HPO Coaches in all parts of the organization. These HPO Coaches take part in an HPO expert program in which they obtain the knowledge and the tools to help their organizational unit develop into an HPO. HPO Coaches work closely together with and support the management of their organizational unit during the execution of HPO activities; act as central coordination of the HPO activities; provide the channel of communication between their organizational unit, other units and central transition management; recruit new HPO Coaches; report the progress of the attention points and HPO activities; communicate best ideas between units; coordinate activities with the other HPO Coaches to ensure a single coherent program of improvement activities; and arrange and conduct follow-on HPO Diagnoses.

An HPO Coaches expert program runs for approximately 18 to 24 months, with one meeting per quarter. In each meeting one of the attention points, derived from the HPO Diagnosis, is discussed extensively and possible courses of improvement actions – based on best ideas from inside and outside the organization and possible input of outside experts – are explored. The last meeting is focused on how the second HPO Diagnosis has to be executed. The meetings are held in rotation at the locations where the HPO Coaches are based.

> "There are several factors for a successful HPO transition. One factor is that there should be someone high up in the organization who already resembles an HPO manager and who is highly motivated to make the organization an HPO. The second factor is that people are willing to face the truth that they are not HPO yet and that they need to do something about it. This is especially important for the management team. The third factor is that you need a transition approach which is built on development and facilitation of people and contains both rewards and punishments: rewards when people do something very nice and punishment when people do not adhere to the agreements. The fourth factor arises from the third: celebrate your successes. Every time we have achieved a milestone in the transition, every time we have an HPO moment of showing the right HPO behavior to customers or to each other, we celebrate this, so the HPO transition is fun. And the last factor is that you have to stick with this approach for as long as is needed."
>
> *Martine Ferment, Ziggo*

KEY POINTS CHAPTER 8

- Just like in the case of the HPO Framework, there is no prescribed way to implement the HPO transition process.

- Looking at the transition approaches that organizations have taken, four HPO transition phases can be distinguished: introduction, preparation, execution and perseverance & arrival. Organizations should design and fine-tune these phases to their specific situation and in accordance with their own views.

- To make sure the transition will run smoothly and to build HPO knowledge throughout the organization, HPO Coaches can be appointed who function as ambassadors for HPO in the organization.

ATLAS Consortium (UK): creating a successful partnership

KEY MESSAGE

Often an organization cannot directly start the HPO transition. First the hygiene factors have to be straightened out otherwise they will become roadblocks during the transition. This straightening out can take anywhere between six weeks – for an organization that is already basically in good shape – to one year – when there is a lot to fix. In the latter case, this means that, when an HPO Diagnosis is done after a year, the average HPO score will probably have improved slightly but this should not be a reason for panic. The ground work for the transition has been laid during that first year, so in the second year the improvement of the HPO factors can really start.

The ATLAS Consortium consists of four leading IT companies: HP (formally EDS, the lead contractor), Fujitsu, Cassidian (formally EADS Defense and Security Systems), and Logica.[89] ATLAS was set up as a project organization in which the partners cooperated, since March 2005, towards the delivery of the United Kingdom Ministry of Defence's Defence Information Infrastructure (DII) project. This contract was the largest IT contract in recent history and required consortium partners with experience in developing and delivering reliable and seamless systems integrations, in both the public and private sectors. The ATLAS headquarters were located in Reading, United Kingdom, and over 2,800 people worked on the DII project. Figure 8.1 shows the organizational chart of ATLAS. The ATLAS Management Board (AMB) consisted of the chief executive officer and the so-called Leads from each partner, which were the highest placed contact persons between the partners and the consortium. The ATLAS Leadership Team (ALT) consisted of the other functions mentioned in Figure 8.1 over the page.

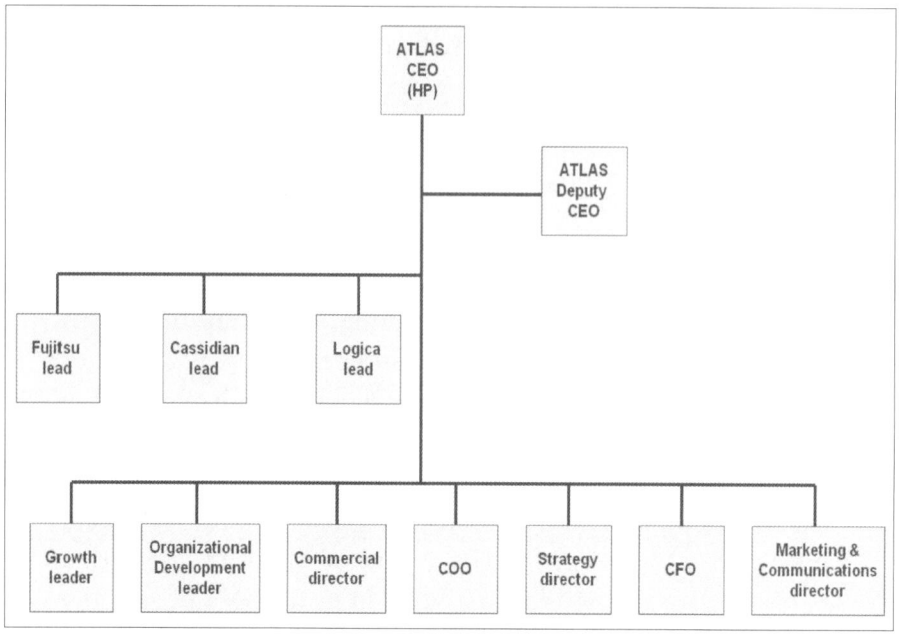

Figure 8.1: Organizational chart of ATLAS Consortium

The DII project was very important to the Ministry of Defence as it was one of the most complex and biggest single infrastructure project rolled out to date in Europe. DII would help make the ministry more agile by creating an effective environment to securely communicate, collaborate and share knowledge and information with 300,000 users on 150,000 terminals (desktop computers, laptops, kiosks for communal areas, etc.) across 2,000 sites worldwide. All authorized personnel across the world would get access to the same information, making decision making more efficient. DII also would realize cost savings of £1.5 billion over a 10-year period. In addition, DII was about saving lives. For example, when someone would be shot on the battlefield the 'golden hour' was activated, which meant that this person needed to get back to base within one hour to receive medical treatment. With DII it would be possible to immediately adapt the medical treatment to the specifics of this person, so when he or she arrived everything would be optimally prepared.

The 2009 HPO Diagnosis

ATLAS could be seen as a unique organization with a huge and important task to fulfill. Since the start in 2005, this uniqueness had however brought tensions in the consortium. From the outset it was assumed that, since each consortium partner had experience with working in long-term partnerships to deliver highly complex military and public sector programs, combining these strengths would bring synergies and lower project risks. However, in reality it turned out that ATLAS combined not only strengths but also differences, such as different country and organization cultures, different ways of working, different incentive systems and performance standards, and different commercial interests. Overcoming these differences required tremendous effort in a hectic environment where there was not always time to reflect on these differences, due to the strong focus on constant delivery of user access devices and realizing targets. ATLAS management decided to ask the HPO Center to conduct an HPO Diagnosis in which specific recommendations had to be given on how to improve the performance of the consortium. The first HPO Diagnosis took place in the summer of 2009, when the HPO Questionnaire was filled in by 902 managers and employees, a response rate of 32.1 percent. The HPO scores were analyzed and in-depth interviews were conducted by the HPO Center. Figure 8.2 gives the HPO status of ATLAS, compared to the HPO status of companies in the ICT industry. The average HPO score for ATLAS was 5.6, which classified the consortium as a medium low performing organization.

ATLAS profiled as a performance-driven consortium, with a highly motivated and cooperative workforce focused on delivering results, which was operating in an environment with clear performance gaps which needed attention so the consortium could achieve

WHAT MAKES A HIGH PERFORMANCE ORGANIZATION

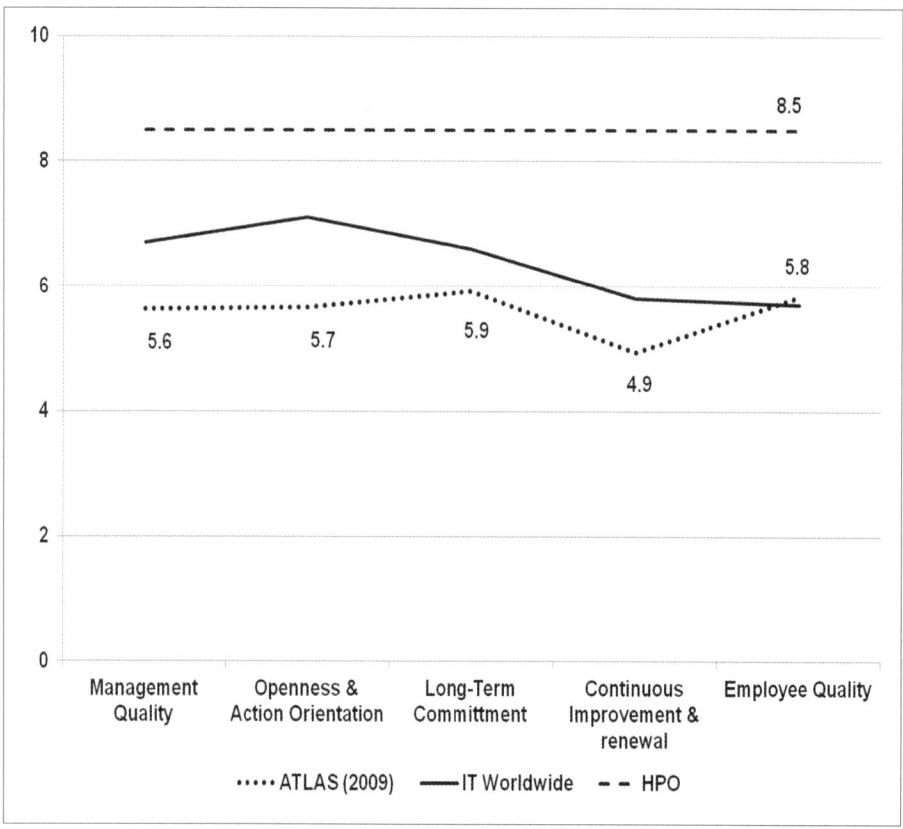

Figure 8.2: HPO status of ATLAS Consortium, compared with the worldwide IT industry

its full performance potential. As ATLAS scored almost one point lower than individual IT companies on average, it was obvious that the potential of the consortium had not been reached yet as the sum of the parts should be higher than the individual parts. Several attention points were identified on which ATLAS needed to work in order to become a high performance consortium:

- *Attention point 1: Create a high performance partnership* – External and internal communications stated that ATLAS was an organization. However, in reality people did not speak about ATLAS as an organization, but looked at the consortium as just another 'account' to work on. As one of the interviewees said, "ATLAS for me is a contractor–subcontractor arrangement. I work for Logica on the ATLAS account. I work for and represent ATLAS to the outside world but inside ATLAS I am a Logica person. Management is trying to treat ATLAS as a one company but it isn't." To address this point, management of ATLAS needed to focus on fostering a culture of trust by stopping the claim-counterclaim culture between partners, fighting protective and defensive behavior, stopping the blaming and shaming between partners, dealing swiftly with the commercial interests of individual partners which hurt the overall interest of the consortium, and helping each consortium partner to improve its quality, attitude and way of working.

▸ *Attention point 2: Strengthen process management* – Different partners brought different ways of working to the table and thus, fostered by the attitude of protecting one's turf and commercial interests, the partner silos in which people operated caused them to lose the view on the importance of an efficient and high quality end-to-end delivery process. One of the interviewees explained, "This silo operating comes from a poor level of understanding of what each partner should be delivering in the end-to-end delivery process, and what the impact of your actions are on the other partners. Also, different ways of working have an impact on the quality delivered. Focus is on getting applications and devices out of the door on time, but setting up efficient process management has been forgotten. There is still no common infrastructure which costs us a lot of time and money." To address this point, management had to focus on increasing project management knowledge and skills, improving process management and planning, preventing cutting corners and compromising quality, create an end-to-end delivery process understanding, and introduce a common IT infrastructure.

▸ *Attention point 3: Increase the quality of leadership* – There existed an attitude within ATLAS of 'making it happen at all costs' which put a lot of pressure on people and caused distrust in management. An interviewee complained: "It is very easy for a senior manager to say 'make it so' and then after a few hours tick off the action. However, for lower levels this behavior creates enormous pressure and we are left doing all the hard work." Employees felt that management generally behaved as if the situation was fine and hence did not show an urgency to change. In the eyes of the employees, management displayed reactive behavior by solving operational issues but lacked proactive behavior in improving the overall working situation. As one interviewee recounted, "Managers create momentum with a focus on priorities and a hands-on attitude. However, currently their communication is depressing: at meetings we only hear we are not performing. But you shouldn't communicate that to your employees in such a way. It is very negative to only highlight problems and talk about budget cutbacks." To address this point, management had to focus on fostering empathic leadership; stimulating pride, ownership and proactive behavior amongst managers; enhancing personal responsibility and accountability; emphasizing unambiguous and accepted role models; stressing more personal coaching from AMB and ALT members; and improving communication skills and a dialogue attitude.

The 2010 HPO Diagnosis

In the Summer of 2010 ATLAS conducted a second HPO Diagnosis to evaluate whether progress was made. This time the online HPO Questionnaire was filled in by 1,185 managers and employees, a response rate of 42.3 percent, and in-depth interviews were again conducted by the HPO Center. Figure 8.3 gives the overall score of ATLAS, which is 0.3 higher than the average score of the first HPO Diagnosis.

THE HPO TRANSITION PROCESS

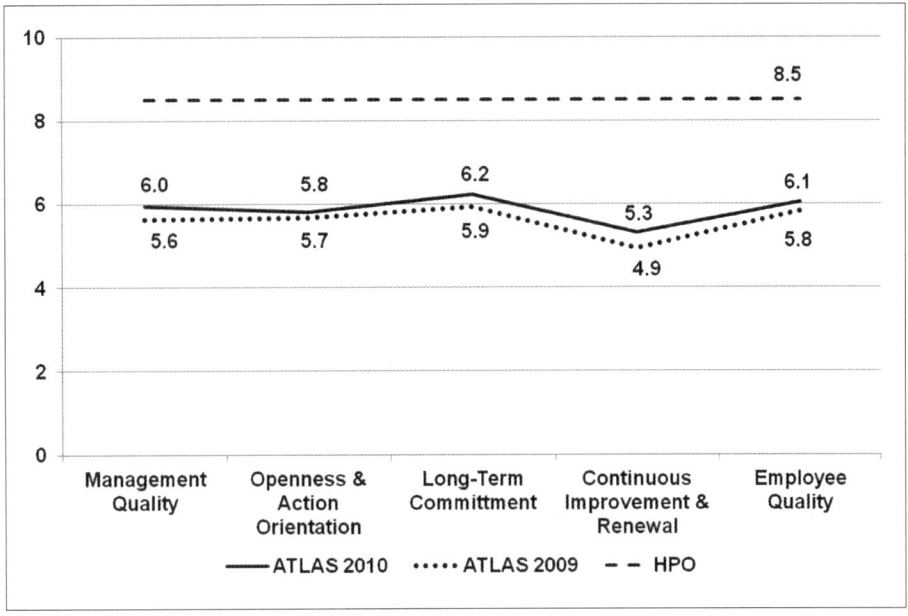

Figure 8.3: HPO status of ATLAS Consortium, in 2009 and 2010

Although it seemed that ATLAS had not made much progress over the past year, the interviews told another story. After the first HPO Diagnosis, the AMB realized that the consortium constituted such a complex environment that the transition to HPO could not be undertaken without considerable preparation, consisting of discussions, negotiations, smoothing out difficulties, and working on setting a common direction. So the AMB decided to use the next 12 months to conduct these conversations, and to also stabilize the consortium by dealing with various ingrained issues – like the commercial interests of the individual partners – and to make headway with an optimization program in which the relation between ATLAS and the ministry was to be improved and cost efficiency measures were to be taken. During the 'preparation' phase, various improvement actions already set in motion were continued leading to the slightly higher average HPO score of 5.9 in the second HPO Diagnosis. Also, this period was spent going round the consortium to talk to people about HPO and its meaning and importance for ATLAS, so people would get more familiar with the HPO Framework and with the role is was going to play in the future development of the consortium.

The second HPO Diagnosis yielded two additional HPO attention points. For the first attention point, the AMB had to deal with the 'communication iceberg.' During the interviews it became clear that the more down one penetrated in the consortium, the less the knowledge about HPO became. Although the AMB and the ALT were very knowledgeable about the HPO Framework and the attention points and were 'waving the HPO flag' on the surface, on the lower levels this 'HPO light' did not filter through enough. It seemed there was a 'clay layer' just beneath the surface, starting in the ALT, which filtered much of the HPO information so that employees were hardly aware of what was happening at the surface. The removal of the clay layer had to have top priority otherwise there would not be enough critical mass among the employees to make the HPO transition. One of the solutions was to appoint people at all sites as HPO Coaches, responsible for spreading the HPO knowledge on site and for helping managers on site in their efforts toward HPO. For the second attention point, ATLAS had to make sure it dealt with the commercial anchors once and for all. As long as the conflicting commercial interests were present in ATLAS, the consortium partners were inclined to look out for their own best interest instead of the interests of ATLAS. Also, the resulting claims and counter claims created an atmosphere of distrust that was not conducive to real and extensive cooperation. When the commercial conflicts could be solved, people all over the consortium would have their hands free to concentrate on the main goal of ATLAS: serving the Ministry of Defence as best as possible, in a profitable way.

The 2011 HPO Diagnosis

The third HPO Diagnosis was performed during the summer of 2011. Again, the response on the HPO Questionnaire increased, this time to 1,903 people giving a response rate of 68 percent. The interviews were conducted this time by the HPO Coaches on all the sites. Figure 8.4 gives the HPO status of ATLAS which, was now a 6.5, constituting an increase of 0.6 points over the 2010 score.

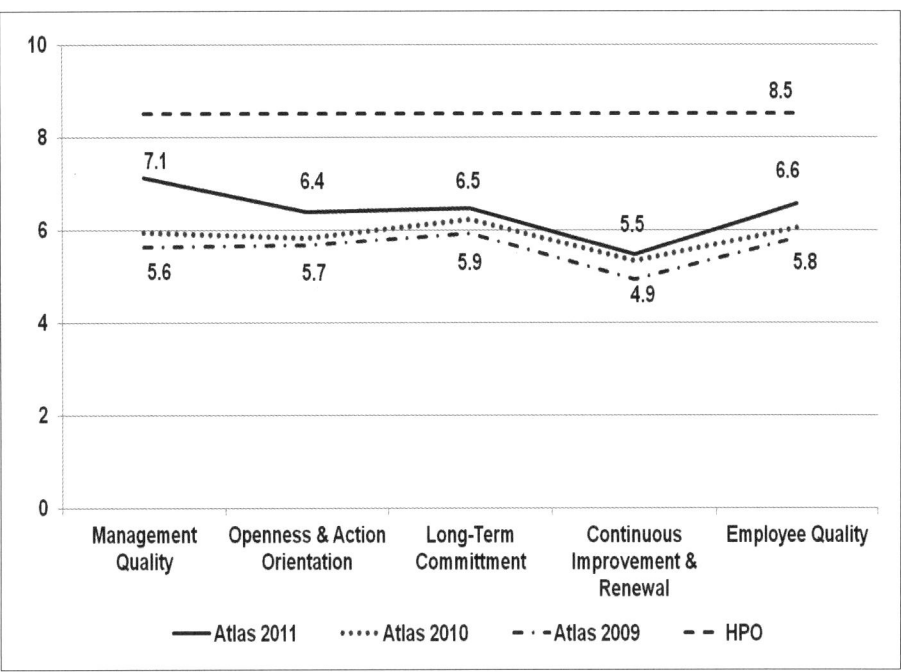

Figure 8.4: HPO status of ATLAS Consortium, in 2009, 2010 and 2011

The core group of respondents (i.e. people who participated in all three diagnoses) saw real improvement and 'felt' they worked in a better organization. Benefits which ATLAS had gained from the HPO transition were that there were better relations, more trust and more communication between the consortium partners. As one interviewee put it: "ATLAS is now the power of four." The engagement of people was rising which could be noticed from the increased response rate on the HPO Questionnaire and from the interviews in which employees said they were now proud about working for ATLAS. Finally, the members of the National Audit Office and Public Accounts Committee, who first were very critical of ATLAS, now expressed that they saw ATLAS as an example of successful cooperation on a grand scale.

The HPO Diagnosis yielded several new HPO attention points. The first attention point was to improve the process of improvement itself. This could be achieved by creating more stability on the middle management level, so improvement efforts could be finalized; creating more slack on management level to create time and energy for improvement; and creating more stability by not adding new processes but first sorting out current processes. In addition, more emphasis had to be put on management discipline so managers would not quit at the bottom of the change curve; and lower-level employees had to be more involved in improvement efforts while not letting them swim without guidance. The second attention point was to foster promotion from within. This could be done by making more time for training of employees and mentoring by managers, so people could progress; daring to take a chance on internal people for promotions and not automatically take outsiders for filling vacancies; and move the HPO Coaches into managerial positions. The third attention point was to increase the involvement of employees. Senior management should have an important role in this by being more visible on the work floor, engaging more with employees, creating more rallying during town hall meetings to boost morale, and providing good feedback to employees on the third HPO Diagnosis. In addition, communication – especially on results – had to be improved by making sure it would take place less in the partner silos and more on overall ATLAS level, and by making it more locally relevant. Finally, more visibility for HPO should be created so it could be kept alive, by communicating the benefits of HPO at ATLAS, formulating all major improvement actions as HPO improvement actions, and creating a dedicated HPO dialogue between managers and employees with the message being: "HPO is here to stay!"

ATLAS' Director of Organization, People & Partners reflected on the HPO transition of the past three years: "We initially thought that with the HPO Framework we bought a change initiative, a methodology which would provide an answer to all our problems. What we actually got was a framework for change which created a common language in the organization and an idea behind which people could rally. To be honest, that felt uncomfortable at the start as sometimes things were said about management which really hit home. But then HPO helped us to start connecting with employees, and employees among themselves, and now I feel it is very satisfying as we see how the framework is helping us to become a high performance consortium!"

The HPO Framework: guideline for mergers

KEY MESSAGE

As is well known by now, the majority of mergers and acquisitions end in failure.[90] Failure in the sense that expected synergies – either in cost savings or complementary portfolios – never materialized and that the sum of the parts turned out to be less valuable than the separate entities. It would therefore be useful to have a diagnostic with which it is possible to evaluate the chance on a successful merger beforehand. This case study shows the HPO Framework can be used as such a diagnostic.

Two companies in the manufacturing business, that were talking about a merger, approached the HPO Center to discuss whether the HPO Framework could help them evaluate their chances of a successful merger. [91] The goal of the merger was to create a single strong organization which would not only be ready for the challenges of the increasingly competitive sector but also would grow to become the industry leader. For this, the strengths and cultures of both organizations should be if not alike at least almost similar. The two organizations had the idea that the HPO Diagnosis would show the strengths and weaknesses, and maybe even more importantly, the HPO statuses (i.e. the curves in the HPO graph) of both companies. This would make it possible for them to compare and see where the organizations complemented each other and

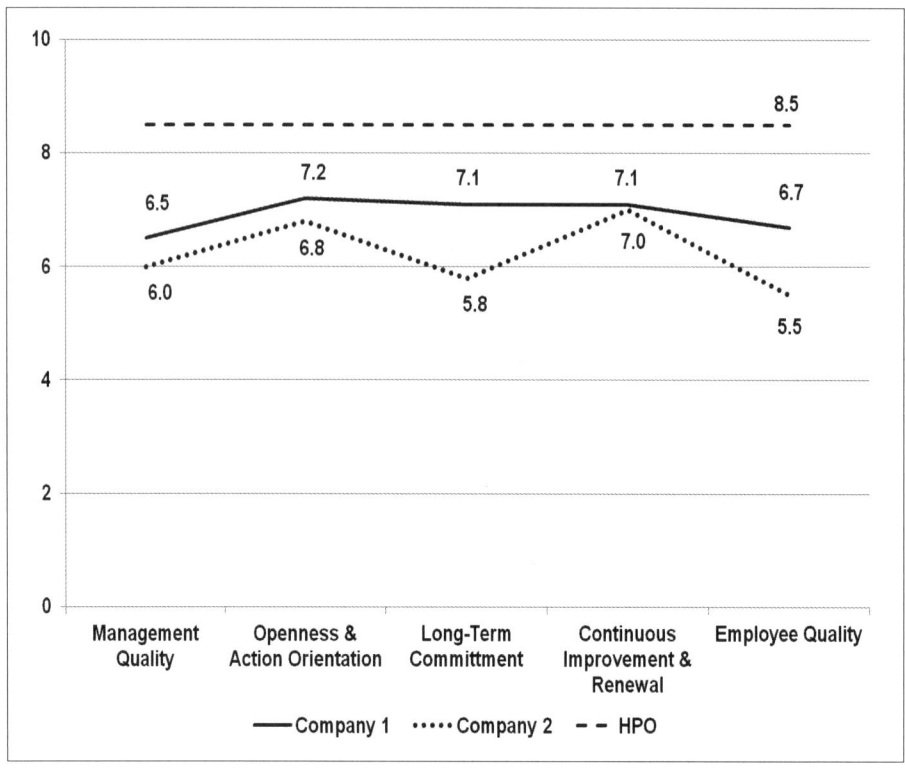

Figure 8.5: HPO status of the two manufacturing companies

if there were any factors in which both were weak and therefore would need special attention.

Managers and employees of both organizations were asked to fill in the HPO Questionnaire. The scores for the HPO factors were calculated and the resulting curves are depicted in Figure 8.5. Company 1 had an average HPO score of 6.9 while the score for Company 2 was 6.2.

Representatives of both companies gathered together to discuss the results of the HPO Diagnosis. Their first conclusion was that, as both companies were not HPO, a merger to create a stronger joint company was quite a good idea. However, the second conclusion was that – because Company 1 had a higher average HPO score than Company 2 (6.9 versus 6.2) – the difference between the two companies was fairly large (for two HPO factors even more than one point) and that because of that they could become unequal partners in the merger, which would negatively affect the merging process. This meant that although Company 1 could be expected to take the lead during the merger, at the same time this company had to be careful not to become too dominant, creating resentment among the people of Company 2. Subsequently, the representatives took a closer look at the detailed scores on the 35 HPO characteristics for both companies, to identify areas of opportunity and areas of potential problems. They distinguished three situations:

1. Both companies scored equally 7.0 or higher on a certain characteristic. This meant the integration between the two organizations during the merger would not be a problem: both companies were strong in this characteristic and should be able to make it work. This was the case, for instance, for the change readiness of management of both companies, and the focus on clients displayed by both companies.

2. One of the companies scored substantially lower (at least 1.5 points) on a characteristic than the other company. The lower-

performing company should then expressly learn from the other company in order to raise the score on this characteristic as soon as possible. Company 1 could learn from Company 2 how to improve its performance management system, and Company 2 could learn from Company 1 how to become more results oriented.

3. Both companies scored equally lower than a 6.0 on a characteristic. This meant there was an integration issue, as both companies were weak and they could not turn to the other company for help and expertise. This characteristic therefore needed specific attention during the merger. For instance, management of both companies were not overly effective and supportive and did not enough involve employees in important processes, and there was rather low flexibility and resilience of employees at both companies.

If too many HPO characteristics ended up in situation 3 it would not be advisable to go straight ahead with the merger. After all, this meant there were too many characteristics that could and probably would create problems and delays in the merger process or would create difficulties afterwards. After reviewing characteristics in situation 3, it turned out that most of these were related to the HPO factor Management Quality. The HPO Center therefore advised that, before the merger was started, top management of both companies should take a long, hard look at their managers to judge whether these were up to the task of making a successful merger happen.

Grohe (the Netherlands): achieving success during times of crises

KEY MESSAGE

Even in tough times, such as an economic crisis, it is possible for an organization to improve itself. In fact, by using the HPO Framework a company can even take a definitive lead on its competitors by working dedicatedly on strengthening the HPO factors and thus achieving a competitive advantage.

Grohe AG is Europe's largest and the world's leading single-brand manufacturer and supplier of sanitary fittings for bathroom, toilets and kitchens, holding roughly eight percent of the world market. As a global brand for sanitary products and systems, Grohe is known for its standards in quality, technology and design aimed at developing products that deliver 'the perfect flow of water'. Grohe strives for a consistently high standard of products to safeguard its reputation as the best value premium brand within the sanitary industry. The company has six production plants worldwide and sales locations in 130 countries. Turnover in 2010 was €980 million, which constituted a 19 percent growth, and an EBITDA (earnings before interest, taxes, depreciation and amortization) of €200 million, a growth of 29 percent, achieved with 5,400 employees worldwide.

In 2008 Rob van den Maagdenberg, Vice President of North Western Europe, decided to conduct an HPO Diagnosis at Grohe in the Netherlands. The reason for this was that, although Grohe was still market leader in that country, the difference with competitors was gradually becoming smaller. The company suffered from a shrinking turnover although it was fortunately still profitable. But Van den Maagdenberg thought the winning spirit had somehow left the company. As people were working too much on automatic pilot and too long in the same departments, there was not enough innovation and too much focus on push marketing instead of pull marketing, and the sales staff were not evaluated on their results so they didn't act aggressively enough. In the second half of 2008, the HPO Questionnaire was distributed among personnel and the average HPO score was calculated. As can be seen in Figure 8.6, Grohe was a good scoring company, not yet an HPO, but performing better than the industry's average.

Subsequent interviews conducted by the HPO Center revealed that Grohe could be characterized as a performance-driven organization with a confident, decisive and action-oriented management, aimed at innovation in order to serve customers as best as possible. The interviews also showed that Grohe should concentrate on several issues to become a full-blown HPO. Chief among these issues was

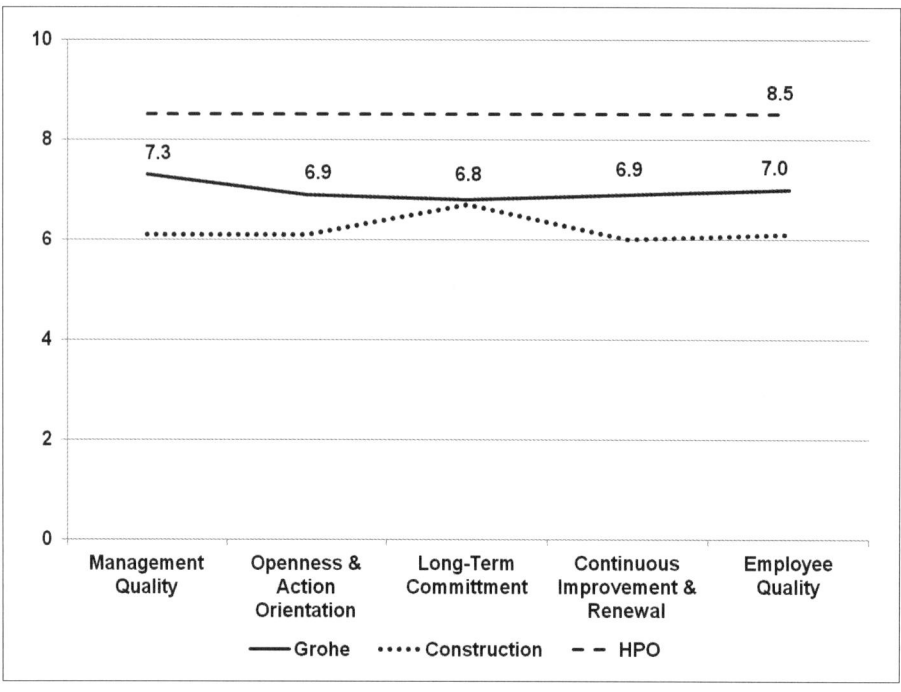

Figure 8.6: HPO status of Grohe in 2008, compared with the construction industry

improving the continuous improvement process by focusing on strengthening process management in the company. Too many process improvements were started but not finished because the various departments in the company were not cooperating well with each other. Each department was working for itself and, as a consequence, improvement results were suboptimal. The lack of cooperation also manifested itself in the fact that knowledge sharing between departments was a difficult process which also was not enough stimulated by management. In fact, managers themselves didn't share much information with employees and thus did not set the right example. Another issue was the quality of both management and workforce, and also the dialogue between these two groups, which had to be strengthened if Grohe was to become high performing. Van den Maagdenberg shared the results of the HPO Diagnosis with all employees in the company, and subsequently several HPO working groups were established which were charged with implementing improvements to address the issues. To improve cooperation, each process improvement activity would from then on only be signed off by management when it was (a) cross-departmental and people from various departments were actively involved; and (b) there were clear innovations to be had from the activity. Knowledge sharing between departments was thus 'automatically' fostered. In addition, knowledge sharing was promoted by organizing quarterly information sessions between management and employees in which company results and on-going and planned actions and activities (such as the HPO improvement actions) were discussed. To increase the quality of management and employees, mini MBA training sessions were organized with a focus on creating a 'we can do' mentality. Also, people got personal performance indicators so they better knew what was expected from them. Finally, the organizational structure was shaken up by moving people around the departments.

In 2010 Van den Maagdenberg asked the HPO Center to conduct a second HPO Diagnosis, to check on the progress and effects of the improvement activities. Figure 8.7 shows the HPO status of Grohe for 2008 and 2010. The average HPO score for Grohe in 2010, compared to 2008, was 0.24 point higher. This increase initially looked disappointingly small until a closer look was taken at what happened in Grohe's industry in the period from 2008 to 2010. The building industry during this period suffered from a severe recession due to which construction activities came virtually to a standstill, with all the negative effects for suppliers like Grohe. Many competitors of Grohe either suffered huge losses or even went bankrupt during this period. Grohe Netherlands however managed to double its sales and profits and won market share which stood then at 45 percent. If one takes into consideration that a HPO transition takes between three to five years, depending on the initial HPO status of an organization, and that an organization needs on average a rise of 1.5 points for this, a yearly increase in HPO status of between 0.3 and 0.5 should be possible. However, in times of crisis the

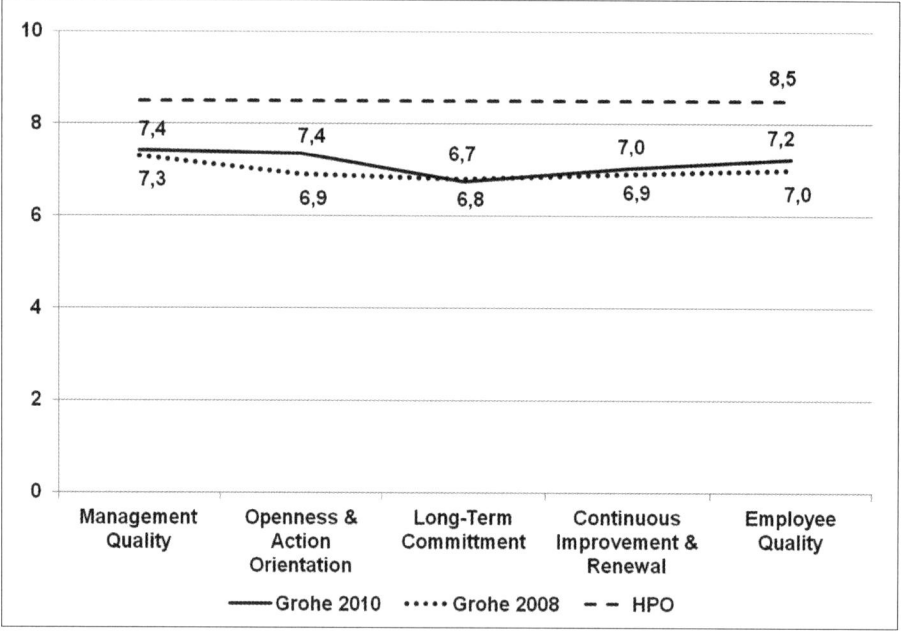

Figure 8.7: HPO status of Grohe, in 2008 and 2010

0.24 increase of Grohe may well have been the maximum that was achievable because of the huge amount of time spent on sales activities and fighting for market share. There was of course much pressure from headquarters and thus not much time and resources were available to apply on strengthening the internal organization. Still, Grohe managed to work on many improvement activities. Looking into more detail at the scores for the five HPO scores, we saw the following effects of these activities:

▸ Openness & Action Orientation went up by 0.5 points from 2008 to 2010: there was an increase in openness because of the quarterly meetings, and more action orientation because departments came together routinely to jointly discuss and take actions.

▸ Continuous Improvement & Renewal went up by 0.1 point: many new products had been introduced successfully during this period and there was a new successful market approach. On the downside, however, processes that had been fully mapped had not yet improved.

▸ Management Quality went up by 0.1 point: new, experienced management had been hired for people who had retired, but the HPO sponsor (the vice president) had to spend much time managing operations in other countries and could not sufficiently direct the HPO efforts and coach the management team.

▸ Employee Quality went up by 0.1 point: a master class for employees had been installed, but they were not part of the working groups that coordinated the HPO improvement activities.

▸ Long-Term Orientation went down by 0.1 point: mother company Grohe AG was in the hands of private equity parties which inclined towards a short term view, consequently there was no vision of the 'Grohe of tomorrow.'

The management of Grohe stated that through applying the HPO Framework the organization had gained a renewed spirit and that the winner's mentality had returned. They knew there still was a lot to improve but there was a broadly shared feeling that Grohe could conquer any challenges because the organization was getting stronger and stronger. At the time of the second HPO Diagnosis we talked to Mr. Van den Maagdenberg once more and we asked him what improvements he was most proud of and what he thought of the role of the HPO Framework in the improvement process. "I am proud of our effective cooperation. We have a much better flow of processes, not only in the departments but specifically over the departments, integrally throughout the company. We now, as a standard practice, look at what we can improve in the whole company, not just in a specific department. So we are gradually breaking down the 'silo thinking' in which every department was only busy and concerned with itself. What helps this new attitude is that we are now much more transparent about the results of the company which we share every quarter with everybody, good and bad. We also share and discuss our plans and involve employees in discussions about these. I have discovered that the way to do the sharing is not in big town hall meetings but in small groups up to 15 people. I meet with these groups in an informal setting and the first 30 minutes I tell them where the company stands. The next 30 minutes is for asking questions and having discussions, a real dialogue in which people can come up with unexpected suggestions and ideas. In small groups people dare more and are really willing to share, in a big group they feel uncomfortable and unhappy to do this. Another thing I am proud of is our increased focus. We have learned to stop starting ten improvement activities without finishing one. We now start with a maximum of two improvements and we round these off completely before we start a new one. In this way, people can follow what is happening and do not get confused because of all the things that are going on. And there are no politics involved in choosing the improvement activities which we are going to do: the ones with objectively the best return are the winners, no matter who proposed them at what organizational level. So what has the role of the HPO Framework been in all this? It started it all. It made us think differently about our business and about how and where we could and should improve it. It helped us think out of the box, be more creative, have the guts to try something different. It brought the openness needed for people to challenge the status quo in the company and it brought much pleasure to people who feel we are on the right track to become an HPO!"

Chapter 9
Benefits of the HPO Framework: *it pays to use it*

The last question which remains to be answered in this book is: What are the benefits of applying the HPO Framework? Section 1.4 discussed the financial and non-financial benefits of being an HPO, based on information found in the literature. It is interesting to see whether the expected benefits are actually realized in practice, after applying the HPO Framework at organizations. Since the first publication on the HPO Framework in 2006, more than 2,000 organizations worldwide have worked with the HPO Framework, and many new research studies have been based on the framework. This made it possible to evaluate the financial and non-financial benefits that applying the HPO Framework can bring to organizations.[92]

Better employee attitude

Employees have a stronger orientation toward improvement. They feel and take more responsibility for improving the organization's products, services and processes. They take more initiative in this area, which results in a continuously improving organization. In addition, the degree of innovation increases as employees dare to experiment more. Because of this, more new products and services are brought to the market place, in shorter time spans, and with more success. There is also a more positive mentality and higher engagement. Employees are more solution-oriented: they think less in problems and more in solutions. They are more proud of their organization and happy to work there. There is a sense of purpose and a renewed spirit in the organization. Employees feel they have a common goal: to become and stay an HPO.

Better cooperation

Employees cooperate more and better, both internally with colleagues of other departments as externally with suppliers and customers. They are more open to ideas from other people and work less in silos as they see themselves as part of an organizational value chain which has to function effectively along all its links. There exists more trust between people which makes it easier for them to build relations and work together. Employees show more interest in each other, and managers are more sympathetic toward employees and really do their utmost to get the best out of them. In addition, there is more openness in the organization. There are better and more frequent dialogues between managers and employees, and also between organizational units.

> ❝One of the most important benefits of implementing the HPO Framework is that everybody in the department takes responsibility to improve month-by-month. They make quarterly improvement plans for their own team and take responsibility for actions and results. Ziggo is a merger company of three separate telecom companies. In the year after the merger Ziggo encountered an unexpected number of start-up problems. That was a huge disappointment for the organization and became the feeding ground for complaints and poor quality with the impact particularly felt within our department. HPO made people realize that even while acknowledging that certain things were not working as well as they should, there was no point in blaming and complaining. They started to ask themselves what they could and should do themselves to fix problems and make things better. And if someone else was involved they should go and meet with that person and solve the problem together. At a certain moment we said something was 'not HPO behavior' to just make clear that something did not work without suggesting solutions for fixing the problems. You could still come forward with your issues but you also had to propose solutions for them and explain what you yourself were going to do about it. Another benefit of HPO is that

people can manage their own issues without having to wait for their supervisors to consent. They are learning that they have the authority to move forward and take action. The nice thing is that people suddenly come up with dozens of ideas and improvement suggestions, just because you give them the space to do so. We also see much more internal cooperation, people who go to colleagues in other departments to fix problems, resulting not only in faster but also better solutions."

Martine Ferment, Ziggo

"The HPO Framework brought a viable facts and data-based framework. It gave us sets of activities that we could undertake to endeavour to improve towards becoming an HPO. It gave us a vision, something to aim for. I think people operate best when they have got that: this is where I am and that is what I need to do to get where I need to be and what I can expect when I get there. With the HPO Framework we had something that we could communicate to people, that people could start biting on, could start believing in. It provided a common language among our people. The HPO Framework was part of the glue that allowed us to stick parts of the ATLAS Consortium together, redirect people's eyes towards an intelligent, believable outcome. It helped to generate the drastic improvement in delivery that we managed to instigate."

Huw Owen, HP D&S

Better organization

The organization has a more unique strategy compared to its peer group. This uniqueness can be found either in the content or the execution of the strategy, and often even in both. This sets the organization clearly apart from its competitors, which raises its attractiveness to new customers and potential employees. There is more focus and discipline. Less projects and initiatives are undertaken and those that are, are finished on time, within budget and with the desired results. Employees also feel a strong corporate social responsibility. As the organization pays dedicated attention to stakeholders, society benefits from activities which the organization's employees undertake in the social sphere. In addition, through better service, less quality problems, less mistakes, more achievement of organizational goals and more fulfillment of promises to clients, the organization gains a reputation of being of a high quality. This makes that the organization enjoys a better reputation both in the business community and in society in general.

Better financial results

The abovementioned non-financial benefits translate into clear financial benefits. Productivity increases as the same people do more, with more success. Profitability also increases as costs are lower and turnover is higher. As a consequence, as the organization rises towards the top of the sector, its market share keeps on growing. Finally, as costs and budgets are better under control, the financial situation of the organization improves and stabilizes.

Competitive advantage

Achieving higher HPO scores means better financial results, and when the organization achieves the highest average HPO score in the sector it also has the best financial results in comparison with its competitors.[93] The same is true for organizational units when these are compared with each other: the units with the highest average HPO scores also have the best financial performance of all the units, and vice versa.[94]

> ❝ Then there are the business benefits. We are almost 50 percent ahead on our budget, our productivity has increased considerably, as have our employee satisfaction and customer satisfaction scores, and we have won an important award for our website two years in a row. Our contracting partners also notice a difference in attitude with Ziggo people, in the sense that we are cooperating better and we look together for solutions, we no longer only discuss performance issues with them and then walk away. Of course we can always improve more, especially in several important customer

processes, and we are planning to pay extra attention to that this coming year. Fortunately, because we have done so well this year, our budget is being increased so that we have more money to spend on improving customer services. Part of this will be to get customer oriented behavior and HPO behavior even more in the genes so that every employee consistently delivers good service. And that in turn will improve the customer satisfaction score. A nice example of the changing behavior is that supervisors now work at least 5 percent of their time on handling phone calls themselves, with the motto: 'customer contact is fun' while last year it was felt that they needed to do 'more important' things than dealing with customers."

Martine Ferment, Ziggo

"Organizations first have got to make up their own minds about whether HPO is the right framework for them. My view is that it ought to be a good framework for almost any business that I can think of, but others might disagree with that. So you need to make up your own mind. Once you have, don't do it half-heartedly. There must be a 100 percent commitment to getting it done, over an agreed and realistic period of time. You have got to truly believe in HPO and commit to it. Because in the early stages, as you are trying to instigate the HPO Framework and get people to buy into it, if you as the leader aren't utterly committed, then it will wither and die very quickly. Communicate, communicate, communicate. Get your top 100 managers absolutely bought into HPO. Get HPO Coaches to spread the story of the HPO Framework throughout the organization. Be evangelical about it. You want people to see that you are taking it very seriously, so let them see that you are acting on it. But remember, it is not a short-term quick win. HPO gives you a framework over a one-two-three-four year period to fundamentally move your business forward. It is a framework that forms the glue that you can use to draw your people together. See it in that way and use it in that way."

Huw Owen, HP D&S

"Think about whether you really understand how the things you are doing will drive value. Question yourself: Am I in the habit of just doing these things because it is what we do, or do I really understand how they drive value? With that knowledge you know what you need to change, how you can go forward and how you should adapt, shape and transform your organization. And don't be afraid to make mistakes along the way to HPO because you will make them, which is okay because you can learn from them."

Alan Clark, SAB Miller Europe

"If you want your organization to become an HPO then *you* have to be the leader of the transition yourself and you should not delegate that task. Not to the management team, nor to external advisers; you yourself have to take responsibility for the transition. You yourself have to organize the resources for the transition, you have to organize complementary skills and talents around you to make the transition. *Create* the impossible instead of *expecting* the impossible. And don't do it half-heartedly, you have to go for it for the full 100 percent. Don't relax, don't think you have explained it often enough, don't expect that it will go automatically, you have to stay on top of it. HPO is too important to stop halfway. It is not: 'this year we'll work on HPO, the next year something else is important, the third year we come back to HPO.' You don't do this in dribs and drabs, it's all the way because it is worth it. **"**

Martine Ferment, Ziggo

The case studies and research studies described in this book illustrate how the HPO Framework can help organizations – profit, non-profit and governmental – step up to a higher performance level and become an HPO. Not only does the framework help organizations pinpoint their HPO status as well as strong points and weak points, it also provides them with clear improvement suggestions which need to be taken up in order to become HPO. In this way, the HPO Framework adds focus to organizational improvement efforts. The HPO Framework has now been so extensively tested in comparative studies and in longitudinal research that it can be safely stated that it provides a lot of certainty: an organization *will* achieve better results when it works dedicatedly on implementing and improving the five HPO factors.

KEY POINTS CHAPTER 9

- Using the HPO Framework to start working on achieving high performance will produce many non-financial benefits for the organization: better employee attitude, more innovativeness, better cooperation, more trust, more openness, more focus and discipline, a better reputation, and in general a renewed spirit in the organization.

- The use of the HPO Framework will also have clear financial benefits for the organization: increased productivity, increased profitability and higher market share.

- Organizations with the highest average HPO scores will have the best financial results in the sector, while organizations with the lowest average HPO scores will rank at the bottom of the industry.

About the author and the HPO Center

André de Waal Ph.D., MSc, MBA (1960) is Associate Professor of High Performance Organizations at the Maastricht School of Management. André is also Academic Director of the HPO Center, an organization which conducts research into high performance organizations. In addition, he is guest lecturer at Vrije Universiteit Amsterdam and Erasmus University Rotterdam, and visiting fellow at Cranfield University (United Kingdom). André holds an MSc in Chemistry (Leiden University, the Netherlands), an MBA (Northeastern University, Boston, USA) and a Ph.D. in Economics (Vrije Universiteit Amsterdam, the Netherlands). He was a partner with Arthur Andersen and Holland Consulting Group for 17 years.

André's Ph.D. thesis was on the topic of the role of behavioral aspects in the successful implementation and use of performance management systems. As an independent researcher, he focuses on strategic performance management and high performance organizations. He has taught and conducted projects in this field in China, Vietnam, Bangladesh, Mongolia, Nepal, Peru, Surinam, Ecuador, the United Kingdom, Poland, Saudi Arabia, Yemen, South Africa, Namibia, Rwanda and Tanzania. André has been selected by managementboek.nl as one of the *Dutch Masters in Management*, ten people who have influenced management thinking in The Netherlands the most in the past decade. Especially his research into high performance organizations and high performance individuals attracts a lot of (international) attention.

André has published over 260 academic and managerial articles and 24 books. These include: *Power of Performance Management, How Leading Companies Create Sustained Value* (John Wiley & Sons, 2001), *Quest for Balance, the human element in performance management systems* (John Wiley & Sons, 2002) and *Strategic Performance Management,*

A Managerial and Behavioural Approach (Palgrave MacMillan, 2007). He has received several awards for his writings. André can be contacted via www.hpocenter.com.

The HPO Center

Customers, employers, employees, suppliers, shareholders, society – everyone benefits when organizations perform as HPOs. At the HPO Center we beam with pride every time we succeed in inspiring and challenging managers and employees to embark on the road towards becoming an excellent organization. We aim to be the source of inspiration and knowledge worldwide when it comes to 'what' makes an organization better and what drives managers and employees within those organizations to improve their performance. We are a knowledge and inspiration center that uses continuous research to work with organizations around the world (including emerging markets) that are driven to improve their performance. Inspiring, rousing and connecting people in a network is our passion. We use the HPO concept to hold a mirror up to organizations and provide a foundation for continuous performance improvement. That is our mission. That is what drives us.

The idea for the HPO Center was born during round-table talks with managers in the profit, non-profit and government sector. During conversations on the scientific research into the success factors of HPOs by Dr. André A. de Waal, the idea arose to establish a center. The goal of the HPO Center would be to create a bridge between this scientific research and its application in practice: "We challenge because we know!" The HPO Center nowadays aims to become the global expert in what makes organizations better. We provide knowledge to this end in the form of diagnoses, interviews, books, articles, lectures, networks and workshops. This knowledge supports organizations in implementing the desired improvements. We have also started new research that looks more in-depth at this subject, including studies into High Performance Managers (HPM) and High Performance Partnerships (HPP).

Based on Dr. de Waal's studies in 50 countries involving 1,470 organizations, an HPO Diagnosis was developed that has been tested extensively in practice. This HPO Diagnosis enables us to hold a mirror in front of organizations, providing a clear indication of their strengths and areas requiring improvement. The diagnosis also provides a clear-cut and broadly based focus for improvement. You can find more information on the HPO Diagnosis and all our HPO writings on www.hpocenter.com.

ABOUT THE AUTHOR AND THE HPO CENTRE

You can also reach and follow us via:

LinkedIn (http://www.linkedin.com/groupRegistration?gid=3383499)
Facebook (http://www.facebook.com/pages/High-Performance-Organization-HPO-Center/179433568763835) and twitter (http://twitter.com/#!/HPOcenter).

New content, blogs, articles, etc. will be published on my HPO Blog: http://www.whatmakesahighperformanceorganization.com/. With the code in this book you can also download extra cases and information on this site. Exclusive for you as the buyer of this book! And finally stay in touch with more and more interesting HPO content by downloading the free HPO app (on iPhone and iPad).

Visit the book website

www.whatmakesahighperformanceorganization.com

Enter login code: AdWHPO12

to obtain more free HPO articles, cases, interviews and other HPO information.

For the HPO Leadership Toolbox app go to:

http://itunes.apple.com/app/hpo-leadership-toolbox/id543205661

Acknowledgments

Writing a book on high performance organizations is not possible without the help of high performing people, and I want to put several of them in the limelight. When I started my research, there were some people who sponsored my studies, both financially and with encouragement. With several of these people I eventually started the HPO Center, which made it possible to conduct many of the case studies included in this book. Thank you very much, Esther Mollema, Chiel Vink and Marco Schreurs, and long may our cooperation continue. Also many thanks to my other colleagues at the center, Lilian Kolker, Eveline Hinfelaar and Alex Meingast, with whom I am writing increasingly more articles on HPO. In addition, I am very grateful to Maastricht School of Management. Through my appointment at this international business school I was able to travel all over the world, collect the data needed for the statistical analysis part of the HPO research, and perform many of the case studies described in this book. Many colleagues and students helped me during the research, either with the statistical work or with a case study, so I am greatly indebted to Bukaza Chachage, Nick Churchman, Hai Duong, Miriam Frijns, Robert Goedegebuure, Tom Groot, Beate van der Heijden, Eveline Hinfelaar, Manley Hopkinson, Paul Jansen, Sandra Linders, Veronica Martinez, Alex Meingast, Giovanna Orcotoma Escalante, Ruben Orij, Michella Oudshoorn, Jantien Rosman, Suhail Sultan, V. Ton, Simon van der Veer and Marijke Zevenbergen.

I am very appreciative of the organizations which not only let me conduct HPO research in their companies but also allowed me to write about it. Without them, obtaining the practical proof of the added value of the HPO Framework would not have been possible. This book is a tribute to you, and to the HPO Leaders with whom I conducted interesting and inspiring interviews. Many thanks also to Ken Lizotte, of emerson consulting group inc, who as my 'thought leader adviser' in the USA got me into contact with several HPOs and with our publisher. I am also appreciative of my publisher Eric Dobby who has turned my scribblings into a very nice looking book. Speaking of scribblings, these have been – together with the support of the excellent 'book review group' consisting of Esther, Lilian, Marco and Ken – made readable by my wife Linda de Waal, who as English editor always does an outstanding job. Thank you Linda, you are a real HPW.

André de Waal
Leiden, June 2012

References

Abrahamson, E. (2004), Avoiding repetitive change syndrome, *MIT Sloan Management Review*, 45, 2: 93-95

Adams, R. (2010), *Ga Vreemd! En onderscheid je door branchevreemd te innoveren, het waarom en hoe van branchmarking*, A.W. Bruna Uitgevers, Utrecht

Adams, M. and Oleksak, M. (2010), *Intangible capital: putting knowledge to work in the 21st-century organization*, Praeger, Westport

Ancona, D., Malone, T.W., Orlikowski, W.J. and Senge, P.M. (2007), In praise of the incomplete leader, *Harvard Business Review*, 85, 2: 92-100

Annunzio, S.L. (2004), *Contagious success. Spreading high performance throughout your organization*, Portfolio Penguin Books, London

Axson, D.A.J. (2010), *The management mythbuster*, John Wiley & Sons, Hoboken

Baker, G.P. and Kennedy, R.E. (2002), Survivorship and the economic Grim Reaper, *Journal of Law, Economics, and Organization*, 18, 2: 324-361

Bakker, H.J.C., M.N.F. Babeliowsky and F.J.W. Stevenaar (2004), *The next leap. Achieving growth through global networks, partnerships and cooperation*, Cyan Books, London

Bagorogoza, J. and Waal, A. de (2010), The role of knowledge management in creating and sustaining high performance organizations: the case of financial institutions in Uganda, *World Journal of Entrepreneurship, Management and Sustainable Development*, 6, 4: 307-324

Bagorogoza, J.K., Waal, A.A. de, Herik, H.J. van den and Walle, B.A. van de (2011), *Improving organisational performance through knowledge management: the case of financial institutions in Uganda*, Paper, First Annual Research Conference, Maastricht School of Management, November 11-12

Barsh, J., Mogelof, J. and Webb, C. (2010), How centered leaders achieve extraordinary results, *McKinsey Quarterly*, 4: 78-88

Barwise, P. and Meehan, S. (2011), *Beyond the familiar, long-term growth through customer focus and innovation*, Jossey-Bass, San Francisco

Bassi, L., Frauenheim, E., McMurrer, D. and Costello, L. (2011), *Good company: business success in the worthiness era*, Berrett-Koehler Publishers, San Francisco

Baumard, P. and Starbuck, W.H. (2005), Learning from failures: why it may not happen, *Long Range Planning*, 38: 281-298

Bennis, W., Goleman, D. and O'Toole, J. (2008), *Transparency: how leaders create a culture of candor*, Jossey-Bass, San Francisco

Berg, C. van der and Vries, R. de (2004), *High performing organizations*, Wolters-Noordhoff, Groningen

Bernasek, A. (2010), *The economics of integrity. From dairy farmers to Toyota, how wealth is built on trust & what that means for our future*, HarperCollins, New York

Bho Group (2009), *Building healthy organizations: transforming organizations through values based leadership*, Trafford Publishing, Bloomington

Blenko, M.W., Mankins, M.C. and Rogers, P. (2010), The decision-driven organization *Harvard Business Review*, 88, 6:54-62

Bond, C. and Seneque, M. (2011), *Locating coaching as an approach to management: an emerging conceptual framework through a comparative analysis of management practices*, Paper, British Academy of Management Conference 2011, Birmingham

Boone James, J., McKechnie, S. and Swanberg, J. (2011), Predicting employee engagement in an age-diverse retail workforce, *Journal of Organizational Behavior*, 32: 173-196

Borchardt, W., Dailey, J. and Rea, I. (2010), *Growth strategies in the new reality: the same success factors really do still apply*, Accenture, ACC10-1145 / 11-1903

Bossidy, L. and Charan, R. (2003), *Execution*, Crown Business, New York

Bower, J.L. (2007), *The CEO within, why inside outsiders are the key to succession planning*, Harvard Business School Press, Boston

Branham, L. and Hirschfeld, M. (2010), *Re-engage, how America's Best Places To Work inspire extra effort in extraordinary times*, McGraw-Hill, New York

Brousseau, K.R., Driver, M.J., Hourihan, G. and Larsson, R. (2006), The seasoned executive's decision-making style, *Harvard Business Review*, 84, 2: 110-121

Brown, S.L. and Eisenhardt, K.M. (1998), *Competing on the edge. Strategy as structured chaos*, Harvard Business School Press, Boston

Bruch, H. and Ghoshal, S. (2004), *A bias for action. How effective managers harness their willpower, achieve results, and stop wasting time*, Harvard Business School Press, Boston

Bruch, H. and Ghoshal, S. (2010), Management is the art of doing and getting done, *Business Strategy Review*, Q2: 70-75

Budman, M. (2011), From like to love, "very good" isn't good enough – your product needs something extra, *The Conference Board Review*, Fall: 54-59

Budman, M. (2012), Still squeezed, austerity and inequality hold back the global economy, *The Conference Board Review*, Winter: 14-19

Campbell, B.A., Ganco, M., Franco, A.M. and Agarwal, R. (2009), *Who leaves, where to, and why worry? Employee mobility, employee entrepreneurship, and effects on source firm performance*, US Census Bureau Center for Economic Studies Paper No. 09-32, http://papers.ssrn.com/sol3/papers.cfm?abstract_id=1484926##, accessed January 18, 2012

Carr, N.G. (2003), IT doesn't matter, *Harvard Business Review*, 81, 5: 41-49

Carroll, P.B. and Mui, C. (2008), *Billion dollar lessons, what you can learn from the most inexcusable business failures of the last 25 years*, Portfolio, New York

REFERENCES

Clayton, B.C. (2010), Understanding the unpredictable: beyond traditional research on mergers and acquisitions, *Emergence: Complexity & Organization*, 12, 3: 1-19

Coffman, C., Gonzalez-Molina, G. and Gopal, A. (2002), *Follow this path. How the world's greatest organizations drive growth by unleashing human potential*, Warner Business Books, New York

Collins, J. (2001), *Good to great. Why some companies make the leap ... and others don't*, Random House, London

Collins, J. and Hansen, M.T. (2011), *Great by choice, uncertainty, chaos, and luck – why some thrive despite them all*, Random House Business Books, London

Collins, J.C. and Porras, J.I. (1994), *Built to last. Successful habits of visionary companies*, Harper Business, New York

Colvin, G. (2009). *The Upside of the Downturn. 10 Management strategies to prevail in the recession and thrive in the aftermath*, Nicholas Brealey Publishing, London

Daley, D.M. (2008), The burden of dealing with poor performers, *Review of Public Personnel Administration*, 28, 1: 44-59

Davidson, H. (2002), *The committed enterprise. How to make vision and values work*, Butterworth Heinemann, Oxford

Davies, H. (2005), The twenty-first century manager book: working on (and on and on ...). In: Cooper, C.L. (ed), *Leadership and management in the 21st century. Business challenges of the future*. Oxford University Press, Oxford

Davis, A. (2009), Are you talking to your people or at them?, *The Conference Board Review*, March/April: 43-46

Davis, R. (2007), *Leading for growth, how Umpqua Bank got cool and created a culture of greatness*, Jossey-Bass: San Francisco

Davis, R.A. (2010), *The intangibles of leadership, the 10 qualities of superior executive performance*, Jossey-Bass, Mississauga

Delbridge, R., Gratton, L. and Johnson, G. (2006), *The exceptional manager, making the difference*, Oxford University Press, Oxford

Delong, T.J., Gabarro, J.J. and Lees, R.J. (2007), *When professionals have to lead, a new model for high performance*, Harvard Business School Press, Boston

Deming, W.E. (2000), *Out of the crisis*, The MIT Press, Cambridge

Deschamps, P. (2008), Innovation leadership in practice: steering innovation, top-down, *Tomorrow's Challenges*, IMD, Lausanne

Detert, J.R., Burris, E.R. and Harrison, D.A. (2010), Debunking four myths about employee silence, *Harvard Business Review*, 88, 6: 26

Dixon, M., Freeman, K. and Toman, N. (2010), Stop trying to delight your customers, *Harvard Business Review*, 88, 7/8: 116-122

Doz, Y., Santos, J. and Williamson, P. (2001), *From global to metanational. How companies win in the knowledge economy*, Harvard Business School Press, Boston

Edmondson, A.C. (2011), Strategies for learning from failure, *Harvard Business Review*, 89, 4: 48-55

Escobar, A. (2011), *Encountering development: the making and unmaking of the third world*, Princeton University Press, Princeton

Favaro, L., Karlsson, P.O. and Neilson, G.L. (2011), CEO succession 2010: the four types of CEOs, *strategy+business*, 63, Summer

Feldman, S.P. (2007), Moral business cultures: the keys to creating and maintaining them, *Organizational Dynamics*, 36, 2: 156-170

Ferguson, A.J., Ormiston, M.E. and Moon, H. (2010), From approach to inhibition: the influence of power on responses to poor performers, *Journal of Applied Psychology*, 95, 2: 300-320

Florida, R. (2010), *The great reset, how new ways of living and working drive post-crash prosperity*, HarperCollins, New York

Foster, R. and Kaplan, S. (2001), *Creative destruction. Why companies that are built to last underperform the market – and how to successfully transform them*, Doubleday, New York

Freeman, E. and Zollo, M. (2009), Re-thinking the firm in a post-crisis world. Special issue – call for papers, *European Management Review*

Furnham, A. and Taylor, J. (2011), *Bad Apples. Identify, prevent & manage negative behavior at work*, Palgrave MacMillan, Basingstoke

Gailly, B. (2011), *Developing innovative organizations, a roadmap to boost your innovation potential*, Palgrave MacMillan, Basingstoke

Garratt, B. (2000), *The twelve organizational capabilities. Valuing people at work*, HarperCollins Business, London

Geus, A. de (1997), *The living company. Habits for survival in a turbulent environment*, Longview Publishing

Gino, F. and Pisano, G.P. (2011), Why leaders don't learn from success. Failures get a postmortem. Why not triumphs?, *Harvard Business Review*, April: 68-74

Gobillot, E. (2007), *The connected leader, creating agile organizations for people, performance and profit*, Kogan Page, London

Godfrey, S. (2010), An Assessment of High Performance Organizations (HPOs) in the Manufacturing Industry in Tanzania, Masters thesis, Tumaini University College, Tanzania

Godin, S. (2010), Redefining failure, *Harvard Business Review*, 88, 9: 34

Goranson, H.T. (1999), *The agile virtual enterprise. Cases, metrics and tools*, Quorum Books, Westport

Grant, A.M. (2008), The significance of task significance: job performance effects, relational mechanisms, and boundary conditions, *Journal of Applied Psychology*, 93, 1: 108–124

Grant, A.M., Campbell, E.M., Chen, G., Cottone, K., Lapedis, D. and Lee, K. (2007), Impact and the art of motivation maintenance: the effects of contact with beneficiaries on persistence behavior, *Organizational Behavior and Human Decision Processes*, 103: 53–67

Griffith, T.L. (2011), *The plugged-in manager: get in tune with your people, technology, and organization to thrive*, Jossey-Bass, San Francisco

REFERENCES

Guest, R. (2011), *Borderless economics: Chinese sea turtles, Indian fridges and the new fruits of global capitalism*, Palgrave Macmillan, London

Gulati, R. and Kletter, D. (2005), Shrinking core, expanding periphery: the relational architecture of high-performing organizations, *California Management Review*, 47, 3: 77-104

Guth, W.D. (2009), Developing new avenues for growth: challenges presented by five trends in the global environment, *Journal of International Management*, 15: 252-261

Hagel III, J. Brown, J.S. and Davison, L. (2009), The big shift, measuring the forces of change, *Harvard Business Review*, July-August: 86-89

Hales, C. (2001), Does it matter what managers do? *Business Strategy Review*, 12, 2: 50-58

Hamel, G. and Välikangas, L. (2003), *The quest for resilience*, Harvard Business Review, September, 81, 9: 52-64

Hansen, M.T. (2009), *Collaboration, how leaders avoid the traps, create unity, and reap big results*, Harvard Business Press, Boston

Harris, F. (2012), *Global Environmental Issues*, 2nd edition, Wiley-Blackwell, Hoboken

Harris, L.C. and Ogbonna, E. (2002), The unintended consequences of culture interventions. A study of unexpected outcomes, *British Journal of Management*, 13: 31-49

Heineman Jr., B.W. (2007), Avoiding integrity land mines, *Harvard Business Review*, 85, 4: 100-108

Henderson, A.D., Raynor, M.E. and Ahmed, M. (2009), How long must a firm be great to rule out luck? Benchmarking sustained superior performance without being fooled by randomness, *Academy of Management Annual Meeting Proceedings*, 2009: 1-6

Henisz, W.J., Dorobantu, S. and Nartey, L. (2011), *Spinning gold: the financial returns to external stakeholder engagement*, Paper, The Wharton School, University of Pennsylvania

Hermalin, B.E. (2005), Trends in Corporate Governance, *The Journal Of Finance*, LX, 5: 2351-2384

Herzberg, F. (2003), One more time: how do you motivate employees?, *Harvard Business Review*, 81, 1: 87-96

Hess, E.D. (2010), *Smart growth. Building an enduring business by managing the risks of growth*, Columbia Business School Publishing, New York

Hickson, D.J., Miller, S.J. and Wilson, D.C. (2003), Planned or prioritized? Two options in managing the implementation of strategic decisions, *Journal of Management Studies*, 40, 7: 1803-1836

Hodgetts, R.M. (1998), *Measures of quality and high performance. Simple tools and lessons learned from America's most successful corporations*, Amacom, New York

Holbeche, L. (2005), *The high performance organization. Creating dynamic stability and sustainable success*, Elsevier Butterworth Heinemann, Oxford

Hollender, J. and Breen, B. (2010), *The responsibility revolution, how the next generation of businesses will win*, Jossey-Bass, San Francisco

Hsieh, T. (2010), Zappos's CEO on going to extremes for customers, *Harvard Business Review*, 88, 7/8: 41-45

Hubbard, G., Samuel, D., Cocks, G. and Heap, S. (2007), *The first XI: winning organisations in Australia*, John Wiley & Sons, Australia

Huyett, W.I. and Viguerie, S. P. (2005), Extreme competition, *McKinsey Quarterly*, 1: 46-57

Ingebretsen, M. (2003), *Why companies fail. The 10 big reasons businesses crumble, and how to keep yours strong and solid*, Crown Business, New York

Jacques, M. (2009), *When China rules the world: the end of the Western world and the birth of a new global order*, Penguin Press HC, London

Johar, G.V., Birk, M.M. and Einwiller, S.A. (2010), How to Save your brand in the face of crisis, *MIT Sloan Management Review*, 51, 4: 57-64

Kaplan, S.N. and Minton, B. (2006), *How has CEO turnover changed? Increasingly performance sensitive boards and increasingly uneasy CEOs*, NBER Working Paper, No. 12465, the National Bureau of Economic Research

Kanter, R.M. (2004), *Confidence, how winning streaks & losing streaks begin & end*, Three River Press, New York

Kanter, R.M. (2011), How great companies think differently, *Harvard Business Review*, 89, 11: 66-78

Kayes, D., Stirling, D. and Nielsen, T. (2007), Building organisational integrity, *Business Horizons*, 50: 61-70

Keller, S. and Price, C. (2011), *Beyond Performance. How great organizations build ultimate competitive advantage*, John Wiley & Sons, Hoboken

Kirkman, B.L., Lowe, K.B. and Young, D.P. (1999), *High-performance work organizations. Definitions, practices, and an annotated bibliography*, Center for Creative Leadership, Greensboro

Kleinbaum, A.M., Stuart, T.E. and Tushman, M.L. (2008), *Communication (and coordination?) in a modern, complex organization*, Working Papers, Harvard Business School Division of Research

Kling, J. (1995), *High performance work systems and firm performance*, Monthly Labour Review, May: 29-36

Knegtmans, R. (2010), *Diversiteit als uitdaging, de zin en onzin van diversiteit*, Uitgeverij Boom, Amsterdam

Kodama, M. (2007), *The strategic community-based firm*, Palgrave MacMillan, Basingstoke

Kotler, P. and Caslione, J.A. (2009), *Chaotics, the business of managing and marketing in the age of turbulence*, Amacom, New York

Kouzes, J.M. and Posner, B.Z. (2010), *The truth about leadership, the no-fads, heart-of-the-matter facts you need to know*, Jossey-Bass, San Francisco

Kreitz, P.A. (2008), Best practices for managing organizational diversity, *The Journal of Academic Librarianship*, 34, 2: 101-120

REFERENCES

Kreling, T. (2011), *Nieuw GM haalt Toyota en VW weer in* [translation: *New GM again overtakes Toyota and VW*], NRC Handelsblad, November 10

Kynge, J. (2006), *China shakes the world: a titan's rise and troubled future—and the challenge for America*, Houghton Mifflin Harcourt, Boston

Lahovnik, M. (2011), Strategic fit between business strategies in the post-acquisition period and acquisition performance, *Journal for East European Management Studies*, 16, 4: 358-370

Laseter, T. and Laseter, L. (2007), See for yourself, *strategy+business*, 48: 1-5

Lawler III, E.E., Mohrman, S.A. and Ledford jr,. G.E. (1998), *Strategies for high performance organizations – The CEO report*, Jossey-Bass Publishers, San Francisco

Lawrence, P. (2002), *The change game. How today's global trends are shaping tomorrow's companies*, Kogan Page, London

Lawrence, S. (2010), What if they don't come back?, *The Conference Board Review*, Winter: 28-33

Lechner, F.J. and Boli, J. (eds.) (2011),*The globalization reader*, 4th edition, Wiley-Blackwell, Hoboken

Lee, T.H., Shina, S. and Wood, R.C. (1999), *Integrated management systems. A practical approach to transforming organizations*, John Wiley and Sons, New York

Lennick, D. and Kiel, F. (2011), *Moral Intelligence 2.0, enhancing business performance and leadership success in turbulent times*, Prentice Hall, Upper Saddle River

Li, C. (2010), The failure imperative, building trust by forgiving mistakes, *The Conference Board Review*, Summer: 60-65

Light, P.C. (2005), *The four pillars of high performance. How robust organizations achieve extraordinary results*. McGraw-Hill, New York

Liker, J.K. (2004), *The Toyota way, 14 management principles from the world's greatest manufacturer*, McGraw-Hill, New York

Liker, J.K. (2011), *Toyota under fire. How Toyota faced the challenges of the recall and the recession to come out stronger*, McGraw-Hill, New York

Liker, J.K. and Hoseus, M. (2008), *Toyota culture, the heart and soul of the Toyota way*, McGraw-Hill, New York

Linder, J.C. (2005), Managing for the upside, *Outlook*, Accenture, no. 2

Loomis, C.J. (2001), *The 15% delusion*, Fortune Magazine, February 5th

Lucier, C., Kocourek, P. and Habbel, R. (2006), CEO succession 2005: the crest of the wave, *strategy+business*, 43, Summer

Mackey, J. and Välikangas, L. (2004), The myth of unbounded growth, *MIT Sloan Management Review*, Winter: 89-92

Maddi, R. and Khoshaba, D.M. (2005), *Resilience at work: how to succeed no matter what life throws at you*, Amacom, New York

Madsen, P.M. and Desai, V. (2010), Failing to learn? The effects of failure and success on organizational learning in the global orbital launch vehicle industry, *Academy of Management Journal*, 53, 3: 451–476

Maister, D.H. (2001), *Practice what you preach. What managers must do to create a high achievement culture*, Free Press, New York

Malone, T.W. (2003), Is empowerment just a fad? Control, decision making and IT. In: Malone, T.W., Laubacher, R. and Scott Morton, M.S. (eds.), *Inventing the organizations of the 21st century*, The MIT Press

Manzoni, J.F. (2004), From high performance organizations to an organizational excellence framework. In: Epstein, M.J. and Manzoni, J.F. (eds.), *Performance measurement and management control: superior organizational performance. Studies in managerial and financial accounting*, volume 14. Elsevier, Amsterdam

Manzoni, J.F., Strebel, P. and Barsoux, J.L. (2010), Why diversity can backfire on company boards, *Wall Street Journal – Eastern Edition*, 255, 19: R3

Marks, M.L. and Mirvis, P.H. (2011), Merge ahead: a research agenda to increase merger and acquisition success, *Journal of Business & Psychology*, 26, 2: 161-168

Marr, B. (2010), *The intelligent company, five steps to success with evidence-based management*, John Wiley & Sons, Chichester

Martin, C. (2002), *Managing for the short term. The new rules for running a business in a day-to-day world*, Currency Doubleday, New York

Matear, S., Gray, B.J. and Garrett, T. (2004), Market orientation, brand investment, new service development, market position and performance for service organisations, *International Journal of Service Industry Management*, 15, 3: 284-301

McGee, K.G. (2004), *Heads up. How to anticipate business surprises and seize opportunities first*, Harvard Business School Press, Boston

McGrath, R.G. (2011), Failing by design, *Harvard Business Review*, 89, 4: 76-83

McGrath, R.G. (2012), How the growth outliers do it, *Harvard Business Review*, 90, 1: 110-116

McLaughlin, M.W. (2010), The worst thing about best practices, *The Conference Board Review*, Summer: 50-54

McNamara, G., Vaaler, P.M. and Devers, C. (2002), Same as it ever was: the search for evidence of increasing hypercompetition, *Strategic Management Journal*, 24: 261-278

Merchant, N. (2010), *The new how. Creating business solutions through collaborative strategy*, O'Reilly Media, Sebastapol

Miller, J.V. (2011), Nobody cared why you messed up, *The Conference Board Review*, Summer: 6

Miller, D. and Le Breton-Miller, I. (2005), *Managing for the long run. Lessons in competitive advantage from great family businesses*, Harvard Business School Press, Boston

Mintzberg, H. (2009), *Managing*, Financial Times Prentice Hall, Harrow

Mische, M.A. (2001), *Strategic renewal. Becoming a high-performance organization*, Prentice Hall, Upper Saddle River, New Jersey

Moss, G. (ed.) (2010), *Profiting from diversity, the business advantages and the obstacles to achieving diversity*, Palgrave Macmillan, Basingstoke

Myatt, M. (2011), Perfectionism vs. productivity, *The Conference Board Review*, Winter: 5-6

REFERENCES

Nagji, B. and Quinn, B. (2010), Shotgun blues, a scattershot approach to innovation guarantees that you'll miss the mark most of the time, *The Conference Board Review*, Spring: 27-31

Nevins, M. and Stumpf, S. (1999), 21st-century leadership: redefining management education, *Strategy+ Business*, 16, 3: 41-51

Niendorf, B. and Beck, K. (2008), Good to Great, or Just Good? *Academy of Management Perspectives*, 22, 4: 13-20

O'Brien, R.C. (2001), *Trust. Releasing the energy to succeed*, John Wiley & Sons, Chichester

Olson, J. (2010), *The little red box of management tools*, Tate Publishing, London

O'Reilly III, C.A. and Pfeffer, J. (2000), *Hidden value. How great companies achieve extraordinary results with ordinary people*, Harvard Business School Press, Boston

Page, S.E. (2007), *The difference, how the power of diversity creates better groups, firms, schools, and societies*, Princeton University Press, Princeton

Parnell, J.A. and Dent, E.B. (2009), The role of luck in the strategy-performance relationship, *Management Decision*, 47, 6: 1000-1021

Pearson, C.A. (ed.) (2012), *The transforming leader: new approaches to leadership for the twenty-first century*, Berrett-Koehler Publishers, San Francisco

Peters, T. and Waterman, R. (1982), *In Search Of Excellence*, Warner Books

Pfeffer, J. and Sutton, R.I. (2006), *Hard facts, dangerous half-truths and total nonsense: profiting from evidence-based management*, Harvard Business Review Press; Boston

Price, C. and Keller, S. (2011), *Beyond performance: how great organizations build ultimate competitive advantage*, Wiley, Hoboken

Quinlan, J.P. (2010), *The last economic superpower: the retreat of globalization, the end of American Dominance, and what we can do about it*, McGraw-Hill, New York

Quinn, R.E., O'Neill, R.M. and St. Clair, L. (eds.) (2000), *Pressing problems in modern organizations (that keep us up at night). Transforming agendas for research and practice*, Amacom, New York

Ramaswamy, V. and Gouillart, F. (2010), Building the co-creative enterprise, *Harvard Business Review*, 88, 10: 100-109

Raynor, M.E., Ahmed, M. and Henderson, A.D. (2009a), *A random search for excellence, why "great company" research delivers fables and not facts*, Paper, Deloitte Development LLP

Raynor, M.E., Ahmed, M. and Henderson, A.D. (2009b), Are "great companies" just lucky, *Harvard Business Review*, 87, 4: 18-19

Resnick, B.G. and Smunt, T.L. (2008), From Good to Great to . . . , *Academy of Management Perspectives*, 22, 4: 6-12

Rhodes, D. and Stelter, D. (2010), *Accelerating out of the Great Recession, how to win in a slow-growth economy*, McGraw-Hill, New York

Richards, D. (2004), *The art of winning commitment, 10 ways leaders can engage minds, hearts, and spirits*, Amacom, New York

Rieger, T. (2011), Turf wars, when rules set "my department" against "our company", *The Conference Board Review*, Fall: 14-17

Ringland, G., Sparrow, O. and Lustig, P. (2010), *Beyond crisis, achieving renewal in a turbulent world*, John Wiley & Sons, Chichester

Rooij, E. de (1996), *A brief desk research study into the average life expectancy of companies in a number of countries*, Stratix Consulting Group, Amsterdam

Rosen, R. (2000), *Global literacies. Lessons on business leadership and national cultures*, Simon & Schuster, New York

Ryan, L. (2010), Ten Signs of a Fear-Based Workplace, *BusinessWeek.com*, 7/12/2010: 8

Sadler, P. (2002), *Building tomorrow's company. A guide to sustainable business success*, Kogan Page, London

Schilder, K. and Teijlingen, H. van (2010), *Veranderen in dialoog*, Scriptum Management, Schiedam

Schoemaker, P.J.H. and Gunther, R.E. (2006), The wisdom of deliberate mistakes, *Harvard Business Review*, 84, 6: 108-115

Seifert, W.G. (2002), Neuer Markt: that damned economic miracle or the return of Dr. Mabuse, *The Finance Foundation News*, 3, July/August

Seitz, J.L. and Hite, K.A. (2012), *Global Issues: an introduction*, 4th edition, Wiley-Blackwell, Hoboken

Seligman, M.E.P. (2011), Building resilience, *Harvard Business Review*, 89, 4: 100-106

Shenkar, O. (2010), *Copycats, how smart companies use imitation to gain a strategic edge*, Harvard Business Press, Boston

Shockley-Zalabak, P., Morreale, S. and Hackman, M. (2010), *Building the high trust organization, strategies for supporting five key dimensions of trust*, Jossey-Bass, San Francisco

Sirota, D., Mischkind, L.A. and Meltzer, M.I. (2005), *The enthusiastic employee. How companies profit by giving workers what they want*, Wharton School Publishing, Upper Saddle River

Skinner, T. (2003), *Beyond the summit. Setting and surpassing extraordinary business goals*, Random House, London

Soene, L. and Duffhues, P.J.W. (2001), *On the relationship between growth, profitability and shareholder value creation*, Tijdschrift voor Corporate Finance, 6, 4: 6-17

Sørensen, C. (2011), *Enterprise mobility: tiny technology with global impact on work*, Palgrave Macmillan, New York

Speijer, J., Veer, S. van de, and Waal, A. de (2010), Organisatievernieuwing: de persoonlijke worsteling en zoektocht van een leider, *Holland Management Review*, 131: 39-44

Spira, J.B. (2011), *Overload! How too much information is hazardous to your organization*, Wiley, Hoboken

Spreier, S.W., Fontaine, M.H. and Malloy, R.L. (2006), Leadership run amok, the destructive potential of overachievers, *Harvard Business Review*, 84, 6: 72-82

Spreitzer, G. and Porath, C. (2012), Creating sustainable performance, *Harvard Business Review*, 90, 1/2: 92-99

Srinivasan, S. (2007), Drucker: On Learning (to learn) management, *The Journal for Decision Makers*, 32, 4: 1-12

REFERENCES

Srnka, K.J and Koeszegi, S.T. (2007), From words to numbers: how to transform qualitative data into meaningful quantitative results, *Schmalenbach Business Review (SBR)*, 59, 1: 29-57

Starbuck, W.H. (2005), Four great conflicts of the twenty-first century. In: Cooper, C.L. (ed), *Leadership and management in the 21st century. Business challenges of the future*, Oxford University Press, Oxford

Steger, M. (2009), *Globalization: a very short introduction*, Oxford University Press, Oxford

Steingraber, F.G., Magjuka, R. and Snively, C. (2011), *"Home-grown" CEO, one key to superior long-term financial performance is managing leadership succession*, A.T. Kearney

Sull, D. (2009), *The upside of turbulence, seizing opportunity in an uncertain world*, HarperCollins, New York

Taylor III, A. (2010), How Toyota lost its way, *Fortune*, July 26: 108-118

Taylor, W.C. and LaBarre, P. (2006), *Mavericks at work, why the most original minds in business win*, Harper, London

Tedlow, R.S. (2010), *Denial, why business leaders fail to look facts in the face – and what to do about it*, Portfolio, New York

Tengblad, S. (2000), *Continuity and change in managerial work*, GRI Report 2000:3, Götenburg Research Institute, Götenburg University, School of Business, Economics and Law

Tengblad, S. (2006), Is there a 'new managerial work'? A comparison with Henry Mintzberg's classic study 30 years later, *Journal of Management Studies*, 43, 7: 1437-1461

Tolmie, P., Hughes, J., Rouncefield, M. and Sharrock, W. (2003), *The 'Virtual' Manager?: change and continuity in managerial work*, Paper, Department of Sociology, Lancaster University, Lancaster, http://www.comp.lancs.ac.uk/sociology/papers/Tolmie-et-al-Virtual-Manager.pdf, accessed March 5, 2010

Toyoda, A. (2010a), *Prepared testimony of Akio Toyoda, President Toyota Motor Corporation*, Committee on Oversight and Government Reform, February 24, available at: http://www.docstoc.com/docs/26641852/PREPARED-TESTIMONY-OF-AKIO-TOYODA-PRESIDENT-TOYOTA-MOTOR

Toyoda, A. (2010b), Back to basics for Toyota, *The Wall Street Journal*, February 23, WSJ.com

Tugend, A. (2011), *Better by Mistake, the unexpected benefits of being wrong*, Riverhead Books, New York

Underwood, J. (2004), *What's your corporate IQ? How the smartest companies learn, transform, lead*, Dearborn Trade Publishing, Chicago

Useem, J. (2005), From heroes to goats ... and back again? In: Leckey, A. and Bogle, J.C. (eds.), *The best business stories of the year: 2004 edition*. Vintage Books, New York

Välikangas, L. (2010), *The resilient organization, how adaptive cultures thrive even when strategy fails*, McGraw-Hill, New York

Veer, S. de and Jong, T. de (2008), Leiderschap met lef zorgt voor succesvol bedrijfsrestaurant, *Kwaliteit in Bedrijf*, september: 12-15

Vermeulen, F. (2010), *Business exposed, the naked truth about what really goes on in the world of business*, Prentice Hall, Harlow

Waal, A.A. de (2003), *On the road to Nirvana, building the real adaptive enterprise*, Hyperion Solutions Corporation

Waal, A.A. de (2006, rev. 2010), *The characteristics of a high performance organization*, Social Science Research Network, http://papers.ssrn.com/sol3/papers.cfm?abstract_id=931873

Waal, A.A. de (2007), *Strategic Performance Management. A managerial and behavioural approach*, Palgrave MacMillan, Basingstoke

Waal, A.A. de (2008a), The secret of high performance organizations, *Management Online Review*, April: 1-10

Waal, A.A. de (2008b), The end of shareholder value thinking, *Business Strategy Series*, 9, 6: 316–323

Waal, A.A. (2009), *Passie voor je vak, hoe gedrevenheid en vakbekwaamheid weer teruggebracht kunnen worden in de financiële dienstverleningssector*, Eureko Academy Life & Pensions, Amsterdam

Waal, A.A. de (2010a), *10 Rituelen van slecht management. Hoe herkent u ze en hoe bestrijdt u ze?*, Van Duuren Management, Culemborg

Waal, A.A. de (2010b), Achieving high performance in the public sector. What needs to be done? *Public Performance & Management Review*, 34, 1: 81–103

Waal, A.A. de (2011a), *Creating high performance organisations: the determinant factors*, Paper, British Academy of Management Conference 2011, Birmingham, September 14-15

Waal, A.A. de (2011b), De resultaatgerichte leider. In: Boonstra, J. (ed.), *De leiderschapsbox*, Managementboek.nl, Schiedam

Waal, A.A. de (2011c), Strategy only matters a bit, the role of strategy in the high performance organization, *Procedures of the Annual International Conference on Business Strategy and Organizational Behaviour (BizStrategy 2011)*: 19-24

Waal, A.A. de (2012a), Characteristics of high performance organisations, *Business Management and Strategy*, 3, 1: 14-31

Waal, A.A. de (2012b), Evergreens of excellence, *Journal of Management History*, accepted for publication

Waal, A.A. de (2012c), Applicability of the high performance organization framework at a multinational enterprise, *Global Business and Organizational Excellence*, accepted for publication

Waal, A. de and Chachage, B. (2011), Applicability of the high-performance organization framework at an East African university: the case of Iringa University College, *International Journal of Emerging Markets*, 6, 2: 148-167

Waal, A.A. de and Frijns, M. (2009), Working on high performance in Asia: the case of Nabil Bank, *Measuring Business Excellence*, 13, 3: 29-38

Waal, A.A. de and Frijns, M. (2011a), Longitudinal research into factors of high performance: the follow-up case of Nabil Bank, *Measuring Business Excellence*, 15, 1: 4-19 (winner of the Outstanding Paper Award 2012)

REFERENCES

Waal, A.A. de and Frijns, M. (2011b), *Applicability of the high performance organisations framework in central Africa: the case of Rwanda's MINALOC*, Paper, 1st Annual research Conference of Maastricht School of Management

Waal, A.A. de and Heijden, B. van der (2012), *Creating customer intimacy through HPO moments*, forthcoming

Waal, A.A. de and Jansen, P.G.W. (2011), *The bonus as hygiene factor: the role of reward systems in the high performance organization*, Paper, 3rd European Reward Management Conference 2011, Brussels, December 1-2

Waal, A. de and Linders, S. (2008), Hoe ziet de excellente sportaccommodatie eruit?, *Sport & Strategy*, 2, 4: 38-39

Waal, A.A. de and Meingast, A. (2011), Determinant Factors for High Performance in the Temping Industry, *Problems and Perspectives in Management*, 9, 4: 35-46

Waal, A.A. de and Orcotoma Escalante, G. (2011), Does the application of corporate social responsibility support a high performance organisation in achieving better results? The case of mining multinationals in Peru, *International Journal of Sustainable Strategic Management*, 3, 1: 33-49

Waal, A.A. de and Oudshoorn, M. (2012), Profielen van de Nederlandse High Performing Employee, *Holland Management Review*, 141: 49-55

Waal, A.A. de and Sultan, S. (2012), *Applicability of the high performance organization framework in the Middle East: the case of Palestine Polytechnic University*, Paper, International Conference on Excellence in Business, University of Sharjah, May

Waal, A. A. de, Duong, H. and Ton, V. (2009), High Performance in Vietnam: the case of the Vietnamese banking industry, *Journal of Transnational Management*, 14:179–201

Waal, A.A. de, Goedegebuure, R. and Hinfelaar, E. (2012b), *Creating the high performance partnership*, Paper, British Academy of Management Conference 2012, Bristol

Waal, A. de, Veer, S. van der and Hopkinson, M. (2010), Working on high performance in the UK: the case of the Atlas consortium. In: Center for Organisational Performance, *Working on high performance in the UK: an overview of current research and practical application*, Chapter 3

Waal, A. de, Orij, R., Rosman, J. and Zevenbergen, M. (2012a), Applicability of the high performance organisation framework in the diamond industry value chain, under review by the *International Journal of Retail & Distribution Management*

Watson, T. J. (2001), *In Search of Management*, London, Routledge

Weick, K.E. and Sutcliffe, K.M. (2001), *Managing the unexpected. Assuring high performance in an age of complexity*, Jossey-Bass, San Francisco

Weiss, A. (2000), *'Good enough' isn't enough ... Nine challenges for companies that choose to be great*, Amacom, New York

Weiss, J. and Hughes, J. (2005), Want collaboration?, *Harvard Business Review*, 83, 3: 93-101

Wiggins, R.R. and Ruefli, T.W. (2002), Sustained competitive advantage: temporal dynamics and the incidence and persistence of superior economic performance, *Organization Science*, 13, 1: 81-105

Wiggins, R.R. and Ruefli, T.W. (2005), Shumpeter's ghost: is hypercompetition making the best of times shorter?, *Strategic Management Journal*, 26, 10: 887-911

Wikipedia (2010), http://en.wikipedia.org/wiki/New_economy, accessed December 22, 2011

Womack, J.P., Jones, D.T. and Roos, D. (1991), *The machine that changed the world: the story of lean production*, Harper Perennial, New York

Wood, D.J. (1991), Corporate social performance revisited, *Academy of Management Review*, 16, 4: 691-718

Wulf, T. (2010), *Performance over the CEO life cycle – A differentiated analysis of short and long tenured CEOs*, Paper, EURAM 2010 Conference, Rome

Yusuph, H. (2010), *Assessment of HPO in banking performance*, Master thesis, Tumaini University College, Tanzania

Zenger, J.H., Folkman, J.R. and Edinger, S.K. (2009), *The inspiring leader, unlocking the secrets of how extraordinary leaders motivate*, McGraw-Hill, New York

Zhang, Y. and Rajagopalan, N. (2010), Once an outsider, always an outsider? CEO origin, strategic change, and firm performance, *Strategic Management Journal*, 31: 334–346

Zook, C. and Allen, J. (2001), *Profit from the core. Growth strategy in an era of turbulence*, Harvard Business Press, Boston

Notes

1. This section is based on and translated from Speijer et al. (2010).
2. The description of the current business environment is based on the following sources: Bakker et al. (2004), Bennis et al. (2008), Colvin (2009), Davidson (2002), Davies (2005), Doz et al. (2001), Escobar (2011), Florida (2010), Foster and Kaplan (2001), Griffith (2011), Guest (2011), Guth (2009), Hagel et al. (2009), Harris (2012), Hollender and Breen (2010), Jacques (2009), Kotler and Caslione (2009), Kynge (2006), Lawrence (2002), Lechner and Boli (2011), Light (2005), Malone (2003), Martin (2002), Pearson (2012), Quinlan(2010), Rhodes and Stelter (2010), Ringland et al. (2010), Rosen (2000), Sadler (2002), Seitz and Hite (2012), Sørensen (2011), Spira (2011), Starbuck (2005), Steger (2009), and Useem (2005).
3. If, for example, the economy prospers HPOs and non-HPOs are given the same advantages. The economic situation can then not be a differentiator between HPOs and non-HPOs.
4. The average life span of organizations on the Fortune 500 list in the 20th century was between 40 and 50 years (Geus, 1997) but declined to under 25 years in the 1990s (Foster and Kaplan, 2001). The probability that a firm would disappear from the Standard & Poor's (S&P) Index in any given ten-year period doubled between 1960s and 1990s (Baker and Kennedy, 2002). Two-thirds of non-financial S&P 500 companies did not survive during the twenty-year period from 1988 to 2007 (Steingraber et al., 2011). Of the Fortune 100 companies in 1966, 66 of those companies didn't exist anymore in 2006, 15 existed but were no longer on the list, while 19 remained on the list (Vermeulen, 2010). The average life span of organizations in Japan and Europe (including start-up companies) decreased to 12,5 years (Rooij, 1996). More specifically, corporate life span in Germany decreased from 45 to 18 years, from 13 to 9 years in France, and from 10 to 4 years in Great-Britain (Seifert, 2002). Many authors since then have remarked that the average life expectancy of organizations has been declining (Bassi et al., 2011; Bho Group, 2009; Mackey and Välikangas, 2004; Srinivasan, 2007). And the chance that an organization will lose its position as leader in the industry tripled between the 1970s and 1990s (Huyett and Viguerie, 2005; Wiggins and Ruefli, 2005).
5. The difficulty of sustaining high growth rates is discussed by Hess (2010), Rhodes and Stelter (2010) and McGrath (2012).
6. The accident, its consequences and causes were widely reported on, among others in Adams and Oleksak (2010), Johar et al. (2010), Kreling (2011), Liker (2011), Olsen (2010), Price and Keller (2011) and Taylor (2010).
7. See for instance the articles and books of Bernasek (2010), Liker (2004), Liker and Hoseus (2008) and Womack et al. (1991).
8. It concerned a statement Mr. Toyoda made before members of the Committee on Oversight and Government Reform on February 24, 2010; this statement was also published in an article in the Wall Street Journal (Toyoda, 2010a+b).
9. The book of Ray Davis, *Leading to Growth* (2007), reads like a case study of how to create an HPO.
10. This quote can be found on page 211 of Davis (2007).
11. The approach to the HPO research is extensively documented in Waal (2006 rev. 2010, 2008a, 2012a).
12. Many thanks to Dr. Veronica Martinez of Cranfield University for repeating part of the research in

this phase, and to professor Tom Groot of the Vrije Universiteit Amsterdam for his help with the statistical analysis.
13 For instance, Blenko et al. (2010) found that fewer than one-third of reorganizations produced meaningful improvements in performance.
14 The fact that ICT is not a decisive factor for creating an HPO was also found by Carr (2003) and Axson (2010).
15 In the past years, there have been quite a few authors, such as Hubbard et al. (2007), McLaughlin (2010) and Pfeffer and Sutton (2006), who warned against the indiscriminate use of benchmarking while trying to improve the organization's result, as this generally leads to copycat behavior.
16 This section is based on the academic paper of Waal and Jansen (2011).
17 This section is based on Waal (2012b).
18 This data can be found on Wikipedia (2010).
19 A similar result was found in a recent study of the stability of success factors for HPOs through time, by Borchardt,et al. (2010).
20 Despite the fact that business writers in general open their writings with a statement that the current business environment is the most challenging ever, many academic researchers (Hales, 2001; Kouzes and Posner, 2010; McNamara et al., 2002; Mintzberg, 2009; Tengblad, 2000, 2006; Tolmie et al., 2003; Watson, 2001) showed that this is *not* the case: every business environment brings its own challenges and managers always have to deal with these.
21 The first management bestseller was *In Search of Excellence*, published in 1982 by Tom Peters and Robert Waterman. Since then especially Peters has done a lot of work on passion and excellence in organizations. Since the 1990s Jim Collins has worked diligently on an extensive oeuvre on high performance (Collins and Hansen, 2011; Collins and Porras, 1994) resulting in the bestseller *Good to Great* in 2001.
22 For instance, academic researchers such as Niendorf and Beck (2008), Raynor et al. (2009a+b) and Resnick and Smunt (2008) showed that the selections made by Jim Collins during his research were not adequate enough to be able to state with certainty that the characteristics of excellence he found are valid for other organizations.
23 Recently a similar extended literature review was done by Keller and Price (2011).
24 In her research, McGarth (2012) showed that industry sector, type of market, level of globalization, and size, age or type of the organization were not determining whether an organization could achieve exceptional growth or not.
25 Until the summer of 2012, the HPO Center has published 14 articles on the HPO research in academic journals and has presented the HPO research results at 17 academic conferences.
26 Absolute guarantees can be given by no model or framework as one can never rule out chance or luck completely. The roles which chance and luck play in achieving high performance are discussed by Gino and Pisano (2011), Henderson et al. (2009), Parnell and Dent (2009) and Sull (2009).
27 'Absolute scale' refers to the fact that if an organization scores a 5 on this scale, it always scores lower than an organization with for instance a score of 7, no matter the industries the organizations operate in or the circumstances they find themselves in.
28 This case was previously published in Waal (2011a). The case company wishes to remain anonymous. Therefore no detailed (financial) information is given about the organization.
29 This case originates from Waal (2012C). The case company wishes to remain anonymous. Therefore no detailed (financial) information is given about the organization.
30 RIG wanted to start with a small group, to get experience with the HPO Diagnosis. After the first nine country divisions, eventually corporate headquarters itself and additional country divisions also participated in the diagnosis.
31 This case study is based on Waal and Frijns (2011b).
32 The first results indicate that MINALOC could be one of the better organizations in Rwanda. This is confirmed by the representatives who state that what distinguishes MINALOC from other ministries

is that MINALOC seems to be better able to fulfill its targets because it has focused on achieving continuous improvement and that in general, because many of MINALOC's employees have direct contact with the constituents, they feel more committed to the organization than is the case at other ministries.

33 For each characteristic a multitude of definitions can be found in the managerial and academic literature. To keep it simple and understandable, we mainly use the definitions as giving in The Concise Oxford Dictionary, The Oxford Dictionary for the Business World, CollinsCoBuild, and www.businessdictionart.com.

34 The 'ideas to get started' have been collected from the literature review that was conducted during Phase 1 of the HPO research, and from recent scientific research studies.

35 The story of the catering manager, Hans Maas from the Dutch company Sodexo, originates from a case study in Waal (2011b). This case study was originally based on Veer and Jong (2008) and is used by permission of these authors (for which many thanks).

36 A manager is defined as someone who is in charge of at least one person.

37 In fact, research shows that trust is not only the most important characteristic for the HPO manager, it also is for the organization. This is because low trust adds significantly to the cost of doing business, restricts the playing field of action and destroys value (O'Brien, 2001). Shockley-Zalabak et al. (2010) show that high-trust organizations considerably outperform low-trust organizations.

38 In a survey, repeated frequently since 1980, on the characteristics of admired leaders the characteristic voted the most important in each survey was honesty (Kouzes and Posner, 2010). Honesty is defined as always telling the truth, having ethical principles and clear standards which are lived up to, and not being afraid to look into the mirror to face up to the truth about oneself.

39 Ideas to foster trust originate from O'Brien (2001).

40 The morally intelligent organization is defined as an organization whose culture is infused with worthwhile values and whose members consistently act in ways aligned with those values (Lennick and Kiel, 2011). Ways to create such an organization are described in Davis (2010), Feldman (2007), Heineman (2007), Kayes et al. (2007) and Lennick and Kiel (2011).

41 This research was performed by Kouzes and Posner (2010). They show that for the younger age category a business leader is still the fourth important role model, so the business leader does play an important role in the age categories that are present in a working environment. Kouzes and Posner also found that this business leader is most often the direct supervisor.

42 The various decision-making styles in combination with the career stages of a manager are described by Brousseau et al. (2006).

43 The difference between 'being active' and 'taking action' is nicely described by Bruch and Ghoshal (2004, 2010). Ways to overcome the traps of non-action that prevent a manager from taking fast action are given by Bruch and Ghoshal (2004, 2010) and Delbridge et al. (2006).

44 In a review of what exactly entails coaching for improved performance, Bond and Seneque (2011) identified the main ingredients of effective coaching and the related activity of mentoring. They defined coaching as 'a holistic process intended to build the capacity of people in organizations to work relationally, socially and organizationally'. Mentoring was defined by them as 'an intervention that is intended to assess and improve individual and team performance, thus enhancing organizational efficiency and effectiveness.'

45 HPO managers in general are driven by a great need for achieving results which makes them a great propelling strength of the HPO. However, they guard against becoming overachievers as this type of managers on the long term does more harm than good to organizations. This is because overachievers often develop a counterproductive management style entailing command and control, and directive and coercive instead of coaching, seeking dialogue and collaboration. Therefore they balance their need for achievement with a need for affiliation. The HPO manager maintains close relationships with the employees and makes sure their needs are looked after as well as those of the organization (Spreier et al., 2006).

46 The tactics to become more effective originate from Ancona et al. (2007), Barsh et al. (2010), Carroll and Mui (2008), Myatt (2011) and Weiss and Hughes (2005).

47 Kanter (2004) has done interesting research into the relation between the types and levels of confidence in an organization and organizational performance. She found that in organizations that are on a 'winning streak', i.e. that beget success after success, management had first created a foundation of confidence that made it possible for people to achieve high levels of performance, as part of a successful team. Each time the team or the organization got a victory, support for confidence increased, and occasional wins turned into a long winning streak.

48 The signs of bad management behavior are based on the ten rituals of bad management, as described in Waal (2010a).

49 Ways to deal with non-performers are described in Daley (2008), Ferguson et al. (2010) and Furnham and Taylor (2011).

50 At the end of the HPO Diagnosis, Craig Cerretani was kind enough to comment on its usefulness for Longfellow: "I had heard about the great work that André de Waal and his HPO Center were doing as it relates to High Performance Organizations but I had no idea the overwhelming effect that they would have on our company. If I can distill the HPO Center's results: Longfellow Benefits is clearly an HPO. That said, we have some work to do to assure we stay there. Their easy to understand recommendations will provide the structure we need to get Longfellow to the next level. Bravo, André and your team!"

51 The interviews were held by a team of the HPO Center and Maastricht School of Management, who had organized this case study research as part of its refresher program for alumni.

52 Ways to start and improve the dialogue in the organization can be found in: Davis (2009), Detert et al. (2010), Gobillot (2007) and Laseter and Laseter (2007).

53 The topic of knowledge management has received a lot of attention in the academic world. The emphasis is shifting from the mechanics of knowledge management to the effects of knowledge management, see for instance: Bagorogoza and Waal (2010), Bagorogoza et al. (2011), Kleinbaum et al. (2008), Kodama (2007) and Rieger (2011).

54 The importance of involving employees to create greater commitment is described by Branham and Hirschfeld (2010), Merchant (2010) and Schilder and Teijlingen (2010).

55 An interesting question to ponder is: What is a mistake? If we undertake an experiment and it goes wrong, is that a mistake? For that matter, what does 'it goes wrong' entail in this respect? Can an experiment ever fail and therefore be a mistake? Or does it just not deliver what we expected or hoped for? Which means that we, although we might not be happy with the outcome, at least learned from the experiment. When Edison invented the long-lasting light bulb after a hundred experiments, he was asked by a reporter: "Mr. Edison, didn't you get very tired of all those failures?" to which Edison replied: "Not at all, I have discovered ninety-nine ways a light bulb doesn't work." This illuminates the essence of a high performance individual! It is important to differentiate three types of mistakes which should be dealt with differently: (a) preventable mistakes in predictable operations, these usually involve deviations from specifications of routine processes and should be prevented or solved as quickly as possible; (b) unavoidable mistakes in complex systems, these are caused by the inherent uncertainty of work and often cannot be avoided but should be managed so that they do not become major problems; and (c) intelligent mistakes, these normally occur in research settings and are valuable because they generate new knowledge and should be welcomed, they are usually called experiments.

56 The importance of experimentation and learning from mistakes is described in Baumard and Starbuck (2005), Delong et al. (2007), Edmondson (2011), Godin (2010), Li (2010), Madsen and Desai (2010), McGrath (2011), Miller (2011), Schoemaker and Gunther (2006) and Tugend (2011).

57 This case study is based on thesis work of two MBA students of Maastricht School of Management, and has been previously published in Waal et al. (2009).

58 This case study is based on Waal and Chachage (2011).

59 This case study is based on Waal and Sultan (2012).

60 An objective is SMART when it is:
- *Specific*: the objective is concrete, unambiguous (susceptible only to one explanation to prevent misunderstandings) and relevant.

NOTES

- *Measurable*: the achievement of the objective can be measured by using critical success factors and key performance indicators.
- *Acceptable*: the objective is acceptable and motivating for the employees.
- *Realistic*: the objective is ambitious yet achievable (with regard to time, money and capacity needed).
- *Time bound*: the objective has to be achieved in a specific timeframe.

61 To be clear, HPO managers don't disagree with the initial idea of shareholder thinking. This thinking originated in the 1970s and 1980s and stated that without an overarching financial goal with which to guide and evaluate management's performance, managers could divert corporate resources to serve their own interests rather than that of the owners. Therefore EVA™, with economic value added, and TSR, total shareholder return, were introduced as the financial targets to focus on, with the explicit notion that long-term value of the organization should be maximized. However, as we have seen, especially in listed companies, this emphasis on shareholder value has often led to short-term thinking and negative organizational results. Organizations started to pay more attention to short-term objectives and targets, such as continuously increasing quarterly profits by delaying needed investments or focusing on mergers and acquisitions, and less attention to the long-term objectives, such as investing in clean production techniques, innovation, the quality of personnel and the environment. Such a short-term focus, however, is not without danger and is a potential threat to the continuity of an organization. The organization will not be able to achieve sustainable growth and will not be innovative enough to keep its customers satisfied with new products and services. In short, a focus on the short-term bottom line prevents a company from becoming and staying a 'living' organization. For becoming such an organization, a balance in focus between short-term and long-term objectives is needed, together with attention for all *stake*holders, rather than just shareholders, of the organization. For ways to build an enduring organization which has stakeholder thinking at its core, see: Kanter (2011) and Ramaswamy and Gouillart (2010).

62 'The myth of economic growth' is based on Waal (2008b), with input from Loomis (2001) in Figure 5.1.

63 This study can be found in Nevins and Stumpf (1999).

64 This study can be found in Soene and Duffhues (2001).

65 Ways to increase customer orientation are described in Barwise and Meehan (2011), Dixon et al. (2010), Gulati and Kletter (2005) and Hsieh (201).

66 This research is described in Waal and Heijden (2012). The research was done in the Netherlands and should therefore be seen as indicative, in other countries other behaviors could be important.

67 There is enough evidence that longer chief executive officer tenure leads to higher organizational performance (Wulf, 2010). Unfortunately the trend in the business world has been toward shorter tenures for especially chief executive officers. During the past decade the length of planned tenures, in which chief executive officers depart on a date that has been prearranged with the board, has dropped from ten to seven years, while the actual average tenure is even shorter, this has decreased from 8.1 to 6.6 years (Kaplan and Minton, 2006; Favaro et al., 2011). This turnover rate however is not sustainable because, as mentioned in Chapter 1, the changing demography will cause many managers in the Western world to retire in the next ten to twenty years, creating a shrinking supply of managerial talent in developed countries. At the same time, the growth in Asia, India and many of the developing countries will quickly deplete the pool of talented managers in those countries. What compounds the problem is that, as recent research shows, talented managers who leave a company increasingly take their talent, experience, ideas and innovativeness with them not to competitors, but to their own entrepreneurial firms. These turn out to be quite successful thereby hurting their former employers considerably (Campbell et al., 2009). It is thus of the utmost importance that organizations succeed in attracting and especially keeping HPO managers as long as possible.

68 In North America, for example, 29 percent of the companies with negative performance in the prior two years had hired an outside chief executive officer versus only 6 percent of well performing companies (Lucier et al., 2006). The externally recruited chief executive officers are the most effective in their first years when they indeed bring in new ideas and also are willing to take more drastic measures as they are not hindered by organizational history. However, after those years their

results drops dramatically while chief executive officers from within show a steady, incremental improvement in organizational results for the length of their tenure (Zhang and Rajagopalan, 2010). In general, externally recruited chief executive officers stay much shorter with an organization than chief executive officers promoted from within (Favaro et al., 2011; Hermalin, 2005).

69 The relationship between Corporate Social Responsibility and the HPO Framework is based on Waal and Orcotoma Escalante (2011), with input from Henisz et al. (2011), Hollender and Breen (2010), and Wood (1991).

70 The telling signs of high performance individuals in the workplace are described by Ryan (2010).

71 This case study originates from Waal and Orcotoma Escalante (2011).

72 Several days after the feedback session with Archway's management, the HPO Center received the following feedback from President, Mike Moroz: "This was the perfect study for Archway to participate in. It pinpointed where we had cracks in our foundation so we can focus on solidifying our foundation before we double in size again. If we had not done this, we would have failed to see gaps as we grew. Thank you for your insights." This feedback strengthened our conviction that Archway not only had the desire but also the capacity to remain a 'great company' and to be an HPO in its sector. The organization planned to repeat the HPO Diagnosis in order to stay on track, so … to be continued!

73 The ideas about the conditions for creating a unique strategy originate from Adams (2010), Shenkar (2010) and Taylor and LaBarre (2006).

74 This section is based on the academic paper of Waal (2011c).

75 This definition and the description and ideas in this section originate mostly from the course book of Waal (2007) and a white paper on the future of performance management (Waal, 2003). For more on facing the facts and what can be done to fight denial to confront the truth in the organization, see Tedlow (2010). For more information on the role of performance management in evidence-based management, see Marr (2010).

76 The ideas to get started with innovation originate from Budman (2011), Deschamps (2008), Gailly (2011), Linder (2005), Nagji and Quinn (2010) and Ringland et al. (2010).

77 This case study is based on Waal et al. (2012a). At their request, the two case companies remain anonymous.

78 This case study is based on Waal and Meingast (2011).

79 This definition, and a description of the characteristics of Dutch high performance employees, can be found in Waal and Oudshoorn (2012).

80 The ideas to get started to increase the motivation of employees originate from Boone James et al. (2011), Grant (2008), Grant et al. (2007), Herzberg (2003), Kouzes and Posner (2010), Richards (2004), Spreitzer and Porath (2012), and Zenger et al. (2009).

81 The ideas to get started to increase resilience originate from Maddi and Khoshaba (2005), Seligman (2011) and Välikangas (2010). The ideas to get started to increase flexibility originate from Waal (2003).

82 Page (2007) explains the concept of cognitive diversity. It means a team of people who have diverse perspectives on situations and problems, diverse interpretations of these perspectives, diverse ways of generating solutions to problems, and diverse ways of looking at and predicting the future. Cognitive diversity can be generated by identity diversity but this is no guarantee. Identity diversity entails differences in race, ethnicity, gender, social status and the like. If identity diversity has resulted in a team of people with different experiences, then cognitive diversity is present. If, on the other hand, the group of people has basically the same experiences there is no cognitive diversity and the organization is still not diverse enough.

83 The ideas to get started to create more diversity originate from Knegtmans (2010), Kreitz (2008), Manzoni et al. (2010), Moss (2010) and Page (2007).

84 The research into the factors of the high performance partnership is described in Waal et al. (2012b).

85 At request the College remains anonymous.

NOTES

86 This case study is based on Waal and Frijns (2009, 2011a).

87 When looking at the overall difference in HPO scores between 2007 and 2008, it is conspicuous that there is a fairly small increase of 0.3. From the interviews it became clear that management did not undertake new improvement actions as a follow-up to the first HPO research performed in 2007. Instead, management decided to continue with the actions already underway, such as applying the new performance management system to the fullest. Although this in itself was a smart decision, the fact that a relatively small headway was made concerning the HPO scores meant that Nabil Bank potentially had not taken advantage enough yet of its resources to achieve even more competitive advantage. At the same time, one can look at the 0.3 increase in a different way. For Nabil Bank to become an HPO, the organization needed to achieve an average score of 8.5, which meant an increase of 1.5 points from the 2007 score. If the transition to an HPO takes on average three to five years, this meant that Nabil Banks should achieve an improvement per year of 0.3 to 0.5 point. In this light Nabil Bank was definitely on its way to becoming an HPO but it seemed to be taking the 'slow road'. If Nabil Bank was able to speed up the transition process to HPO it could gain even more advantage over its competitors in the increasingly competitive Nepalese market place.

88 The four phases of the HPO transition process have been shaped with the help of information drawn from Abrahamson (2004), Harris and Ogbonna (2002), Hickson et al. (2003) and Skinner (2003).

89 This case study is based on Waal et al. (2010).

90 Information on the number of mergers and acquisitions that fail, and the reasons for this, can be found in Axson (2010), Clayton (2010), Hess (2010), Ingebretsen (2003), Lahovnik (2011), Marks and Mirvis (2011), and Vermeulen (2010).

91 The two manufacturing companies asked to remain anonymous.

92 These benefits have been noticed at organizations which have applied the HPO Diagnosis at least twice and have used the diagnosis results to work on becoming an HPO. Some of these organizations are described in this book: ATLAS Consortium (Chapter 8), Grohe Netherlands (Chapter 8), Iringa University College (Chapter 4), and Nabil Bank (Chapter 7).

93 This observation is based on four sector comparisons. The first study was in the banking sector in Vietnam (Chapter 4). The second study was conducted in the Tanzanian banking sector where employees from ten banks in the Tanzanian capital Dar Es Salaam received and completed the HPO Questionnaire (Yusuph, 2010). The subsequent average HPO scores, calculated for the ten banks, were ranked and matched with their financial performance. The final matching showed that Tanzanian banks with the highest HPO ranking also had the best financial performance. Tanzanian banks with the lowest HPO ranking displayed the worst financial performance. The third study was performed in the manufacturing sector in Tanzania (Godfrey, 2010). In this study, employees from ten manufacturing firms in Dar Es Salaam filled in the HPO Questionnaire and their scores were averaged. The subsequent HPO ranking was matched with the financial performance of the ten manufacturing firms and the matching showed that the Tanzanian manufacturing firms with the highest HPO ranking also had the best financial performance, while Tanzanian manufacturing firms with the lowest HPO ranking reported the worst financial performance. In the fourth study, the HPO scores and financial results of two Dutch swimming pools were compared, with as outcome that the highest-scoring swimming pool had the best financial results of the two swimming pools and also the highest reputation as a client-oriented swimming pool (Waal and Linders, 2008).

94 This observation is based on seven studies comparing the average HPO scores, financial results and non-financial results of organizational units. The first study was at a division of an international bank in the Netherlands (Chapter 2). The second study was at an European temping agency (Chapter 6). The third study was at the multinational Retail International Group (Chapter 2). The other four studies were basically conducted in the same manner as the first two (note: most of the organizations in these studies asked to remain anonymous). At a Dutch hospital, four laboratories were examined. These laboratories participated in an independent benchmark in which laboratories of all hospitals in the Netherlands were compared for productivity per employee. The results of this benchmark study were matched with the average HPO scores of the laboratories and the matching showed that the laboratory with the highest productivity per employee also scored highest in HPO status. For a Dutch university, the average HPO scores of its eight faculties were compared with the financial

results, absenteeism, student satisfaction scores and employee satisfaction scores of these faculties. The matching showed that the faculties with the highest HPO scores also had the highest financial and non-financial results, while faculties with the lowest HPO scores showed the worst financial and non-financial results. At a Dutch accountancy agency, with seven locations, the HPO Questionnaire was filled in at each location. The average HPO scores for the locations were matched with the net operating profit per employee. The HPO ranking corresponded for almost 100 percent with the financial ranking. A Dutch care giver, specializing in care for the elderly, conducted the HPO Diagnosis at its five locations and compared the resulting average HPO scores per location with the financial results and client satisfaction. The location with the highest average HPO scores also had the best financial and client satisfaction scores.

Index

A
Accountability 9, 24, 55, 82, 89, 90, 91, 92, 95, 97, 144, 190, 195, 234, 270
Action-taking 24, 50, 75, 76, 112, 132, 133, 143
Adkinson, Bob 178
Air France - KLM 10, 120, 160, 163, 165, 187, 191, 193, 195, 197
Allowing Mistakes 121, 123, 178
Amanco Plastigama (Ecuador) *see* CASE STUDIES
Amsterdam 206
Antamina 171
Archway Marketing (USA) *see* CASE STUDIES
ATLAS Consortium (UK) *see* CASE STUDIES
Atrion Networking Corporation (USA) *see* CASE STUDIES
Attention Points 268
    Longfellow Benefits (USA) 102
    Ministry of Local Governance and Social Affairs (Rwanda) 59, 60

B
Belgium 206
Berger, Pim 12, 117, 121, 123, 129, 152, 155
Better Employee Attitude 287
Bonus: HPO Characteristics 32, 33
    Rewards 34
Boogaard, Lennard 14, 80, 84, 114, 116, 124, 148, 221

Business Environment, Current 3
Business Leader 70

C
Canada 178
CASE STUDIES
    Amanco Plastigama (Ecuador) 199
    Archway Marketing (USA) 173-179
    ATLAS Consortium (UK) 265-273
    Atrion Networking Corporation (USA) 229-232
    Dealer Antwerp 207
    De Beers Marine (South Africa) 105-110
    Diamond companies (Europe) 204-207
    Grohe (the Netherlands) 279-282
    Intermediate Amsterdam 207
    International bank (the Netherlands) 44
    Iringa University College (Tanzania) 134-139
    Longfellow Benefits (USA) 97-103
    Mining multinationals (Peru) 170-171
    Ministry of Local Governance and Social Affairs (Rwanda) 58-59
    Nabil Bank (Nepal) 240-242
    Palestine Polytechnics University (Palestine Territories) 141-144
    Retail International Group (Europe/Asia/South America) 51-56
    South American College of Higher Education (SACHE) 235
    Temping Agency Nearby (TAN) 208-213

Toyota 8
Umpqua Bank (USA) 16
Vietnamese banking industry
 (Vietnam) 131-132
Cassidian 265
Catering Manager 65, 68, 70
 coaching 78
 confidence 87
 decision-making 75
 decisiveness towards non-performers 92
 managment style 95
 role model 70
Cerretani, Craig 101
Clark, Alan 12, 67, 70, 94, 119, 157, 217, 292
Coach 70
Coaching 55, 77, 78, 79, 80, 83, 95, 102, 121, 137, 231, 238, 261, 270
 catering manager 78
Collins, Jim 36
Colombia 202
Communication vs dialogue 112
Competitive Advantage 290
Confidence 36, 39, 55, 86, 87, 88, 216, 252
 catering manager 87
Conflict Management 227
Continuous Business Improvement (CBI) initiative 107
CONTINUOUS IMPROVEMENT & RENEWAL – HPO FACTOR 4
 innovation 195
 introduction 183
 performance management 192
 process alignment 189
 process improvement 189
 process simplification 189
 unique strategy 184
Cooperation 288
Corporate Social Responsibility (CSR) 146, 171
 HPO characteristic 166

HPO framework 166
Courtesy 156
Customer
 HPO interaction 155
 understanding 156
Customer Orientation 151, 153

D
Dactylo 2
Davis, Ray 16
Dealer Antwerp see CASE STUDIES
De Beers Marine (South Africa) see CASE STUDIES
Decision-making 50, 64, 73, 74, 112, 132, 133, 143, 226
 catering manager 75
Decisiveness toward Non-performers 17, 27, 60, 92, 93, 94, 233
 catering manager 92
Delprete, Melissa 232
Dialogue 25, 27, 31, 46, 56-57, 69, 95, 102, 108, 111-115, 137, 144, 147, 161, 176, 226, 243, 254, 257, 261, 270, 275, 281, 284, 288
Diamond Companies (Europe) see CASE STUDIES
Diversity 115, 196, 223, 224

E
Ecuador 199
Effectiveness 4, 24, 26, 28, 29, 58, 59, 73, 75, 81, 82, 83, 84, 87, 92, 95, 114, 115, 117, 120, 121, 128, 129, 215, 249, 278
 catering manager 87
Employee Involvement 38, 119, 120, 121, 274
EMPLOYEE QUALITY – HPO FACTOR 5
 inspiration 216
 introduction 215
 partnership 225
 resilience and flexibility 220
 workforce - diverse and complementary 223

INDEX

EMPLOYEES
  complementary workforce 223
  cooperate more 288
  curiosity 215
  customer orientation 151
  diverse workforce 223
  flexibility 220
  high-quality 156
  inspiration 216
  involvement 119
  ideas to get started 120
  more solution-oriented 287
  motivation 217
  motivational conditions 218
  resilience 220
  secure workplace 163
  turnover 164

F
Factors, non-distinguishing *see* NON-DISTINGUISHING FACTORS
Fad Surfing 157
Ferment, Martine 14, 39, 42, 252, 262, 263, 289, 291, 293
Financial Results 290

FIVE FACTORS (HPO)
  continuous improvement & renewal 26
  employee quality 26
  long-term orientation 25
  management quality 24
  openness & action orientation 25
  table of characteristics 27
  see individual entries
Flexibility 12, 25, 26, 28, 125, 193, 220, 221, 222, 278
Fujitsu 265

G
Gazda, Kevin 101
General Motors 9
Grohe AG (the Netherlands) *see* CASE STUDIES
Growth, myth of economic growth 148

H
Hayward, Lani 13, 72, 85, 122, 125, 127, 155, 220
Hebron 142
Heitlager, Ilja 12, 117, 121, 123, 129, 152, 155

HIGH PERFORMANCE
  consistent growth 6
  relative 5
  performance drivenness 127
  performance management 192
  Performance Review Scorecard 176
  sustained 6
  System 193

HIGH PERFORMANCE ORGANIZATION (HPO)
  definition 5
  five factors 24
  Framework 4
  growth expectations 6, 7
  improving an existing HPO 97
  non-distinguishing factors 29
  practical application 39
  research 21
  returns vs peer group 7
  the role of reward systems 32

HPO CENTER
  work and methods 5, 38, 39, 40, 41, 46, 107, 170, 212, 232, 242, 245, 259, 267, 276, 278, 281, 295

HPO FRAMEWORK
  HPO Framework 5, 205, 245, 272
    based on comprehensive literature study 37
    basis of original reporting 37
    benefits 6, 287
    competitive advantage 290
    cooperation 288
    employee attitude 287
    financial results 290
    organization 289
    certainty of results 293
    comprehensive basis of research 37

cooperation 205
corporate social responsibility (CSR) 166
definition 5
development 21
distinguished from model 38
HPO Factors 23, 238, 259, 283
  improving 136
  is it all too much? 94
  link with positive performance 23
  management quality 63
  possible changeability? 35
  graphic 23
  improving through use 134
  mergers guidelines 275
  scientific validation 4
  unique factors 36

HPO FIVE FACTORS
continuous improvement & renewal 26
employee quality 26
long-term orientation 25
management quality 24
openness & action orientation 25
table of characteristics 27
See **individual entries**

HPO LEADERS
Air France KLM 10, 120, 160, 163, 165, 187, 191, 193, 195, 197
Berger, Pim 12, 117, 121, 123, 129, 152, 155
Boogaard, Lennard 14, 80, 84, 114, 116, 124, 148, 221
Clark, Alan 12, 67, 70, 94, 119, 157, 217, 292
Ferment, Martine 39, 42, 252, 262, 263, 289, 291, 293
Hayward, Lani 13, 72, 85, 122, 125, 127, 155, 220
Heitlager, Ilja 12, 117, 121, 123, 129, 152, 155
HP D&S 11, 29, 113, 251, 262, 289, 292
Jong, Arend de 11, 120, 160, 163, 165, 187, 191, 193, 195, 197
Maas, Jan 13, 86, 125, 147, 159, 186, 227
Microsoft Netherlands 89, 116, 161, 192, 219, 226
Microsoft, the Netherlands 11
Microsoft USA 71, 78, 91
Microsoft, USA 11
Owen, Huw 11, 29, 113, 251, 262, 289, 292
Rinsema, Theo 11, 89, 116, 161, 192, 219, 226
SAB Miller Europe 12, 67, 70, 94, 119, 157, 217, 292
Schuberg Philis 12, 117, 121, 123, 129, 152, 155
Sørensen, Mikael 13, 35, 80, 113, 128, 152, 163, 185, 189, 216, 223
Svenska Handelsbanken 13, 35, 80, 113, 128, 152, 163, 185, 189, 216, 223
Tata Steel 13, 86, 125, 159, 186, 227
Umpqua Bank 13, 72, 85, 122, 125, 127, 155, 220
Unilever 14, 80, 84, 114, 116, 124, 148, 221
van der Kooi, Rik 11, 71, 78, 91, 223
Ziggo 14, 39, 42, 252, 262, 263, 289, 291, 293

HPO MANAGERS
accountability 89
business leader 70
coach 70
coaches 77
confidence 86
conflict resolvers 82
creating partnerships 225
creating secure workplace 163
discussing 64, 67
fighting complacency 127
four decision-making styles 73
highly effective 82
innovativation 122

INDEX

knowledge sharing and exchange 116
leader of change processes 125
leadership 84
learning from mistakes 121
longevity in organization 157
management style 95
mentoring 77
popularity 68
purposeful action 75
recruitment of employees 220
results oriented 81
risk taking 121
role model 70
sharing 116
tough decision-making 92
using dialogue 112

HPO Process and Examples
  HPO Analysis 40
  HPO Challenger 248
  HPO Characteristics 212
    corporate social responsibility (CSR) 166
    identifying in an industry 131
    mining multinationals (Peru) 171
    stability over time 36
  HPO Coach 42, 259, 262, 272
    program 263
  HPO Diagnosis 39, 108, 178, 179, 199, 211, 248, 267, 272, 274, 281
    analysis 40
    Archway Marketing (USA) 174
    assessment workshop 40
    ATLAS Consortium (UK) 267, 270, 273
    Atrion Networking Corporation (USA) 230
    coaches 42
    De Beers Marine (South Africa) 105
    detailed analysis 41
    full debrief 41
    Longfellow Benefits (USA) 98
    reasons for starting 249
    Retail International Group (RIG) 53
    sample interview answers 46

  steps graphics 40
  HPO Improvement
    Retail International Group (RIG) 55, 56
  HPO Questionnaire 40, 59, 131, 170, 174, 200, 209, 230, 242, 273, 277
  HPO Ranking
    international bank (the Netherlands) 45
    Temping Agency Nearby (TAN) 211
  HPO Research 21
    Phase 1 187
  HPO Scores
    diamond companies (Europe) 207
    Temping Agency Nearby (TAN) 210
    Vietnamese banking industry (Vietnam) 132
  HPO Sponsor 247
  HPO Transition Process
    Introduction Phase 246
    Execution Phase 256
    Perseverance & Arrival Phase 259
    Preparation Phase 252
  HPO Workshop 59, 135
    Iringa University College (Tanzania) 135, 138

HPO Status
  Amanco Plastigama (Ecuador) 200
  Archway Marketing (USA) 174
  ATLAS Consortium (UK) 268, 271, 273
  Atrion Networking Corporation (USA) 230
  De Beers Marine (South Africa) 106
  Grohe AG (the Netherlands) 280, 282
  Iringa University College (Tanzania) 136
  Longfellow Benefits (USA) 99
  Nabil Bank (Nepal) 242
  Palestine Polytechnics University (Palestine Territories) 142
  Retail International Group (RIG) 53
  South American College of Higher Education (SACHE) 236
  two companies pre-merger 276

327

HPO Transition
  attention points 256
  changing/improving culture 257
  communication 254
  creating trust 65
  identify the core competencies 252
    process 245
  execution phase 256
  introduction phase 246
  openness about progress 257
  overview 260
  perseverance & arrival phase 259
  preparation phase 252
  role model of management 254
  training 254
  transition plan 253
High Performance Partnerships (HPP) 225, 226
HP (Hewlett Packard) D&S 11, 29, 113, 251, 262, 265, 289, 292

I

Ideas to Get People Excited
  execution phase 258
  introduction phase 248
  perseverance & arrival phase 259
  preparation phase 255
Ideas to Get Started
  action-taking 76
  allowing mistakes 123
  becoming a role model 71
  coaching 79
  confidence building 87
  creating trust 65
  customer orientation 153
  dealing with non-performers 93
  decision-making 74
  dialogue 114
  diversity 224
  effectiveness 83
  employee involvement 120
  flexibility 221
  fostering accountability 90
  fostering integrity 68
  improving processes 190
  innovation 196
  inspiration 217
  knowledge sharing 117
  leadership 85
  longevity of organization 158
  partnership 226
  performance management 193
  promotion from within 161
  resilience 221
  results orientation 81
  secure workplace\ 164
  stakeholder orientation 147
  strategy, unique 185
  welcoming change 126
Improvement Suggestions
  Archway Marketing (USA) 178
Innovation 11, 107, 109, 128, 147, 195, 196, 203, 233, 280, 281, 287
Inspiration 108, 137, 192, 216, 217, 218, 245, 248, 255, 256, 258, 260, 296
Integrity 24, 27, 50, 52, 67, 68, 69, 70, 95, 166, 170, 231
  catering manager 68
  fostering 68
Intermediate Amsterdam *see* Case Studies
Iringa University College (IUCo) *see* Case Studies

J

Jerusalem 142
Jong, Arend de 10, 120, 160, 163, 165, 187, 191, 193, 195, 197
Just-in-time (JIT) 189

K

Key Points
  Chapter 1 15
  Chapter 2 43
  Chapter 3 96
  Chapter 4 130

INDEX

Chapter 5 169
Chapter 6 198
Chapter 7 228
Chapter 9 294
Knowledge Sharing 56, 61, 108, 116, 117, 118, 119, 203, 281
Kooi, Rik van der 11, 71, 78, 91, 223

L

Leadership 1, 27, 29, 30, 42, 72, 84, 86, 87, 95, 98, 103, 110, 113, 114, 125, 160, 167, 187, 231, 234, 270
Leading to Growth 16
LEAN Methodology 234
Logica 265
Longevity of organization 25, 72, 157, 267
Longfellow Benefits (USA) *see* CASE STUDIES
Long-term Commitment 146
LONG-TERM ORIENTATION – HPO FACTOR 3 - 145
    customer orientation 151
    longevity 157
    promotion from within 159
    secure workplace 163
    stakeholder orientation 146

M

Maas, Jan 13, 86, 125, 147, 159, 186, 227
Maastricht School of Management 135
MANAGEMENT QUALITY – HPO FACTOR 1
    accountability 89
    action-taking 75
    coaching 77
    confidence 86
    decision-making 73
    decisiveness toward non-performers 92
    effectiveness 82
    integrity 67
    leadership 84
    results orientation 81
    strong role model 70
    trust 64
Management Style 95
Market Share 290
Mentoring 77
Mergers
    guidelines from HPO Framework 275
Mexichem 199
Microsoft 11
    Netherlands 89, 116, 161, 192, 219, 226
    USA 71, 78, 91
Minera Yanacocha 171
Mining Multinationals (Peru) *see* CASE STUDIES
Ministry of Defence's Defence Information Infrastructure (DII) project 265
Ministry of Local Governance and Social Affairs (Rwanda) *see* CASE STUDIES
Minneapolis 173
Moroz, Mike 177

N

Nabil Bank (Nepal) *see* CASE STUDIES
National Audit Office 274
Nepal 240
Netherlands 11
NON-DISTINGUISHING FACTORS
    benchmarking 31
    bonuses and reward systems 31
    communication 31
    employee autonomy 30
    ICT 31
    organizational design 30
    strategy 30
    structure 30
    technology 31
Non-performer, decisiveness towards *see* Decisiveness toward Non-performers

O

OPENNESS & ACTION ORIENTATION – HPO FACTOR 2 111
  allowing mistakes 121
  dialogue 112
  employee involvement 119
  knowledge sharing 116
  performance drivenness 127
  welcoming change 125
Organization 289
Owen, Huw 11, 29, 113, 251, 262, 289, 292

P

Palestine Polytechnic University (PPU) see CASE STUDIES
Palestine Territories 141
Partnership 25, 26, 28, 100, 147, 168, 171, 202, 204, 225, 226, 227, 259, 265, 267, 268
Partnership, high performance partnerships (HPP) 225
PDCA cycle 239

PERFORMANCE
  Performance Drivenness 127
  Performance Management 192
  System 193
  Performance Review Scorecard 176
Peru 170
Peters, Tom 36
Pope, Michelle 231

PROCESS
  alignment 189
  improvement 187, 189
  simplification 189
  Temping Agency Nearby (TAN) 213
Profitability 290
Profit-sharing System 34
Promotion from Within 159
Public Accounts Committee 274

R

Randstad Group 2
Reading 265
Reengineering 189
Reporting
  organization-wide 192
  performance 192
Research 21
Resilience 220
Responsiveness 156
Results Orientation 81
Retail International Group (RIG) see CASE STUDIES
Rinsema, Theo 11, 89, 116, 161, 192, 219, 226
Risk Taking 121
Role Model, Strong 70
  catering manager 70
Rollercoaster Management 149, 150
Rwanda 58

S

SAB Miller Europe 12, 67, 70, 94, 119, 157, 217, 292
Schuberg Philis 12, 117, 121, 123, 129, 152, 155
Secure Workplace 163
Service Quality 156
Setup of this Book 10
Shareholder Thinking, limitations 146
Silo Thinking 284
Situational Leadership 95
Sørensen, Mikael 13, 35, 80, 113, 128, 152, 163, 185, 189, 216, 223
South American College of Higher Education (SACHE) see CASE STUDIES
Speijer, Jonard 2
Stakeholder Orientation 146
Strategy 184
  HPO organization's better 289
  relative importance 187
Strategy, Unique 184
  Temping Agency Nearby (TAN) 212
Svenska Handelsbanken 13, 35, 80, 113, 128, 152, 163, 185, 189, 216, 223

INDEX

T
Tanzania 134, 139
Tata Steel 13, 86, 125, 147, 159, 186
Temping Agency Nearby (TAN) *see* CASE STUDIES
Tim Hebert 231, 233
Toyoda, Akio 8

TRANSITION PROCESS
  Introduction Phase 246
  Execution Phase 256
  Perseverance & Arrival Phase 259
  Preparation Phase 252
Trust 64
    catering manager 65
Trustworthiness 156
Tumaini University 134

U
Umpqua Bank 13, 72, 85, 122, 125, 127, 155, 220

Unilever 14, 80, 84, 114, 116, 124, 148, 221
United States (USA) 11, 178

V
van den Maagdenberg, Rob 279, 281, 284
Vietnamese Banking Industry (Vietnam) *see* CASE STUDIES

W
Waal, André de 295
Warwick 229
Welcoming Change 125
Workforce, Diverse and Complementary 223

Z
Ziggo 14, 39, 42, 252, 262, 263, 289, 291, 293